THE FENCE AND THE BRIDGE

THE FENCE AND THE BRIDGE

Geopolitics and Identity along the Canada–US Border

Heather N. Nicol

WLU PRESS

WILFRID LAURIER
UNIVERSITY PRESS

Wilfrid Laurier University Press acknowledges the support of the Canada Council for the Arts for our publishing program. We acknowledge the financial support of the Government of Canada through the Canada Book Fund for our publishing activities. This work was supported by the Research Support Fund.

LAURIER
Inspiring Lives.

Library and Archives Canada Cataloguing in Publication

Nicol, Heather N. (Heather Nora), 1953–, author
   The fence and the bridge : geopolitics and identity along the Canada–US border/ Heather N. Nicol.

Includes bibliographical references and index.
Issued in print and electronic formats.
ISBN 978-1-55458-971-5 (pbk.).—ISBN 978-1-77112-059-3 (epub).—
ISBN 978-1-77112-058-6 (pdf)

   1. Border security—Political aspects—Canada. 2. Border security—Political aspects—United States. 3. Geopolitics—Canada. 4. Geopolitics—United States. 5. Canada—Boundaries—United States. 6. United States—Boundaries—Canada. 7. Canada—Foreign relations—United States. 8. United States—Foreign relations—Canada. I. Title.

FC249.N53 2015   327.71073   C2014-905440-8
                                                               C2014-905441-6

Front-cover photo by Bob McCarthy, Sarnia, Ontario. Cover design and text design by Angela Booth Malleau.

© 2015 Wilfrid Laurier University Press
Waterloo, Ontario, Canada
www.wlupress.wlu.ca

To Peter G. Goheen

CONTENTS

LIST OF FIGURES

ACKNOWLEDGEMENTS

This book is the result of a long process of research and writing. I would like to acknowledge not only the help I receive from the Social Science and Humanities Research Council and a research grant to develop what I called Border Stories, but also the financial assistance of Trent University and the Borders in Globalization Project (lead by Emmanuel Brunet-Jailly and Victor Konrad) for the preparation of this manuscript.

I received considerable assistance from personnel at the Vancouver Public Library, Queen's University Special Collections, Trent's Bata Library, the Public Archives of Canada, and the McCord Museum in finding suitable materials, texts, cartoons, and other images for this volume. Two excellent reviewers read the manuscript and made suggestions, and the staff at Wilfrid Laurier University Press were incredibly accommodating of both my schedule and my writing process. Research assistance was provided by Trent students Blair Cullen, Adam Blacklock, and Daphne Dobbin, while James Dobbin provided some excellent photography. Thanks to all who helped, and thanks also to my patient family, especially Rupert. Any errors and omissions in this volume are my own, and for those I must take sole responsibility.

INTRODUCTION

Just over two decades ago, there was much celebration as the Berlin Wall top-pled. It represented to many the end of an era—the end of borders, the victory of Western liberal democracy, and the launch of a truly global world. But in many ways, this dream has not been realized. Instead, we have seen an increase rather than a decrease in the number of borders and border fences throughout the world, and the promise of truly transnational, perhaps even cosmopolitan, society has begun to fade as the fences and walls grow higher. The process is fed by political, economic, and cultural as well as social uncertainty and distrust, proving to many that borders, besides being real, durable, physical structures, are virtual ones imposed by our imaginations. They are located as much in the mind as at a particular place or site (e.g., between two countries). The phrase "borders are everywhere" (Balibar, 2002) has been the mantra of the borderless generation, reflecting the irony that the more we celebrate the demise of the "wall"—most famously, the Berlin Wall dismantled in 1990—the more we devise borders among and between ourselves, in our daily lives. In doing so, we risk losing the vision that overcame the two solitudes of "East" and "West" in the Cold War as well as the shared vision of a world united rather than divided by ideologies, religions, and standards of living.

Take the US–Mexico border. Here, since 11 September 2001, an enhanced "Homeland Security" initiative has built hundreds upon hundreds of miles of fencing and border obstacles, all designed to reify a boundary between what was at one time two indistinguishable territories. Now towers and surveillance cam-eras are also being installed. Similarly, the Israeli government continues to build a separation wall in the West Bank to provide "security" to Israelis and Palestin-ians alike. The Israelis are now considering a wall along their border with Egypt. India's famous border fence with Pakistan is nearly 2000 kilometres long, and recently the US Department of Homeland Security has even considered build-ing a security fence along the Canadian border. The media have made these examples familiar to us, but there are less familiar and equally important border

1

walls in Saudi Arabia, Cyprus, Korea, and Western Sahara as well as between Pakistan and Iran and Iraq and Kuwait, to name only a few. We also see them *within* states and sometimes even cities (in Belfast, Northern Ireland, border walls remain in the form of "peace lines," with murals and memorials demarcating the border between Protestants and Catholics). It is unclear whether these new walls have succeeded in fostering friendly and orderly relations between or within nations.

But not all border walls are physical. They proliferate and develop even where the barbed wire and watchtowers are not so visible. We also have walls between Canada and the United States. Canada's Conservative Government led by Stephen Harper began negotiating common borders a few years ago, beginning with the Security and Prosperity Partnership (SPP). That effort has since culminated in the Beyond the Border initiative and the signing of a Canada–US security perimeter accord. Both Americans and Canadians have been forced to concede that they no longer maintain the "world's longest undefended border." Moreover, it seems that the security perimeter of the future as presently being proposed will result in heavier surveillance and more onerous documentation standards than any of us have experienced so far in our cross-border travels.

So even though we live in the era of globalization and of engagement with the "other," the resulting "threats" are defined and border management initiatives are developed in ways that project state power. This state-centred approach dictates how states respond to perceived threats. For Popescu (2012: 77), it means that we live in a world in which "one of the most significant impacts that re-bordering and re-territorialization processes have on the geography of interstate borders is to move attention beyond territorial border lines." In North America in particular, this has meant the development of a multitude of programs that secure passengers and cargoes well behind borderlines, at airports and other secure facilities. There has been unprecedented harmonization between Canadian and American policy-makers in the area of cross-border management. At times this has been a bone of contention, given that the two countries define threats to themselves in different ways and view them quite differently. As a result, one nation's demands can raise problems for the other. Nonetheless, the two nations have developed a securitization agenda that is mutually constitutive as well as independent, reactive, and reflexive.

All of this has created a new security industry that provides technologies for enhancing existing walls in some places and creating new ones in others. The problem of how to manage the risk presented by border control protocols has hugely expanded. Today, not just the probability but the remote *possibility* is being assessed that criminals, terrorists, or unauthorized immigrants might breach borders. Nowadays, anything that can be "imagined" must be "controlled." This new approach to dealing with what de Goede calls "premeditated risk" (de Goede, 2008) has fostered an age of self-induced terror, even "neurosis" (Isin, 2004). All of this means that even as we open up to the world, making time and distance shrink, and even as we become more frequent travellers, the need to provide walls and barriers to protect ourselves, as well as checkpoints and surveillance tools to document and control all travellers, grows proportionately.

For some, especially long-time citizens of North America, the new technologies will have little impact; retina scans and fingerprints will be an inconvenience at most. But for others, the new "biometric" technologies will be much more invasive and thus more problematic (Magnet, 2011)—the walls they raise will be as difficult to cross as barbed wire or brick. Moreover, as those walls have become thicker, the penalties for breaching them have become more serious. In the wall-building discourse, even high rates of *legal* immigration are viewed as problematic. Immigrants are increasingly suspected of wishing to cause "harm"; their entry into the country, even when authorized, is seen as inimical to nation-building (Popescu, 2012; Huysmans, 2006).

Because of these issues, borders have become an important field of study in the early twenty-first century. The ways in which borders are understood have also changed. Before the 1990s, those who studied borders focused mainly on how to demarcate them, that is, how to transcribe borders from maps onto the landscape itself (see Nicol and Minghi, 2005). Today, all aspects of borders are being scrutinized (de Goede, 2008; Salter 2006; Walters, 2006; Popescu, 2012; Nicol, 2011). We now ask questions such as these: "What role do borders play in immigration policy?" "Is the enhancement of borderlines creating or protecting us from a more general state of insecurity?" "Are border walls good or bad?" "Do they enhance or detract from peace, human rights and democracy?" "What is the role of the border wall more generally, and how does it manifest itself in modern democracies and other types of states?" "What role does a wall play in the development of security and insecurity?" Ever since 9/11, that last question has become a critical one for scholars, politicians, and policy-makers.

THE CANADA–US BORDER

This book is an effort to answer the questions and issues raised in this introduction, especially for Canadians. The main focus here is on our contemporary Canadian border. This book explores the emerging border security relationship between Canada and the United States in terms of the recent history of that border but also in the context of the longer history of border security in North America as a whole. As Donnan and Wilson remind us in their seminal work on borders, although boundary lines may not actually shift, "relations across it as well as within it between a border people and their political core may be subject to repeated re-definition" (Donnan and Wilson, 1998: 21).

This allusion to "repeated redefinition" embeds the borderline in the geopolitical and biopolitical narratives which have positioned Canada within North America, in relation to the United States but also in relation to the historical understandings that have long defined and depicted the Canada–US border. This book explores the geopolitical perceptions and representations that continue to define and depict the Canada–US border for Canadians and Americans and that strongly influence border policy. These perceptions affect laws and political activities in each country, as well as how the public understands those laws and activities.

For Canadians, borders have always been active symbolic sites: they speak to identity in ways that transcend regions and that attach Canadians to a specific national space or territory, albeit often in very different ways (Berland, 2009). The meaning of that space is provided by national narratives that at times are inclusive and at other times are much more exclusive, referencing attributes of race, gender, and power. All of this is at times reinforced, and at times challenged, corresponding regional narratives (Helleiner, 2009; Konrad and Nicol, 2008). This border space is also chameleon-like: Canada's border initially marked out the edge of a dependent colonial place defining the limits of French and British Empire, then a tentative North American nation, and finally a symbol of both independence and cooperation, marking the extent of Canadian sovereignty in North America. This trajectory has important implications for both how Canadians see themselves and their place in the world and how they are metaphorically represented in a geopolitical sense, through borderlines.

The malleable symbolic role of borders can also be seen in the changing significance of the mantra that for many years linked Canadians in their search for a national identity. This mantra repeated the sentiment that Canadian identity was based on the fact that Canadians were "not American." Historically, maintaining the border with the United States was read as a deliberate act to promote "Canadianness" by resisting "Americanness," by thwarting US ambitions of territorial control (Aitken, 1959), and American perceptions of Canada as a weak nation prepared to transfer its dependency from Great Britain to the United States (see Chapter 1). Depending on which side of the border was referenced, these symbolic renderings of the border created a line that supported or resisted these dependency and annexation discourses, in order to separate two peoples and two political communities. In Canada, these differences were often personified in cartoon figures like Maid Canada, Jack Canuck, and Brother Jonathan. This symbolism held even as thousands of Americans and Canadians "flooded" over the line in both directions (Widdis, 1998; Bukowczyk et al., 2005).

This historical border and its symbolic representation played to Canadians' sense of being different from Americans. Still, the symbolism of "not American,"

does not necessarily reflect a "negative identity" on the part of Canadians (Berland, 2009). It also signifies a positive one that offers a different version of "destiny" in North America than that provided by American culture and economy.
This fact reminds us of the malleable geopolitical nature of the border, which has
most recently been seen to symbolize and reinforce a "Canadianness" that, while
acknowledging American hegemony and a continental economy, promotes its
own sovereignty as non-negotiable.

For Americans, too, borders have played an important role, and not just
since 9/11. In past times, when a young "America" was seeking to exert its power
and influence over all of North America, borders were made to be broken. For
Americans, the border was at first an irritant, marking the edge of US influence
and thwarting its "manifest destiny"; this remained the case until the state's territorial edges were firmly negotiated and accepted as the limits of Europe's "intrusion" in North America (represented by Great Britain and its nineteenth-century
Canadian colony). Today, the border is as important as ever, but in a different
context: the United States maintains borders in order to defend itself against the
world, especially against terrorism and drugs, violence, and illegal immigration.
This mistrust of the world beyond the United States is attributed to the fear of
terrorism and the events of 9/11, but it actually predates the current post-9/11
situation by several centuries. This is clear from the historical record, however
prone we are to think of it as a recent phenomenon. Yet—and this is perhaps
one of the most important points made in this book—neither Americans nor
Canadians can now survive independently on this continent, despite the border
walls they have made for themselves. The current geopolitical "reality"—sup-
posing there can be only one—is that power asymmetries and American economic hegemony have reinforced a North American if not global brand of neoliberalism that challenges walls but relies on the maintenance of differences—be
they economic, cultural, political, or social, real or perceived—to provide the
motivation for the much needed "connections" (Konrad and Nicol, 2008).

This connectivity acts against a one-way flow of power and influence
(Gilbert, 2007). Indeed, the border is a highly symbolic and malleable site that
functions in reflexive ways (Helleiner, 2009), as we will discuss in the following
chapters. Until recently, this reflexivity was often described in ways that attested
to the ambivalence of the Canada–US relationship (Thompson and Randall,
1994), or even Canadian antipathy and "anti-Americanism" (Bélanger, 2011;
Granatstein, 1996), the latter viewed as "dysfunctional" (i.e., as an "irrational"
force speaking to fears that have long been assuaged). However, understanding
the border as "reflexive" speaks to how walls and gates are mutually constitutive
(Gilbert, 2007; Nicol, 2012); how each is part of the other, and how the sum of
the two creates a specific transnational identity that is the outcome both of US

hegemonic practices (present and past) and Canadian nation-building narratives that resist American hegemony. In this way, borders modulate themselves, and this modulation can be explored with reference to constructions of "us" and "them" using theoretical constructions of cosmopolitanism and universalism (Brennan, 1997; Harvey, 2003, 2009; Beck, 2006; Beck and Grande, 2007).

Initially described as "hospitality to strangers" by philosopher Emmanuel Kant, cosmopolitanism has taken on a new lease on life in the twenty-first century. According to Beck (2006; Beck and Grande, 2007), cosmopolitanism is a global vantage point that is highly inclusive and beyond "transnational." It is a European social attribute or, more specifically, an attribute of the European Union. In the EU, Beck argues, borders do not "close off" cosmopolitan spaces but instead create them. This notion is much contested, however. For Brennan (1997), cosmopolitanism is American as much as European, although American cosmopolitanism is different. Brennan (1997: 308) agrees that American cosmopolitan traditions have at times engaged with the other in ways that are truly open; but more often than not, it is "also jealously supportive of ... American cultural hegemony, an imperial myth about the portable ethos of the United States as an idea." Such a tradition promotes "universalism" and subscription to American values. This universalization, which Beck calls Pax Americana, precludes the development of a truly cosmopolitan society and instead creates a sort of reflexive transnationalism (Beck, 2006). For Beck, Brennan, and others, what often passes for cosmopolitanism is not; the outcomes are made in America and designed to promote the American way. While the ways in which US practices and concepts have been universalized on a global scale are beyond the scope of this volume, we will, however, explore how this process has transpired in terms of Canada–US border metaphors and the border practices thereby generated. This is because seeing cosmopolitanism as a successful outcome is extremely important to our understanding of reflexivity itself.

Because of the relationship between openness or cosmopolitanism and othering or bordering, I prefer the concept of "reflexive transnationalism" rather than "anti-Americanism" or "anti-Canadianism," and I prefer to discuss border relations with reference to cosmopolitan or critical cosmopolitan theory (Delanty, 2009). While Canada has not been occupied by the United States, like Iraq, nor has it been made an official dependency like Puerto Rico, there is still an American presence in the Canada–US relationship that goes beyond the bounds of normal relations between states. When it comes to understanding what has happened along (or rather because of) the Canada–US borderline and the institutionalized power relationships it narrates, the idea of reflexive transnationalism better captures the way in which nationalism has been constructed and connected by borderlines. It also allows us to see North America, and its borderlands and security agendas (including moments of US and Canadian mutual antipathy), as part of a relatively normative process. This process has created a shifting, reflexive and evolving, and increasingly global twenty-first-century geopolitical narrative, rather than some kind of dysfunctional aberration or deviation from an "ideal" bilateral relationship as Granatstein would hold (1996). Indeed, as Brennan (1997) and Harvey (2009) remind us, we cannot embrace the idea of cosmopolitanism as a US or EU goal without also encountering a cosmopolitan world of retrenching nationalisms.

Why this book now? It is a response to the fact that a tremendous amount of literature has been produced over the past decade or so in response to the Canada–US relationship, particularly since 9/11. Much of this work has focused strongly on "functional outcomes," such as the development of new security protocols or emerging national security threats. In focusing mainly on these issues, the Canada–US relationship is viewed in ways that belie its historical complexity. Often the product of think tanks and commissions reflecting the viewpoints of particular stakeholders, US security perspectives are increasingly seen as normative, standard-setting, and "best practice," for managing North American border relations. Instead of questioning US security hegemony and its underlying motives, however, we increasingly see Canada–US border arrangements in normative ways, on a fairly shallow time horizon, and in terms of fairly limited policy-oriented goals designed to resolve immediate post-9/11 problems. Still, there has been considerable work focusing on how the border embeds both meaning and identity in contradictory ways (Helleiner, 2009; Nicol, 2012) and through the lens of critical theory (Walters, 2006). As a result, the current Canada–US border, which is often treated through the lens of "applied" studies, has been met by a critique concerning technologies, discourses, geopolitics, and security. In contrast to the literature concerned with pragmatics, or with defining and rationalizing recent security agendas, a more critical scholarship situates Canada–US border security in broader governmental and bilateral relations and examines the governance rationales and logics of new security spaces in North America (Muller, 2010; Konrad and Nicol, 2008). There is also a growing interest in borders as a result of the work of those engaged in understanding security and securitization in Canadian contexts, from scholars like Côté-Boucher (2008), Bell (2006, 2011), and Salter (2008). Meanwhile, critical security studies undertaken by Muller (2010), Magnet (2011), Walters (2006), and others, explore issues of borders and biometrics in North American contexts, again speaking to the impacts of exceptionality and securitization. So if for much of the "normative" school of border experts, the border is something that must be managed, controlled, and presented as a functional site whose meaning is uncontested; a new and sustained critique of this approach is also emerging.

This book takes the more critical approach. It asks what I believe are the "right" questions, and it questions what traditional scholarship has long taken to be the "right" answers. We begin with the premise that the security motifs that are now attached to the Canada–US border are but the most recent manifestations of a much longer process through which the meaning of borders shift over time (Donnan and Wilson, 1999) and through which a changing roster of broader geopolitical narratives are referenced (Agnew, 2003). They have developed and evolved at different points over time and have become part of a larger mosaic, or quilt, whose patches have been stitched together to create a new design. Yet the pieces are familiar, like bits and pieces taken from clothing utilized in the past and recycled into new patterns. As we will see, many of the security motifs that currently characterize perceptions of the Canada–US border have precedents in Canada–US border management strategies; indeed, they restate in different terms the discourses and metaphors of border relations from earlier periods. Many of these have roots dating back not just years or decades but in some cases centuries. They are part of an evolving North American geopolitical logic, or what Depledge (2013), Dittmer and colleagues (2011), and Stuhl (2013) would call a geopolitical "assemblage"—that is, a collection of shifting thoughts, narratives, discourses, representations, and histories that orient how borders are perceived, how they function, and what they mean. The themes of free trade, illegal immigration, cross-border crime, terrorism, and territorial sovereignty, for example, may read like a laundry list of current cross-border relations, but they have also always been important and constituent building blocks of the Canada–US relationship (see Granatstein, 1996; Lee, 2002; Thompson and Randall, 1994; Woodcock, 1989).

The ongoing geopolitical imaginings of generations of Canadians and Americans, popularized in political texts, newspapers and editorial cartoons, literature, film, television, and other discourses, reflect these deep roots. That said, while the understandings of what constitute the existential threats of our time may be unique in terms of their referent objects and themes, they are not so unique in terms of the "othering" and "securing" processes they reflect. There is a "déjà vu" quality to much of the Canada–US border security discourse. For example, Americans are more concerned than Canadians about "illegal" Mexican immigration and potential terrorist infiltration. A century or so ago, it was the common fear of "Oriental immigration" and of other non–Anglo Saxon immigrants that created unease and prohibitive border security legislation. Today, "Orientalism" (Said, 1978) still exists in North America, but instead of Chinese and Japanese bearing the near total brunt of inflammatory racist constructions, Middle Eastern and Mexican ethnicities (Magnet, 2011) have been constructed as "problematic" by border discourses. This is a response both to high levels of undocumented migration and to the enhanced risk of terrorist activity in the early twentieth-first century.

How can we understand these commonalities and differences in geopolitical ways? One is by looking more closely and critically at how threats and differences are represented. This includes examining texts and illustrations generated by politicians, policy-makers, scholars, the media, and others. The metaphors used to describe, illustrate, and cartoon borders bring to light the reflexive nature of the Canada–US affairs. Those metaphors situate this political relationship in context of the larger geopolitical rationales that sustain North American territory and sovereignty arrangements (Laxer, 2003). But these metaphors are also important for how they critique continental power and hegemony. They help us understand why, for example, border walls are believed to be necessary. They also indicate for whose security those walls have been constructed, and how biopolitics intersects with geopolitics, by asking whose management directives are embedded in border security arrangements, or, are "best practices" best, and for whom?

THEORETICAL APPROACHES

Today, Canada and the United States cooperate on cross-border security and negotiate security threats by utilizing existing institutions or creating new ones. The Canada–US border is now mainly a location or even a testing ground for implementing security measures. But the border was not always covered by security agreements, nor was it seen in terms of being a front line against terrorism and criminality in the way it is today. The border's meaning and functions have developed over more than two centuries. In fact, in North America, the border between Canada and the United States began as a vague geopolitical "frontier" that divided the interests of European nation-states from each other, and its evolution into a security barrier by the late twentieth and early twenty-first century was dramatic and even violent. North American borders have been transformed from mere lines on a map into fences and walls on the ground and into sites of securitization with cogent national meaning (Salter, 2006, 2008). Indeed, the Canada–U.S border today can be seen as a multi-faceted institution, or anchor, for a bundle of related security technologies and institutions (Walters, 2006). In this sense, the Canada–US border is not, even today, an *a priori* security institution, fully developed to mediate existing security threats. Rather, it is the still-evolving institutionalized outcome of boundary-making processes and is continually being modified by those processes (Popescu, 2012: 24; Konrad and Nicol, 2008).

Furthermore, the functions of border security and the implementation of security technologies today are highly site-specific as well as sensitive to context. North American borders have developed quite differently from those of the EU, for example. Why is this so? Some scholars argue that there are very specific organizational reasons for these differences (Brunet-Jailly et al., 2006; Farson, 2006); others suggest that the reasons have to do with American hegemonic control of globalization and that "empire building" has been key to North American security responses in the late twentieth and early twenty-first centuries (see Beck, 2006; Nicol, 2005, 2006, 2011, 2012). Moreover, the border is an institution as well as a site, an agent and an object of security, which complicates things. Borders contribute to the construction of security discourses through their collective agency and their function as security actors. Borders are also the *prima facie* object of securitization and the place where such securitization takes place, which creates spaces of exceptionality (Salter 2006; 2008). Borders may be lines on the ground or sites within a territory, or they may pass through the body of any given individual who is treated by contemporary technology as an assemblage of codes and risk probabilities. As such, borders both hide and define power; they exclude and include simultaneously (see Popescu, 2012). They have no agency because they are inanimate sites, yet they have as much agency as if they were actors themselves, through the power of social and political constructions.

Because there are various complicated understandings of the role, function, and significance of borders, as well as different ways of understanding how borders figure into the territorialization of nation-states, it is worthwhile to explore how borders function in terms of normative political theory, as well as the limits of doing so. By "normative" theories, I mean institutional, realist, and constructivist theories as encountered in political science and international relations. Beylerian and Lévesque (2004) argue that from the perspective of international relations, "institutionalist theory considers that the principal powers use security institutions to gain tangible advantages" (2004: 9). This means that security institutions exchange information with regard to defining a "threat" (ibid.) and what constitutes its remediation. Popescu (2012: 24) argues that understanding borders using an institutional approach will reveal "the multiple and changing meaning of borders in different historical and spatial circumstances [because] borders as institutions develop their own history."

It is through an institutionalized, policy-related understanding of borders that the image of the border as a security apparatus has gained so much recent traction. In the case of Canada and the United States, it is clear that security institutions have done prominent work in developing the meaning and establishing the functions of the post-9/11 border. The Canada–US border is seen as a threat, but that threat is mediated by security discussions and cross-border communications. All of this has been institutionalized through border agreements and cooperating departments, leading to the most recent round of "Beyond the Border" negotiations.

Moreover, if in the process of developing security arrangements between Canada and the United States, an institution-building discourse has been adopted, its outcome has been to soften the edges of the hard realities of power asymmetry and hegemonic relations currently existing between the two nations, recasting these arrangements as important deterrents to those who would do harm. For example, the Canadian and US governments have both produced online texts that portray current border security arrangements as mutually beneficial and as "harmless" to the general public. There is, here, a degree of bravado and congratulatory discourse, in that these same texts speak of integrated border management teams working together with the Canadian Border Services Agency (CBSA) and the US Border Patrol (USBP), while state and provincial police coordinate across the border.

But institutional approaches do not exhaust the ways in which the Canada–US border can be understood. There is still room for conventional international relations theory, which focuses on the *realpolitik* of security, and there is still a need for insights obtained from post-structural and deconstructive critiques of the geopolitics of border building. Realist discourses, for example, remain important. They situate border-making within well-defined state interests and presume that state agencies and actors respond and act in light of them. They also generate state-centred narratives.

But can we take the interests they examine at face value, thus furthering the idea that monolithic, power-oriented geopolitics is a "human condition"? Probably not. This is why critical post-structural and constructivist approaches set out to "unpack" the certainties surrounding the meaning of space and place and recast power as a narrative that is both cultural and politically constructed. The latter approach contributes to our understanding of how narratives of power and border, and their corresponding representations, are often reifications of wishful thinking. Their deconstruction also helps us consider how, in recent times, a coupling of border management and security, or a "security/border" nexus, has formed to replace other ontologies of border function and meaning. In North America today, for example, borders are increasingly closed, and the tipping of the balance of power from open to closed borders is surely rooted in a geopolitical narrative that reinforces the idea that there are two worlds: the one "inside" and the one "outside" national spaces. But this was not always the case. North American borders have, in the past, been relatively open and indeed have facilitated high levels of immigration and large flows of goods and products with the encouragement of state-centred agencies. Clearly, then, the current realist border narrative is one of many.

This leads us to the idea of using constructivist and critical analysis. A critical approach to issues of power and security enables us to look more closely at the landscape through which security discourses and security institutions have been constructed, to deconstruct them and to see how they have became dominant ways of analyzing borders. Why for example, do we insist that we have "open borders" in the early twenty-first century, even as undocumented immigration and detention grows by leaps and bounds? Deconstruction through a critical lens requires not just the evidence of political texts, but everyday texts as well, the banal evidence of newspapers and cartoons. These represent a different way of seeing.

Given these differences in theoretical approaches, although we do not adopt a specific international relations theory in this book, we do acknowledge that a combination of institutional, realist, and constructivist approaches is very useful; see, for example, Beylerian and Lévesque (2004). Our discussions proceed mainly from the point of view of a "critical geopolitics" approach. But exactly what is meant by "critical geopolitics"? Clearly, it is not a "normative" international relations theory.

Critical geopolitics acknowledges the realist and institutional ramifications of international relations but relies on a critical reading of those relations. In this sense, it is a constructivist approach that acknowledges the limitations of normative theories. Political geographers (Dalby and Ó Tuathail, 2002: 3) go so far as to suggest that a critical understanding of geopolitics explores "the spatial practices, both material and representational, of statecraft itself." In other words, it is not a prescriptive approach or mindset based on empirical and objective criteria but rather a way of seeing how geopolitical narratives have profoundly spatial consequences. Moreover, geopolitics "engages the geographical representations and practices that produce the spaces of world politics" (2). In this sense, a critical geopolitics approach lends itself very well to understanding the representational elements of geopolitical discourses and the identities and world views on which they draw (Ingram and Dodds, 2009). Indeed, as Flint (2006) reminds us, such discourses are ongoing encodings of the world, which, although they promote meaningful and commonly accepted perceptions, are often incredibly self-serving as far as nations and international relations are concerned. Take the Bush administration's "War on Terror," which relied on colourful images, extreme rhetoric, and fear mongering to make its foreign policies palpable. Clearly, these representations were rooted in both perception and power and were subjective in their self-conscious and self-referenced understandings ("whoever is not with us is against us"), all of which fostered a course of thinking and of action that translated easily into foreign policy (Flint, 2006; Nicol, 2011). Two important outcomes of this process were the geopolitical discourse itself and its prescription for action. Both were revealing, for their assumptions about power, gender, race, and civilization were ones that we take for granted, act out in our daily lives, and support in the ballot box and online (Ingram and Dodds, 2009). But this understanding of geopolitical processes is rather different from we might have encountered only a few decades ago. In the nineteenth and early twentieth centuries, it was believed that geopolitics could be understood as "scientific" and "rational." Today, most of those who study geopolitics are no longer bent on discovering essential truths about the relationship between geography and security; instead, they assess the world and its peoples in an attempt to understand how politics are naturalized and "essentialized." Geopolitics today is a critical, deconstructive field of study. Building on Dalby and Ó Tuathail (2002: 2), we can define it as a field that critiques "normative" foreign policy-making: "we begin from the premise that geopolitics is itself a form of geography and politics, that it has a con-textuality, and that it is implicated in the ongoing social reproduction of power and political economy. In short, our perspective is a critical one, our practice a critical geopolitics."

Like other contemporary critical geographers (see Agnew, 2003; Depledge 2013; Dodds, 2007; Ingram and Dodds, 2009; Flint, 2006), Ó Tuathail and colleagues (1998) insist that critical geopolitics remains relevant and important, even though the "poster child" era of geopolitical thought (i.e., the Cold War) has ended. They have arrived at this conclusion in response to the popularized belief, dating back to the early 1990s, that geopolitics itself has gone the way of the Cold War and the Cold Warriors themselves, in that it represents an outdated understanding of the relationship between geography and politics, one that saw the world as divided into strategic places that were differentially valued in terms of their location and resources. Today, no one would argue that politics are geographically determined, but this does not mean that the geopolitical perspective is irrelevant. Instead, geopolitics has retained its importance, but as a critical field rather than a prescriptive one. Indeed, Agnew (2003) suggests that geopolitics has endured beyond the Cold War years because it is now informed by post-structural scholarship. He argues that while "the term geopolitics has long been used to refer to the study of the geographical representations, rhetoric and practices that underpin world politics ... the term is now used freely to refer to such phenomena as international boundary disputes, the structure of global finance, and the geographical patterns of election results" (5). Building on this understanding of the analytical value of geopolitical approaches, he has argued that we should expropriate the term "geopolitics" and ascribe to it "a more specific meaning: examination of geographical assumptions, designations and understandings that enter into the making of world politics" (ibid.).

Kuus (n.d.) reinforces this perspective. She suggests that critical geopolitics "approaches geopolitics not as a neutral consideration of pre-given 'geographical' facts, but as a deeply ideological and politicized form of analysis." It is because of the importance of geopolitics in constructing borders as a discursive phenomenon or relationship that I begin this study by outlining the perspective of critical geopolitics. Critical geopolitics affords a vantage point for reviewing some of the "taken for granted" understandings we have about Canadian, American, and indeed North American integration more generally. It is a great leveller, for it decouples the linked assumptions that represent the power and territorial relationships we are familiar with today, exposing them not as facts but as at times hegemonic discourses or even wishful thinking. As such, a critical geopolitics approach is a more robust way of identifying and assessing how "realist" national narratives are constructed to serve specific interests in ways that further authorize unequal understandings of power. Such geopolitical approaches are thus highly critical of the state, even if they privilege state-centred analysis. Kuus writes: "In terms of the state, the key questions to address are not about the 'real' sources, meanings or limits of state sovereignty in some general or universal sense, but, more specifically, about how state power is discursively and practically produced in territorial and non-territorial forms … The task is to decentre but not to write off state power by examining its incoherencies and contradictions." This approach, which Kuus so succinctly defines, opens the door to an understanding of the complex influences and contexts in which border making is situated, because from a critical geopolitics perspective, borders are not simply state lines or objective "facts" but ongoing ideological, national, and even hegemonic understandings and assumptions about territorial spaces and the processes that produce such spaces. (This will become clearer in Chapter 2, which explores the concept of Manifest Destiny as a hegemonic American boundary discourse through a critical geopolitics lens.)

Along these same lines, Ingram and Dodds (2009) suggest that "critical geopolitics is a most important and increasingly suggestive area of inquiry, unfolding at the conjuncture of social theory, political geography, international relations and cultural studies" (xi), while Depledge (2013), speaking more generally about this type interaction as a way of seeing and knowing, calls the result an "entanglement" of perspectives and practices, or an "assemblage."

It is this understanding of geopolitics as an approach rather than a set of nomothetic theories, as a series of assemblages of locutionary and political activities and practices or a suggestive type of inquiry rather than a methodology, that is adopted in this book, and it is one that builds on the ground broken by many others whose geopolitical theories inform contemporary boundary work (see Ó Tuathail, 1992, 2000; Agnew, 2003; Ó Tuathail and Agnew, 1992; Dalby, 2008; Flint, 2006; Dodds, 2007; Newman and Paasi, 1998; Depledge, 2013; Ingram and Dodds, 2009; Dittmer et al., 2011). And as Dalby (2008) tells us, it is high time—there are indeed "imperial themes … in need of criticism" that have "proliferated in the current decade." Among the most important of these are "the link between geographical specifications of cultural identity, and the invocation of specific geographies of danger linked to matters of military strategy" (415). Dalby is referring here, of course, to arrangements concerning "security" that have proliferated since the "War on Terror" discourse emerged late in the twentieth century. So it is important to combine a critical reading of borders and geopolitics with a critical reading of securitization (see Chapters 5 and 6).

Following this same vein of thought, we also need to tip our hat to the seminal work of Ingram and Dodds (2009), whose understanding of how popular cultures, perceptions, security concerns, and foreign policies relate to one another has also been groundbreaking. In discussing the link between representation and geopolitical thought, Ingram and Dodds suggest that geopolitics is an active process, one through which "the geographical complexity and richness of the world gets reduced to schematic spatial templates … Critical geopolitics has not only explored how those templates are embedded within foreign policy and security discourses, but also how they reverberate through popular culture and particular media such as films, newspapers, cartoons, and television" (4).

Representations, as Ingram and Dodds remind us, shed light on how geopolitical discourses are normalized and given broader societal meaning. So another important advantage to a critical geopolitical approach is that it allows us to examine how geopolitical templates "reverberate through popular culture and particular media" so that we can challenge our own deeply rooted logic about "causality." Critical geopolitics problematizes assumptions about the "bipolar world" and "globalization" and asks "Why now?" and "Why here?" It links geopolitical templates, both textual (newspaper stories, political speeches) and representational (political cartoons, films, TV news), to broader discourses that render the world intelligible.

THE BIG PICTURE

What do we mean by "a broader discourse that renders the world intelligible"? Agnew (2003) suggests that geopolitical narratives and strategies must be understood in the context of the intellectual and technological characteristics of their time, with reference to orienting discourses that generated overarching belief systems, explanations of facts, and even truth itself. The intellectual paradigms, world views, and ontological frameworks of any time period are reflected in the dominant narratives of societies themselves (even though societies are neither uniform nor monolithic in terms of beliefs). Building on this understanding, Agnew argues that there have been at least three great geopolitical "ages," each of them linked to the emergence of dominant civilizational and ideological narratives that informed the foreign policies of powerful nations. Each of these ages had at its foundation normative attitudes about geography, foreign relations, society, and indeed knowledge itself. Each era reflected specific widespread discourses that oriented ontological "truths" regarding the world order and the meaning of life.

For example, those who conducted geopolitics in the "Age of Civilization" understood the world as a field for imprinting empire, and the political map as an outcome of power whose expression was justified by theology, race, and superior military technology. In the late nineteenth century, as social Darwinism captured the geopolitical imagination, power relations among states were viewed as reflecting the natural order, which was understood to be based on "survival of the fittest." In later decades, international relations would be infused with ideological beliefs about the "free" versus the "communist" world. Similarly, Agnew argues, the geopolitical era that followed the Cold War saw the emergence of new understandings of world politics (Agnew, 2003).

Today, neoliberalism is generally accepted as the dominant discourse in international relations and as increasingly informing border institutions and technologies (see Sparke, 2006; Ó Tuathail and Luke, 1998; Herod, Ó Tuathail, and Roberts, 1998; de Goede, 2008; Agnew, 2005). There is a renewed focus on US centrality and global capitalism, as well as an assumption that the United States will remain the political and economic fulcrum in a new era that is no longer divided into two opposing ideological camps (Agnew, 2005).

Yet it is also now very clear that assumptions about US centrality have also been manufactured by American think tanks, politicians, and even academics, just as much as they reflect a consensus among students of political geography and international relations, among international governments, and even in popular perceptions. US hegemony, then, is an ongoing socio-political construction. It is also highly contradictory, in that it is based on ideas that authorize policies that legitimize thinking violently about the "clash of civilizations" and the "War on Terror" even while they validate the notion that the United States is a peace-loving nation and a "beacon" for the world.

A CRITICAL GEOPOLITICS OF US HEGEMONY

The idea of the United States as a moral beacon has been prominent for the past half century. As we apply a critical geopolitical perspective to the Canada–US border, we must remain aware that most dominant geopolitical understandings of the current world order today—those that postulate a Pax Americana—are Ameri-centric, that is to say, they are discourses that position the United States as the moral and political centre of a system with almost no significant competition. Generally, it is Americans who construct these discourses, although non-Americans tend to reinforce them through powerful media and political narratives. For example, this is evident in the way in which, in the first decade of the twenty-first century, these "realist" assessments have uncritically embraced the "clash of civilizations" (Huntington, 1996) and the "War on Terror" as hegemonic discourses in international relations. Bear in mind, though, that while these discourses produce the context for understanding international relations in terms of American hegemony, they may also be contributing to resistance to that hegemony. Why? To better understand the practice and meaning of hegemony in this context, we need to examine its foundational concepts more closely.

Antonio Gramsci (1973), whose writings were seminal in this respect, links hegemony to a drive to create intellectuals and elites who speak for classes. The ideology of these elites then fosters a class-based society that is coterminous with the national society. According to Gramsci, the "moment of hegemony" arrives with the growing awareness that one's own corporate interests can transcend the corporate limits of the purely economic class and become the interests of other subordinate groups. Hegemony thus creates a necessary tension between civil society and political societies. For Gramsci, however, achieving hegemony is not always a conflicted process, nor does it necessarily result in armed violence. Rather, it can be understood as values and goals that have been institutionalized so that they become norms that explain and perpetuate hegemonic orders.

So the question is how does hegemony influence civil society, which Gramsci has identified as the "entire complex of social, cultural and political organizations and institutions within a society" (42)? What is hegemonic, not just in domestic contexts but in international ones? How has US hegemony gained traction through the implementation of geopolitical discourses that authorize certain types of power? Are these discourses restricted to the national level—or can they also be larger, an example being the hegemonic order imposed by advanced capitalism on what Agnew (2005) has called "marketplace society"? American marketplace society, he argues, sees hegemony as "the enrolment of others in the exercise of your power, by convincing, cajoling, and coercing them that they should want what you want" (2). For Agnew, globalization is an outcome of US hegemonic marketplace society, which has imposed its territorial logic and socio-economic discipline worldwide. The result has not been hegemonic empire in a military sense, but rather networked hegemony through diffuse practices of globalization. New bordering practices demand harmonization with American standards, thus fostering American hegemony.

Yet there has been historical resistance to this hegemony project. As we will see in Chapters 2 and 3, in the eighteenth and nineteenth centuries, strong national discourses marshalled Canadian resistance to US territorial ambitions (including annexation), and after a struggle, firm borders were created as tools of resistance. Today, of course, while territorial conquest is extremely unlikely, American hegemony is nonetheless being exerted through a multitude of networked cultural, economic, and political institutions and organizations. Borders have become more than just lines or even borderlands; they have come to mean all kinds of transnational agreements, too. The resistance of many Canadians to the Canada–US Free Trade Agreement (FTA) in the late twentieth century, for example, was less about American territorial ambitions than about greater American control of Canadian economic and cultural institutions.

HEGEMONY OR EMPIRE?

In the second decade of the twenty-first century, there is more speculation than ever regarding how "real" American hegemony and empire actually is. The global financial meltdown of 2008 and the apparent decline in US economic power both continue to resonate, although since then recovery has occurred and perceptions of American power are that it is once again strengthening. So it is important to bear in mind, as Agnew (2003) does, that geopolitical ideas are neither absolute truths nor eternal truths. The notion that the United States is the world's leader is not Holy Writ, nor is it carved in stone, however strongly Americans may believe in "Manifest Destiny." Such seeming truths must be seen in the context of their time and place. The United States became a global power only in the mid-twentieth century, for example, after a series of events that saw the demise of the European empires, two world wars on foreign soil, and the rise of North American military power and economic markets. Its rise also paralleled the rise of neoliberalism as a market and governance strategy, as well as the collapse of the Soviet Union. So this moment in time can be equally well understood as reflecting broader international conditions rather than the outcome of a reality created by a nation's unshakable faith in its destiny as inevitable and unstoppable.

Few would argue, however, that today globalization is not strengthening American power. It seems to be promoting an American empire that embraces all corners of the earth. Agnew (2005) suggests that one reason for the success of what some have called the "American empire" is that the US has changed the nature of the competition upon which global competition has long rested. It brought its home-based focus on economic expansion to bear upon its boundaries. In this sense, since the Second World War, American global hegemony has created a new type of geopolitical age. Agnew sees a new geopolitical map that, even as it centres control on the United States, has also created a series of threats. It is "an emerging geopolitical order dominated by a US attempt at pushing globalization but frustrated by US national economic weaknesses, widespread nostalgia for a putative past of 'secure national territories' (not least in the United States) and an inability to come to terms with non-state adversaries such as global terror networks and drug traffickers" (12).

Agnew's work is part of a trend. US hegemony has been well studied by scholars who understand hegemony as a political project and who advocate hegemonic relations as the basis for world order. A key question addressed by these scholars is whether US hegemony has created an American "empire" (Dalby, 2008; Agnew 2005; Harvey, 2003) or whether the United States is actually in decline. Indeed, critical readings of this era see it alternatively as the US on the rise, in decline, or an era in which the US is challenging all of the rationales on which preceding epochs were based with its network of influence. Some also see the emergence of a border security regime that is differentiated from that of the EU but equally substantive. With regard to this question, Dalby (2008) has explored recent US militaristic ventures, focusing on the formal hard power of hegemony and empire, while Harvey (2003), for his part, suggests that US hegemony is not hard but soft, now primarily economic, fashioned from shifts in the "material basis" of American power that have been under way since the late nineteenth century. This includes, of course, industrialization and economic growth, as well as American deficit difficulties and the contraction of the US economy in the first decade of the twenty-first century: these global growth and contraction patterns stem from what Agnew (2005) sees as the diverse network of American capitalism worldwide. For Agnew, globalization is Americaniza-tion and is a product of American corporations, which have internationalized the world's production and financial systems. Both Harvey and Agnew see the extension of what Gramsci (1973) referred to as "leadership" or even "direction" over civil society based on consent, to be consistent with US domination in international affairs and markets. Harvey (2003), in particular, believes the latter to be particularly consistent with Gramsci's concept of hegemony as "political power exercised as domination through coercion. On other occasions it seems to refer to the particular mix of coercion and consent embedded in the exercise of political power" (36).

This mix of coercion and consent, or even domination, has also been explained as an increasing tendency towards unilateralism on the part of the American state (Adamson, 2005). In the twenty-first century, a new literature has emerged that links US unilateralism to broader processes of empire building, imperialism, and globalization. This literature was spurred into existence by the rise of the Asian economies as well as by new challenges to American economic and military power in the late twentieth and early twenty-first centuries (Agnew, 2005; Harvey, 2003; Hardt and Negri, 2000). Hardt and Negri, for example, explore the emergence of empires representing a coalition of powers, leading to an empire that cannot be contained by a single nation-state.

So despite significant consensus on American might post-9/11, by no means do all agree on the concept of empire. There is disagreement about what empire means, even among those who evoke the term. David Harvey (2003) suggests that in the case of the United States, "empire" means neither world government nor territorial control but rather the exercise of economic power on a deterritorialized basis—power that is diffuse, dispossessing, and ultimately imperialistic. For him, globalization and imperialism reflect networked control resulting from the configuration of American capitalism and political power, exercised through global institutions.

Like Beck (2006) and Agnew (2005), David Harvey suggests that the basis for US hegemony is a view of the world that does not seek to address global problems in a cosmopolitan sense (i.e., by creating a common sense of investment in global problems and solutions among all nations); rather, it seeks to reduce issues to those of American national interest so as to extend and embed American marketplace norms worldwide. This reflects a general societal model rather than a military project. Civil society is thereby instrumentalized and expanded through the ideal of "consumer society." Overall, Harvey (2003), Hardt and Negri (2000), Agnew (2005), and others argue that in today's world, "hard" territorial control is unnecessary. Global capitalism has created the conditions for domination or even "dispossession"—for a virtual empire, so to speak. A variety of managerial, financial, and institutional arrangements exist to strengthen the hegemony of the advanced Western powers, specifically the US and the EU but especially the former. These arrangements include the World Bank and the International Monetary Fund (IMF), both US creations, the North Atlantic Treaty Organization (NATO), and the World Trade Organization (WTO). In fact, Harvey suggests that this institutional hegemony developed hand in hand with "capital bondage" over the last three decades of the twentieth century.

Thus, there is a consensus of sorts that promoting global capitalism—now generally seen as an increasingly US-based process—has done much to shape an American imperialism, more so than for any other nation. The coupling of neoliberalism with hegemony has created the dynamic force of US global power and interest as the foundation for current mappings of power and territory. For Hurrell (2005), US hegemony can best be understood, historically, as one means of achieving "order through hierarchy, hegemony, or even empire" (158). But even Hurrell acknowledges its limitations, arguing that the concept of American "empire" may not be the best way of understanding or positioning current US hegemony, at least not in the classic sense that empire involves hard military power and direct territorial control. Hurrell argues instead that "it is analytically more useful to understand the United States as a hegemonic rather than an imperial power, because doing so forces the analyst to focus directly on the crucial questions of negotiation, legitimacy, and 'followership'" (153). Yet he understands that "hegemony" can have important structural results: "Compared with empire, hegemony is commonly seen as a shallower and less intrusive mode of control" (153). Moreover, the structural forces "which have pushed the United States towards deeper and more intrusive involvement are likely to continue to complicate the exercise of U.S. power" (153).

TECHNOLOGIES OF EMPIRE

Despite points of divergence with respect to the perspective of "empire" and its meaning, there is a consensus that neoliberalism, with its cross-border hegemony, has contributed greatly to US economic and security domination in the early twenty-first century. So it is necessary to understand how border technology has become instrumental in managing security and perceptions of security in ways that promote both hegemonic and strong neoliberal agendas. In other words, we need to examine not just the technical programs that promote objective and normative security results, but also how these programs advance specific geopolitical and geo-economic agendas, recognizing that borders are rapidly becoming a particular type of security technology. Popescu (2012) argues that border "security" is nowadays derived from the utilization of a series of machines that read encoded data in passports, manifests, and ID cards; from technologies that detect radioactive materials, contraband, and human cargoes; and from electronic data-sharing systems that identify suspect individuals or that track cargoes and people who cross borders. These technologies, where introduced, require new border infrastructure as well as new institutional arrangements for implementation, enforcement, and management. Flows of individuals, goods and services, money, and information are all being filtered, monitored, and tracked across borders. Indeed, since 9/11, flows of people, goods, and services have all become so vulnerable to all concerns generated in the arena of international relations that border policies are now the equivalent of foreign policies in many ways.

For academics engaged in the critical analysis of contemporary Canada–US border arrangements, the work of scholars like Deleuze (1990) and Foucault (2007) has provided an important analytical lens for understanding how border technologies affect individuals and societies. According to Sohoni, for example, Foucault asked how we understand what we know, describing how "discourses"—that is, ways of thinking and talking about topics—shape what constitutes "knowledge" at particular historical times. For Foucault, however, discourses are not closed systems of meaning; rather, they draw upon meanings and values constructed by other discourses. Foucault (2007) also stresses that what we consider "knowledge" reflects the power of individuals or groups to determine cultural meanings" (Sohoni, 2006: 828).

Following from Foucault, those who deconstruct border security practices tend to focus on the diffuse agency of security as it is enacted through new technologies, including biopolitical technologies that inscribe individuals' information into larger data sets. This approach signals a break with past readings of border management and mobility as well as with "disciplinary society" as Foucault defined it. Indeed, Walters (2006) argues that new technologies have brought about a new mode of political agency and governance by implementing what he calls a "control society."

For Canadians, Walters is describing a control and hegemony that is almost entirely embedded in US border security writ large, making it diffuse and networked and extending its reach to all corners of North America. This means that in matters of border management, US hegemony has come to exert territorial control over extraterritorial spaces in North America. Why? Because the new technologies, being one-size-fits-all, tend to universalize the security practices and concerns of well-developed states like the U.S, making their security agenda and rules global. Consider here the "no-fly lists" and passenger manifests that have been introduced to North America (see Konrad and Nicol, 2008; Walters, 2006; Muller, 2010). Consider also the biometric data and machine-readable information chips that are currently being inscribed into passports and driver's licences, the harmonization of visa requirements, and the development of "best practices" at a growing number of jointly policed Canada–US border posts.

So a new spatiality has come to be associated with control society. This is why we need to take pains when positioning US hegemony as "territorial empire" or "network of influence." The idea advanced here that the United States is a hegemonic power rather than an imperial one addresses recent developments in border technologies as well as grand geopolitical narratives at the global level. As any number of scholars have pointed out (Walters, 2006; Nicol, 2011; Popescu, 2012), new border technologies tend to deterritorialize border control—they can be implemented at sites like airports or secure zones outside borderlands (including detention centres), and they foster harmonization and standardization. They build on the understanding that power is diffuse, that it is embedded in spatially diffuse social networks and practices, and that it is strongly linked to communications and information technologies (rather than bounded institutional enclosures). These technologies do not seize territory but merely extend it in a number of highly fungible yet real and important ways.

READING THE GEOPOLITICS OF POPULAR CULTURE

Most current critical readings of geopolitics proceed from an appreciation that perceptions, images, and framings of important events are linked in important ways. This book is no exception and argues that those links are strong and perhaps even mutually constitutive. Like Dijkink (1998), it argues that there is very often a correlation between popular values and the foreign policy goals constructed by political elites. Agreement is fomented by the media, and this fosters a convergence of public perceptions and foreign policy. Indeed, it is from the media that many people draw their opinions about foreign policy (see Sharpe, 1996). According to Dijkink, this process creates a sort of "popularized" geopolitics that reinforces the state and its status quo. Television, films, newspapers, and social media—among other sources—all reflect attitudes and perceptions that fuel self-identity, which becomes writ large in terms of both domestic agendas and foreign relations (Dittmer, 2005; Dittmer et al., 2011; Ingram and Dodds, 2009; Dodds, 2007). But these television episodes, films, and other media venues do more than reflect a consensus—they also help *create* consensus, or even "codes" (Flint, 2006). That is, they generate metaphorical and stereotypical representations, images, and attitudes that are shortcuts for the actual "thing." They are sites of production, as Sharpe (1996) suggests in her critical study of *Reader's Digest,* and they are important in large measure because the Gramscian concept of hegemony (see above) relies on popular culture to create a consensus. As Sharpe remind us: "Gramsci understood social norms and rules of behaviour to be reproduced by and through the actions of every person, but not equally" (558). For her, this means there are key institutions that create and maintain the consent of the majority of society and that ensure they conform to the actions of dominant classes. But Sharpe also recognizes that hegemony is a construct rooted not simply in political ideologies, "but more immediately through detailed scripting of all aspects of everyday life" (558). She reminds us that popular culture plays a "significant role" and "any political analysis of the operation of dominance must take full account of the role of institutions of popular culture in the reproduction of cultural (and thus political) norms" (558). Sharpe's analysis challenges the idea that "the location of agency in geopolitics is solely in the hands of intellectuals of statecraft," maintaining instead that "geopolitics is a discursive practice constructed out of cultural norms and standards" (557). In this sense, the "production of discursive practices of geopolitics" can be found outside the "formal area of the state" as well as within (557).

Such discursive practices "do work," as Sharpe (1996), Dodds (2007), and Dittmer (2005) demonstrate. They create consensus or even, as Flint (2006) has argued, contribute to geopolitical "codes" of meaning. These codes, however, can be extremely biased or pejorative (see Flint, 2006), since they do not reflect any geopolitical reality that can be empirically verified, but rather are discourses linked to social practices. Equally important, some geopolitical codes, such as those embodied in cartoons or even fanciful images and metaphors (Dodds, 2007), create "structures of expectation" as Dittmer (2005) describes them, in that they "influence the way readers view the world and locate their own place ... within it" (627). Because they are simple and repeated, they tend to become familiar and uncritically accepted. In this way, the texts and images produced by popular culture represent "one of the ways in which people come to understand their position both within a larger collective identity and within an even broader geopolitical narrative, or script" (626). These structures of expectation thus influence foreign relations and how "others" are viewed.

This is what makes texts and images highly cogent geopolitical venues: they do a great deal to orient popular as well as more schooled perspectives on places and processes. For instance, one remarkably resilient and common perception held by Americans is that Canadian Inuit live in ice or snow houses. This is a recycling of incomplete knowledge and stereotypes acquired from now hoary films and images produced in the early and mid-twentieth century in the United States. *Nanook of the North,* the famous 1922 silent documentary made by Robert J. Flaherty, promoted such stereotypes among Americans, and so do other assessments from earlier and later eras. These have proven to be enduring. For example, in the twenty-first century we see that the Canada–US border has become an important metaphor depicting "danger" in US Congressional border hearings. But it is well to remember that this perception merely reinforces a previously constructed understanding of Canada–US relations that (as we shall see soon) originated in British–American hostilities in the eighteenth and nineteenth centuries, as well as in mid-twentieth-century Hollywood films, where dangerous French trappers were chased by "Mounties" across a snowy wilderness. Today, many accounts in the popular media, including films, television programs, and newspaper articles, portray America's northern neighbour in ways that reinforce rather than challenge such a stereotype. A case in point is the film *Frozen River,* which portrays the Canada–US border as a dangerous, frozen, and uncivilized frontier, complete with police chases and backwoods criminality. Such visions have often been accessed and reinforced in post-9/11 texts that portray the "northern" border as "dangerous." Contrast this with the meaning of border in the Canadian film *Gunless,* in which the border, instead of depicting a dangerous frontier, reflects a place of entry into a more civilized realm than the United States and its Wild West: the Dominion of Canada. You can begin to see how divergent border stories have embedded specific meanings and identity narratives.

Today, both "defensive expansionism" and "Manifest Destiny"—two themes we identify as powerful national constructions of the meaning of the Canada–US border—remain important influences in border scholarship as well as in popularized understandings of cross-border relations, border management, and border security. Although less shrilly advocated than in previous eras, these still amount to national discourses concerning sovereignty and state, and indeed they reify the category of "state as actor" for each. Even in an era of globalization and fast-tracked neoliberal interactions between the two nations, these discourses continue to provide both identity and "othering" contexts for Canada–US relations. Because of this, our discussion of the Canada–US border will, in the chapters to follow, begin with a historical and critical understanding of how the border relationship was constructed in the nineteenth century and how it has encouraged separate nationalisms in North America, even while it has celebrated the "joining" of these nationalisms in borderland spaces. As much as possible, we will be accessing evidence provided by "structures of expectation" and popularized accounts to highlight how hegemonic national discourses were constructed from geopolitical events and how these informed different understandings of the meaning of border. This is because, as Sharpe (1996), Dodds (2007) and Dittmer (2005, 2011), in particular, remind us, hegemony is rooted in everyday understandings and practices, both political and representational.

COSMOPOLITANISM AND NORTH AMERICAN BORDERS

We now need to consider how the Canada–US border can be understood as a reflexive and transnational site—as not just dividing but joining. In this regard, we need to return to the idea of cosmopolitanism introduced earlier in this chapter to consider what "cosmopolitanism" is and its relevance for the study of North American borders. The idea of cosmopolitanism was developed by the ancient Greeks but more recently, and famously, by Immanuel Kant through his concept of universal community. Recent debates in the European literature, particularly with reference to the EU, view cosmopolitanism as a European idea (Rumford, 2008; Beck, 2006; Beck and Grande 2007; Delanty, 2009; Harvey, 2009). The concept of cosmopolitanism has been injected into borderland studies through Balibar (2002) in particular, with his writings about methodological nationalism and "polysemic" borders. A general understanding has developed that Europe is cosmopolitan or is embarked on a cosmopolitan project (Beck and Grande, 2007), whereas the United States is not and has not (Beck, 2006), or has done so to a lesser extent. David Harvey (2009) and Rumford (2008) challenge both these assertions, suggesting that the United States is more cosmopolitan than generally supposed (see also Brennan, 1997) and that the EU may be less so, or that the idea of cosmopolitanism itself is fraught. Nonetheless, Beck's (2006) and Brennan's (1997) understanding that there is something different about how the United States engages with the globe is captured in the argument that decades if not centuries of "Pax Americana" represent a one-way universalism rather than a truly global encounter with others.

Harvey disagrees, however, both with Beck's universalism and his definition of cosmopolitanism. Harvey (2009) argues that Beck's cosmopolitanism represents a form of neoliberal globalization, but, like Rumford (2008), he is skeptical about most cosmopolitan theorists. Indeed, according to Harvey we might better understand American cosmopolitanism as an anti-cosmopolitan force (Harvey, 2003; Beck, 2006; Brennan, 1997). Similarly, Rumford (2008) and Delanty (2009) suggest that we develop a critical cosmopolitanism, in part to explore the surprising and unexpected areas where different worlds engage and to situate new spaces of cosmopolitanism, although neither discusses the issue of European–North American differences directly. While its central focus is historical and geopolitical, this book will, in the final analysis, attempt to argue that cosmopolitanism in North America has historically been an American state-centred socio-political process that also and inevitably facilitates US hegemony. As such, it is an extremely useful way to position some of the transnational influences and assemblages that characterize Canada–US cross-border relations and imagery, especially with reference to the way in which Beck has positioned cosmopolitanism and "Pax Americana." In other words, cosmopolitanism provides a useful vehicle for examining how hegemony has been articulated and interacts with transnational narratives of American power and influence.

ORGANIZATION OF THE BOOK

To engage with these questions, in this book we examine Canada–US border relations and practices beginning from the premise that North American borders need to be understood from a critical geopolitical lens, one that questions the political assumptions reflected in present-day border security. In Chapter 1, we examine the late-eighteenth- and nineteenth-century border relationship between Canada and the United States. Around that time, notions that the border was a "wall" emerged to serve an important purpose, which was to recast Canada–US relations in reflexive and dialectical ways so that the border was more than a flimsy barrier to US continental expansion (which is how American geopolitical rhetoric had defined it). In its alternative metaphorical role as wall, door, and line, the Canada–US border has evolved both in response to and in cooperation with American imperatives. Its creation was not simply the result of treaties, judicial agreements, and the occasional border skirmish. Intertwined in this development were the force of US Manifest Destiny sentiment, the desire to annex Canada, resistance to that desire, and (eventually) the burgeoning imperatives of free trade and continental markets.

Chapter 2 examines how borders contributed to hegemonic relations in North America. Borders did not simply set the terms for identity, citizenship, and inclusion; they also helped establish the need to control populations and develop and enforce exclusionary policies. The rise of naturalized geopolitics as a national discourse reinvented the Canada–US relationship and has strongly influenced immigration and profiling practices to this day. As they established a naturalized geopolitical discourse, Canadians and Americans reassessed their relationship, which had previously been based on classic geopolitical struggles for territory, framed by civilizational discourses that encouraged "othering." "Othering" was now to take place along racial lines, and meanwhile, a complex set of metaphors defined the border as a site where the two nations were divided yet simultaneously "sutured" together (see Berland, 2009).

Chapter 3 is about the economic border between Canada and the United States, which, in the late nineteenth and early twentieth centuries, divided the two nations in terms of their national economies. This was the precursor to today's "smooth" or cooperative border (Chapter 4), which reorganized border management to referee the conflict between immigration and trade by establishing border management institutions, which in turn involved a broad set of discourses for promoting harmonious and cooperative relations. This chapter examines how twentieth-century security arrangements promoted a "borderless" North America for defence and market integration purposes. It positions the NAFTA and the rise of neoliberalism as forerunners of the present-day post-9/11 securitization initiatives.

Chapter 5 examines the interplay between border management and security by deconstructing the discourses that have led to the problematization of the Canada–US border since 9/11. A "dangerous Canada" discourse has been fostered with the goal of strengthening US-defined security measures along the line. Chapter 6 explores the twenty-first-century border in the post-9/11 era, during which a multitude of new technologies are pushing the border back into neighbouring spaces. This has required close cooperation and data sharing. Such technologies had changed perceptions about border control; indeed, they are challenging the very notion of borders. Post-9/11 border practices and management regimes have become embedded in US hegemony and in more general practices of "control" with regard to North American cross-border relationships (Walters, 2006).

Chapter 7 addresses reflexive nationalism, globalization, Pax America, and, ultimately, hegemony. It describes how the Canada–US border has contributed to an ongoing relationship of hegemony and resistance, a relationship that has so far bedevilled US attempts to thoroughly control North America. This "continentalism," in tandem with the broader tenets of "Pax Americana," has precluded the development of a North American cosmopolitan vision.

Chapter 8 summarizes the book, arguing that the border had always been a site of US hegemonic "impulses." The border is a hegemonic institution, one that over the past two centuries has been transformed in ways that promote an unequal relationship and that discourage more open, mutually representative arrangements for national security.

This book has its limits, and it is well to acknowledge them. It does not analyze European cosmopolitanism in depth; instead it evaluates different versions of it as they have been developed in the literature (see, for example, Beck, 2006; Rumford, 2008). Are European concepts of cosmopolitanism (at least, the mainstream ones) robust enough to capture the historical and contemporary development of seemingly transnational spaces in North America? Is critical cosmopolitanism a useful concept for examining North American boundary spaces and processes? And after all is said and done, how do North American border and border security discourses—as reflected specifically in the changing impact, meaning, and diversity of national boundary spaces and processes— relate to the broader issue of the relationship between cosmopolitan space, transnational space, and Canada–US "relations"? Is it possible to explain US hegemony in North America in terms of spatial diffusion processes, or do those processes merely provide a rendering of Canada–US relations consistent with those already extant, which reinforce the primacy of "methodological nationalism" approaches? These are the topics of interest and they remain quite specific to a (Central) Canadian perspective.

Second, and unapologetically, this book has been written from a Canadian academic perspective by a researcher whose interests lie in how political constructs are embedded in popular geopolitical perceptions. It is written primarily for Canadians with the implicit understanding that the national narratives it describes are not necessarily viewed as such on the opposite side of the line. There is already a large literature on American perspectives, as well as a large literature on border policy. Most North American literature deals with American issues, American hegemony, and American global interests without examining, more critically, how hegemonic processes have been shaped in the context of a continental border along which the United States remains the more visible of the two nations but still a separate one. In North America there are two other nations that have very different perspectives on borders, continental integration, and North America's place in the global community. Using American literature to understand these positions does not necessarily result in great insights, for even where "Canadian issues" are included in American discussions, the result is generally an American perspective on Canada, a "utility statement" rather than a cosmopolitan Canadian perspective (see, for example, Warner, 2010).

Reducing the Canadian perspective to a sidebar in text that is focused on broader American issues simply perpetuates the idea of a "Pax Americana" or a US "Manifest Destiny." Such perspectives encourage rather than critically explore the present-day security rhetoric and thus become devices for furthering such discourses. They also, unfortunately, further the idea that there is no significant difference between Canada and the United States, no push-back from Canada that would help expose hegemonic processes. Canada has been "erased" in this sense. So this book examines the issue from a Canadian perspective, decentring and problematizing the American approach, in an attempt to identify how hegemonic processes contribute to a reflexivity that is mediated by border security and border metaphors and that is shaping (indeed, impeding) the development of a North American cosmopolitan society.

As a final caution, it is well to remember that this book was written at the very beginning of the Beyond the Border process and does not attempt to capture the complexities of this newly emerging and potentially enduring relationship. Its goal is more to place in context the developments that have led to Beyond the Border and to contextualize this potential next step in the Canada–US border relationship.

Chapter 1

WARS AND WALLS
THE EARLY CANADA–US BORDER

This chapter explores how the Canada–US border evolved in the late eighteenth and early nineteenth centuries. We are particularly interested in how the border reflected both the hegemonic aspirations of Manifest Destiny and a "resistant Canada" north of the line. How did Canadian and American perceptions of their continental relationship evolve? And what impact did those perceptions have on US hegemony and Canadian resistance to it?

To answer these questions, instead of relying on political speeches and documents (which is the more common approach), we will seek out and analyze popular culture images and texts that generated stereotypes and metaphors that became the building blocks of a "bordering" process. These will be given the same weight as more formal texts and academic works. Flint (2006) calls these types of representations or metaphors "codes," and as we will see throughout this book, such codes create attitudes towards the border and colour its importance to national and transnational identity. This is because, as we have discussed, geopolitical perceptions and discourses are translated into popularized accounts that reinforce the symbolic importance of borders. Cartoons, newspaper, films, and television programs all contribute by creating imaginary snapshots that position ideas and understandings about self and other and that reify those understandings with reference to geography, space, and power.

Manifest Destiny, for example, reflected the American aspiration for continental hegemony—that is, the belief that America had a divine role to play as ruler of the North American continent. Americans constructed this powerful and engaging concept in the eighteenth century and came to view it as a "normative" and (even more importantly) morally "correct" reading of geopolitics in the western hemisphere. The ideology of Manifest Destiny drove generations of Americans to push for control over the North American continent and to attempt to procure it—by purchase or conquest. Art and images contributed to the manufacture of "American exceptionalism." Figure 1.1, one of the most famous artistic renderings of American destiny, painted by John Gast, suggests a people led to the Promised Land by divine intervention: an angel guides them west across the frontier to establish a new civilization. This land offers an alternative to the class- and conflict-riven political cultures in which Europe remains steeped, and it is theirs for the taking.

But this ideology, this foundational intellectual concept, influenced more than American domestic politics. It also informed a geopolitical outlook, one that perceived American politics as the most important geopolitical agenda in North America. This amounted to a call for empire, raw and unbridled. US territorial expansion was necessary in order to create that empire, and to that end, the United States purchased or conquered lands previously held by European nations, including Florida (purchased from Spain in 1819), Alaska (purchased from the Russians in 1867), and Oregon (acquired by treaty with the British in 1846).

In the early nineteenth century, border metaphors developed in the context of a palpable sense of America as a centre of material progress, indeed, as a new "civilization" (Agnew, 2003: 90). The strong, deep roots of the belief in American exceptionalism and Manifest Destiny also influenced how the United States saw

Figure 1.1. George A. Crofutt's 1873 chromolithograph *American Progress*, based on the 1872 painting of the same name by John Gast. *Source*: Library of Congress, Washington, DC.

its neighbour to the north. It should not surprise us that in American texts of the early to mid-nineteenth century, the Canada–US border is usually represented as little more than a thin and inconvenient line thwarting the exercise of US continental hegemony (see Figure 1.10). During this same period, in Canadian texts, however, the Canada–US border was more often framed using the symbolism of a wall or fence protecting Canada against the threat of American military "takeover." So while we have focused thus far on the American perspective, arguing that there is a US hegemony project that uses border practice as a means to extend its own political and economic influence in an extraterritorial way, we need to remember that the border has also been central to Canadian understandings of continental geopolitics. Clearly, there were profound differences in each nation's understanding of the meaning of border.

The rest of this chapter examines how the border relationship was constructed in the nineteenth century and how that history has encouraged separate nationalisms in North America even while celebrating the joining of these nationalisms in borderland spaces. As much as possible, we access popular accounts in order to highlight how hegemonic national discourses were constructed from geopolitical events and the impact of those discourses on how the border was understood, because, as Sharpe (1996) and Dittmer (2005) in particular remind us, hegemonic practices are reflected also in everyday understandings and practices.

OPENING LINES: INSCRIBING TERRITORY

The first border established between what is now Canada and what is now the United States was perhaps more accurately a frontier, for it represented little more than a geopolitical front that shifted back and forth depending on the state of affairs among distant European nations (Laxer, 2003). In general terms, it demarcated the edge of European power in the New World. Figure 1.2, the 1780 Raynal and Bonne Map of the North American continent, suggests a less than precise understanding of where territories ended, although the nations that claimed the continent were well known. Even after the American Revolution and the withdrawal of France from its North American territories, Britain retained a strong imperial presence in North America, which it stoutly defended. Increasingly, Britain was the single most important European power in North America (Laxer, 2003). For much of the nineteenth century, British forces continued to man a number of fortified outposts, including Kingston, Niagara, Quebec, York, and Halifax, ostensibly because geopolitical tensions remained along the frontier, although after the War of 1812, those tensions did not escalate into a more general armed conflict. So in the late eighteenth and early nineteenth centuries, the border was a de facto geopolitical border, one that demarcated the territory

Figure 1.2. Rigobert Bonne and Guillaume Raynal's 1780 map of the North America Continent. Reproduced with permission. *Source*: Courtesy of Geographicus Rare Antique Maps.

and sovereignty of distinct American and European civilizations, even before cooperative border arrangements were institutionalized through treaties and other agreements.

Making a border subsequently engaged American and British policy-makers for over a century. Maps were important to this project—indeed, mapping represented the original "border technology" dividing North America into national spaces and territories. The processes of treaty making and empire building, and the resulting boundary lines, were not necessarily based on intimate knowledge of the actual territory, however (Nicholson, 1979). In the late eighteenth and early nineteenth centuries, for example, borders were little more than agreements regarding what heights of land and bodies of water divided nations. Ownership among European nations was geopolitically determined and was settled by treaty, sometimes with the help of third-party arbitrators, as was the case with the Maine Boundary Dispute, mediated by the King of the Netherlands in 1820, while in the Pacific Northwest, Britain, the United States, and Russia all claimed control of the same territory for a protracted period extending from Captain James Cook's voyages to the Oregon Treaty of 1846 (Findlay and Coates, 2002: 12). National territory and identity were defined with reference to the continental powers rather than to any strong regional attachments. It was sometimes unclear where the borders between such powers actually ran and which nation was in control. Nicholson (1979) notes that even as the provinces of Upper and Lower Canada were drawing internal boundaries for administrative purposes, well after the American Revolution, "precise boundaries were not mentioned because of the difficulty of describing the boundaries between the two provinces and the United States, which depended upon the clarification of certain matters arising from the Treaty of Paris of 1783" (33). A case in point was the Maine–Canada border, which remained unresolved well into the mid-nineteenth century.

Despite sincere efforts by both sides, neither the Definitive Treaty of 1783, nor Jay's Treaty of 1814, nor the Convention of 1818, succeeded in crafting a border agreement from sea to sea between the United States and Canada. Disputes continued well beyond the end of the Revolutionary War. Boundary negotiations after the American Revolution—and there were many—both reflected and reified the hegemonic roots of territorial arrangements as they stood in the late eighteenth century. Claims were made on areas and regions where substantive control was virtually impossible. For both the United States and Britain (Canada), the process of drawing boundaries—on land if not on paper maps—was incremental and ongoing rather than "instantaneous." The Alaska boundary, for example, was negotiated only in 1903, and even today, although there are no continental land boundaries left to be delineated, maritime ones are still being established.

When boundary-makers in early times focused on what today is the Canada–US border, it was territory rather than people that initially concerned them. The border was a concept rather than a place. Early mappings reflected the general geopolitical interests and imperatives of not one but two continental powers, which clashed through the discourses of Manifest Destiny and British dominion. Findlay and Coates (2002) write that in the Pacific Northwest, "the lines had no geographic significance, ignored First Nations territories, ran roughshod over existing patterns of trade and commerce, and paid no heed to the needs and aspirations of the handful of non-indigenous peoples living in the region" (13). Actually, the lines *did* have geographic significance, but from a geopolitical perspective rather than a local one. "Canada" was not yet an independent state, and thus Britain's mapping of North America, unlike that of the United States, served the purpose of creating a colonial space for empire to fill. This very much complicated issues relating to territorial control. Still, the vagueness of boundary delineation and demarcation in late-eighteenth-century North America meant that the elements of boundary-making that reinforced territorial definitions of nationhood were imprecisely developed. In many ways, this reflected the reality on the ground, where no border posts marked the landscape. Not until 1844 did an article appear in what is now *The Globe and Mail* (Toronto) announcing that boundary markers had arrived to delineate the Canada–US border along its "long undisputed boundary line" between Canada and the United States.

Figure 1.3   J.W. Glass Jr. sketch of the Quebec–Maine borderlands region, titled "Camera Lucida Sketch—Junction of the DuLoup with the Chaudière—near Semples. Sketches From Surveys Led by Talcott, N° 1-16; Item N° 104; Series 11; Record Group 76." *Source:* Cartographic and Architectural Branch, National Archives, College Park, MD.

Rodrigue's (1997) study of the Maine–Quebec borderlands and the Canada Road also suggest that imprecision was common on both sides of the border, paving the way for tremendous intermingling of people, activities, and markets. Figure 1.3 illustrates that in general terms, this border was understood to be a highland frontier region, although this was not precisely delineated or demarcated. Both sides maintained the connecting road, and contemporary artists' renderings of the borderlands offered bucolic vistas (Rodrigue, 1997). Similarly, the Maine border with present-day New Brunswick, which was so contentiously framed by the Aroostook War, was initially left unresolved, to the delight of Americans in the northeast, among whom war was unpopular and for whom links to British markets in Canada were important.

For Craig (2005), the seamlessness of the Saint John River Valley that demarcated the border between New Brunswick and Maine allowed a unique society to develop along the margins of Canadian and American society, one that was oblivious to international boundaries. She argues that the river was, until the railway was finished in the 1870s, "the only convenient means of communication within the settlement and between the settlement and the outside world. People did their business wherever it suited them, and the lumber interests particularly ignored the boundary … Local people even voted where they resided with scant attention to citizenship" (74). Craig insists, though, that this was not a case of transnational borderland society in the making, but rather a case of society pre-existing the construction of borderlines.

But as we shall discuss at greater length in the next sections of this chapter, in the early-nineteenth-century North American borderlands, this peaceful inter-connectivity was increasingly anomalous (Craig, 2005). New World national identities remained geopolitically referenced, and as a result of cultural and ideological differences, those identities often served as a flashpoint for disputes. In the 1820s, for example, the peaceful coexistence between New Brunswick and Maine in the Saint John River Valley ended with Maine taking "a hardline position in the northeastern boundary dispute as they tried to assert sovereignty over these very remote and not so accessible northern reaches. The state sent agents to the disputed territory to investigate 'trespasses' and 'aggressions' by the British" (76). The Aroostook War of 1839 saw the border dispute magnified by nationalistic rhetoric that encouraged Americans to "twist the lion's tail" and a British–US border dispute; negotiation and settlement followed. Imprecise borders thus meant that boundary negotiations were often difficult and protracted.

NEGOTIATING THE LINE

To explain why all of this was so, let us backtrack momentarily. In 1794, "Jay's Treaty" attempted to resolve disagreements over boundary lines in the Oregon Territory and between Maine and New Brunswick, which had been left incomplete by the 1783 "Definitive Treaty." Jay's Treaty did not resolve all boundary issues, and the Canada–US border remained an unfinished project. This is suggested in Figure 1.4.

Not until after the War of 1812 did boundary cooperation resume between Britain and the United States. The Treaty of Ghent of 1814 and the Convention of 1818 continued to struggle with the problem of establishing a "definitive border" between Canada and the United States. Perhaps this protracted struggle is not surprising, considering that bloody memories of the American Revolution and the War of 1812 were still fresh. The Definitive Treaty had called for amicable relations, and mapping projects and border negotiations were opportunities to foster them, but this was a thin veneer. Peaceful cooperation would have to wait until later in the nineteenth century.

By then, of course, the discourses of Manifest Destiny and American exceptionalism, after having suffered a setback by the failure of the American invasion of Canada, were being transformed. They were increasingly being recast through the "Monroe Doctrine," which declared the western hemisphere, not just North America, to be a US "sphere of influence." This fused Manifest Destiny's more organic, nationalistic, and even religious ideologies about Divine Right and exceptionality with geopolitical and continental ideals. The Monroe Doctrine is associated with President James Monroe's seventh annual message to Congress on 2 December 1823, in the course of which he advocated that with respect to

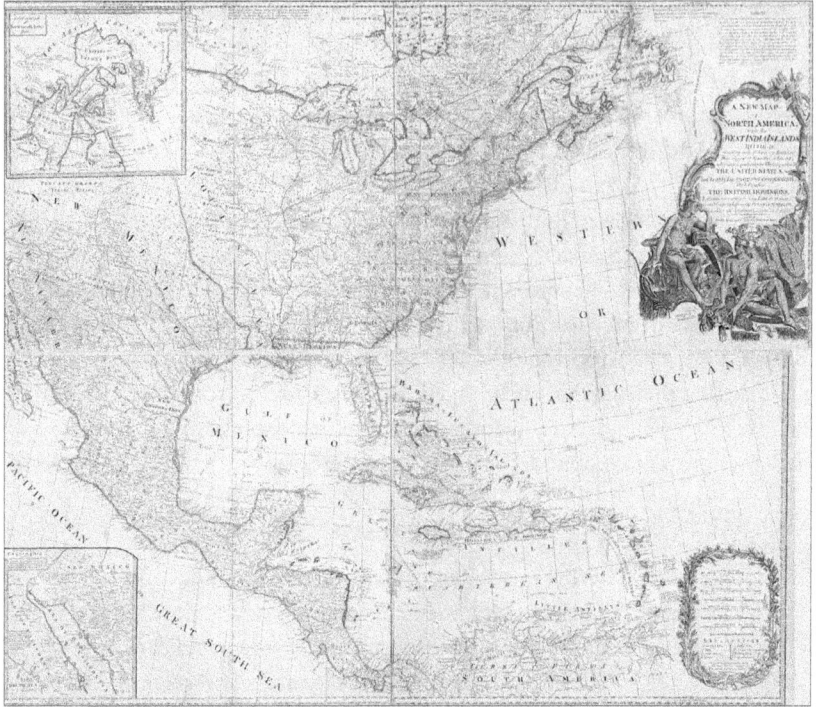

Figure 1.4 This map, titled "A new Map of North America with the West India Island," is dated 12 May 1794. It is drawn "according to the preliminary articles of peace, signed at Versailles January 20, 1783." *Source:* Lionel Pincus and Princess Firyal Map Division, New York Public Library, Astor, Lenox and Tilden Foundations.

European powers, "we owe it, therefore, to candor and to the amicable relations existing between the United States and those powers to declare that we should consider any attempt on their part to extend their system to any portion of this hemisphere as dangerous to our peace and safety" (Avalon Project, 2012).

The fact of a boundary with Europe (Britain in particular), and the fact that more than one national power occupied North America, grated against the American belief system, which rejected European influence. Canada was a thorn in the side of the newly incubated America because it so obviously rendered Manifest Destiny a fiction. American geopolitical narratives rooted in the Monroe Doctrine and Manifest Destiny now became more than general anti-British discourses and began to take specific aim at the Canadian colonies. But recall that American founding father George Washington had argued, with regard to Canada, that "if that country is not with us, it will, from its proximity to the eastern United States, its intercourse and connection with the numerous tribes of the western Indians, its communion with them by water and other local advantages, be at least a troublesome if not a dangerous neighbour to us" (Pratt,

1925: 41). Although Washington was speaking well before Monroe developed his doctrine, here we see the idea begin to take shape.

In some ways this rhetoric is reminiscent of George W. Bush's twenty-first-century mantra, "if they are not with us, they are against us," in that it naturalized and universalized American interests. According to Pratt (1925), the desire to absorb British North America continued as a historical force and was combined with racist logic reflecting public fears about British aggression and the "Indian threat" even after the War of 1812 ended. And it proved resilient. In 1845, for example, an influential American, John O'Sullivan, argued in aggressive rhetoric (in the *United States Magazine and Democratic Review*):

> Away, then, with all idle French talk of balances of power on the American Continent. There is no growth in Spanish America! Whatever progress of population there may be in the British Canadas, is only for their own early severance of their present colonial relation to the little island three thousand miles across the Atlantic; soon to be followed by Annexation, and destined to swell the still accumulating momentum of our progress. And whosoever may hold the balance, though they should cast into the opposite scale all the bayonets and cannon, not only of France and England, but of Europe entire, how would it kick the beam against the simple, solid weight of the two hundred and fifty, or three hundred millions—and American millions—destined to gather beneath the flutter of the stripes and stars, in the fast hastening year of the Lord 1845!

Increasingly, during the first half of the nineteenth century, American independence from Britain, but *without* Canada, was being cast as a serious security problem for the United States. At least it was constructed as such by a series of "speech acts" that called for extreme measures to counteract the threat of European imperialism, represented by the existence of a border itself. We will return to the idea of security as a "speech act" later in this book. Here, the point is that although American geopolitic rhetoric was relatively hostile to Britain and Canada well into the mid-1800s, there are plenty of indications that Canadians and Americans lived peacefully side by side in the borderland areas once boundaries were established (see Konrad and Nicol, 2008). These relations have been described by numerous historians, and will be discussed shortly here. But, in the context of the national geopolitical sabre-rattling of border discourse related to Manifest Destiny, the fact of good local border relations was rather insignificant. This just reinforced the idea that Manifest Destiny faced impediments to its success: indeed that any border was an impediment. (In Chapter 2 we trace how this attitude was furthered in the context of high rates of cross-border mobility.) Even where amicable, these local borderland relations only fuelled the American expectation that the US would ultimately absorb the people "north of the line."

CONTESTING THE LINE

To understand all of this, we again need to backtrack to the years just after the American Revolution. As already noted, one of the earliest boundary treaties, the Definitive Treaty" of 1783, attempted to specify permanent borders between Canada and the United States. Besides providing the terms for resolving outstanding boundary issues in the aftermath of the American Revolution, that treaty attempted to reaffirm the undying friendship and common ancestry of American and British subjects. In its preamble it declared:

> It having pleased the Divine Providence to dispose the hearts of the most serene and most potent Prince George the Third, by the grace of God, king of Great Britain, France, and Ireland, defender of the faith, duke of Brunswick and Lunebourg, arch-treasurer and prince elector of the Holy Roman Empire etc., and of the United States of America, to forget all past misunderstandings and differences that have unhappily interrupted the good correspondence and friendship which they mutually wish to restore, and to establish such a beneficial and satisfactory intercourse, between the two countries upon the ground of reciprocal advantages and mutual convenience as may promote and secure to both perpetual peace and harmony. (Avalon Project, 2012)

But Benjamin West's unfinished painting of the same event is quite revealing about the tentative nature of the peace (see Figure 1.5), for it suggests that deep geopolitical antagonisms remained after the American Revolution. The painting, titled *American Commissioners of the Preliminary Peace Agreement with Great Britain,* is incomplete because the British commissioners who signed the treaty refused to sit for the recording of the event on canvas, while important American politicians who were not actually at the signing, like Henry Laurens and Benjamin Franklin's grandson, William Temple Franklin, were incorporated into it, ostensibly to create a fictitious narrative. Thus, the declaration of goodwill was only one strand of the post-revolutionary geopolitical discourse: the fuller discourse was captured accurately by the artist in a work the British refused to commemorate in an American national gallery. The incomplete painting echoed the very real problem of a peace with incomplete borders during which underlying geopolitical acrimony continued to simmer.

The first challenge was the War of 1812. As West's painting suggests, geopolitical contests generated in North America took their toll even after the conflict and bloodshed had ended. Memory and perceptions continued to play an important role in the politics of boundary-making. In the United States, animosity towards the British was memorialized by images and texts that demonized the British and extolled the American project in ways that referenced the Revolutionary War. Such images encouraged a belief in Britain's villainous intentions

Figure 1.5 Benjamin West's 1783 unfinished painting of the Definitive Treaty of Peace Commissioners, sans the British, who were to appear on the right side of the canvas. *Source*: Library of Congress LC-USZ 62-70531.

and reified the American martyrs. For example, Figure 1.6 illustrates the Boston Massacre of 5 March 1770, during which five American men died. This genre of depicting the British as a military machine wielding violence on an innocent people, accompanied by copious quantities of gushing blood, would resurface even after the Definitive Treaty had been signed and amicable relations had supposedly been resumed. The same theme is evident in Revolutionary and War of 1812 illustrations of violent events, where the British and their native allies are shown massacring and scalping Americans.

Moreover, and we will return to this point later, Native peoples were often seen as accomplices of the British. British savagery was coupled with racialized discourses targeting Indigenous peoples on the Canada–US frontier. In this way, American popular culture not only racialized but epitomized the Canadian frontier as a dangerous place. As a border with Britain it was thus a de facto location of violence, slaughter, and contestation—a border of civilization indeed. Figure 1.7 captures this metaphor of civilizational abyss: it depicts a violent border and violent "other," a place where the "savage" and the "British/European" wreak cruelty on innocent Americans. This cartoon protests the British support for Native people during War of 1812, a time when—so Americans believed— Native people were committing atrocities in the name of the British king.

Figure 1.6 The Boston Massacre. *Source*: Courtesy of the
Library of Congress, Washington, DC.

This sense of danger, reinforced by racialized and indeed civilizational geopolitical discourses, created a field of metaphors and codings for the Canada–US
frontier. Images like the one in Figure 1.7, emanating from constructions of
danger at the US–Canadian border, were typical of the art and media renderings
of the day. Pratt (1925) tells us that at the time, newspapers in the northwestern
United States were preoccupied with the "Indian problem." Little wonder, then,
that in 1812, after warfare resumed between the Americans and the British and
Canadians, the Canada–US border took on a renewed significance as a geopolitical marker. Through rhetoric, representations, and images, the border was
constructed as an existential threat, one that coupled the personification of evil
represented by "British Empire" with savage racial stereotypes of Indigenous
peoples. As a consequence, Manifest Destiny became a coherent and cogent
political discourse for securitizing the border.

Figure 1.7 An American cartoon attacking the alliance between the "Humane British" and the Indians during the War of 1812. William Charles (1776–1820), artist. *Source*: Courtesy of the Library of Congress, Washington, DC.

This is not mere conjecture. American political discourses of the time stressed that there was reason for national concern, and prescribed action. Pratt (1925) tells us that "the idea of taking Canada from the British, as the only way of assuring peace with the Indians[,] had been announced in Congress at the beginning of 1809" (44). Furthermore, "in the summer and fall of [1810], and throughout the year following, government officials, the western press, and the resolutions of public meetings voiced their sense of danger and [that] the British were responsible for it" (44). The result was that American newspapers often referred to "British savages," and to the War of 1812 as the "Anglo-savage" war, again underscoring the racialized and civilizational foundations of the prevailing discourse.

These perceptions generated support for hostile representations of the British (now Canadian) border in North America. In geopolitical terms, then, Manifest Destiny fuelled a logic that pitted American "civilization" against both Europe and Indigenous peoples and called for the border to be erased. But also in play were elements of connectivity—a point reinforced by historians of the North American borderlands.

Summarizing a rather developed literature on the Upper Canada/New York State/Michigan borderlands, Murray observes that for much of the nineteenth

century, peace and tranquility alternated with war and rebellion. The resulting
tensions created discourses of difference: "visitors and inhabitants alike commented knowingly on the contrasts between British America and the United
States" (341). In reinforcing its reflexive role, Murray suggests that regional perceptions of the border were always flexible. Geopolitics notwithstanding, people
moved across the line in both directions. The frontier with Upper Canada was
perceived as a relatively fluid space for most of Canada's pre-Confederation
history. In this sense, the boundary's significance as a firm dividing line waxed
and waned, but generally, except during the years of open conflict, it allowed
for remarkable connectivity: "There has always been a constant interaction
between the systems of justice on both sides of the boundary and the border
itself. Throughout its history, the border has been used by people in the United
States and in Canada to circumvent laws or societal norms seen to be inconvenient" (341). Indeed, Murray suggests that perceptions of the border were flexible, that even when it was imbued with geopolitical significance, it might have
little effect on restraining mobility and identity. There was, he points out, much
drawing them across, despite

> a vividness born in Upper Canada by a Loyalist culture strongly reinforced by
> the experience and memories, first of the American Revolution and then of the
> War of 1812. Underlying it, of course, was a boastful pride of Britons and many
> colonists in the unquestioned superiority of the monarchy and British institu-
> tions, matched no less on the other side of the border by an equally aggressive
> pride held by Americans in their Republican ideals and institutions, as well as
> the conviction held by many that the inevitable destiny of the Canadas was to
> become part of the United States. (343)

So, for Murray, the fact that the border was a geopolitical construct did
not supersede its other functions, particularly those that facilitated connectivity
between Americans and Canadians. Others have made similar observations,
particularly as the nineteenth century progressed. This was to become an era
characterized by the tremendous movement of people, so that in some places,
including northeastern North America, connectivity was the norm (Widdis,
1998). The border's geopolitical significance grew in the sense of taking its
root as the marker between two separate nations; but all the while, the frontier
areas on both sides witnessed increased traffic as a result of growing trade and
population momentum. Moreover, despite any number of rivalries and armed
incursions during wartime, and despite the heightened tensions in 1812–14,
Murray (1996) argues that ambivalency was normative and that local allegiance
and national identity operated at, and indeed referenced, different geopolitical
scales, often simultaneously:

When we strip away the layers of British-American hostility and Upper Canadian loyalism what we find underscored for many ... is a reaffirmation of
the idea of a common North American nationality or individualism, a ready
willingness of many individuals to move when their interests or circumstances
dictated, regardless of whether this meant switching national allegiances. This
does not diminish the importance of the border, but it raises the question
of how deep-rooted these allegiances were. Re-examining the early frontier
relations between Upper Canada and the United States from the perspective
of the people themselves may lead us to see this period in larger, more continental terms, an important supplement to the view through a more partisan
British imperial lens ... Apart from periods of war and armed rebellion when
restrictions on the usual access to the border were expected, if not always
totally accepted, the normal peacetime expectation was that movement across
the border was untrammelled and open to anyone. Individuals freely crossed
the border, including immigrants, but legal commerce was tied up in the tariffs of the old colonial system until the middle of the century. When anything
occurred to interrupt this, the reaction was quick and forceful. (343)

This passage helps us understand the conflicting narratives about North
American borders in the early nineteenth century. The geopolitics of the time
emphasized difference, and parts of the continent had been laid claim to by
various nationalities, including the French, Spanish, Russians, Dutch, and British—indeed, many of these colonies, including the Canadas, remained intact
in the early nineteenth century. Yet in 1811, US President John Quincy Adams
assured Americans that

> the whole continent of North America appears to be destined by Divine Provi-
> dence to be peopled by one nation, speaking one language, professing one gen-
> eral system of religious and political principles, and accustomed to one general
> tenor of social usages and customs. For the common happiness of them all, for
> their peace and prosperity, I believe it is indispensable that they should be asso-
> ciated in one Federal Union. (http://en.wikipedia.org/wiki/ManifestDestiny)

Adams's claim was rooted in the idea—a popular one among borderlanders—
that North America was indivisible.

Support for Adams's 1811 position was not dampened by the American
failure to take control of Canada in the War of 1812. Indeed, the eruption of
the so-called Aroostook War of 1839, although hardly a major war (it cannot
even be called an armed conflict), draws attention to how resilient discourses
advocating confrontational geopolitics ("empire by armed force") remained in
the United States even while border negotiations were being conducted. Hannay
(1990) tells us that this war had its roots in the 1830s, when US domestic politics
and international relations, steeped as they were in the certainties of Manifest

Destiny, drew strength from anti-British sentiment. The dispute arose from a highly localized confrontation between Canadian lumberjacks and an American land agent, to which approximately 10,000 state troops were dispatched. At issue was where the Canada–US boundary should be located in this particular part of the Madawaska Valley. It was agreed that the boundary dispute at the heart of the conflict would be resolved through a boundary commission. While this commission was carrying out its task, the conflict continued to simmer, fuelled by a decade of acrimony on both sides of the line. It also drew from a war-mongering discourse that reified internal state politics and recycled past anti-British sentiments. One metaphor in this discourse was the British lion, which referenced "empire" and positioned this minor boundary dispute within a broader geopolitical contest. Indeed, in the United States, "twisting the lion's tail" became a popular metaphor in the nineteenth century, one that parodized the symbol of British Empire (Moser, 1998):

> Anti-British feeling was strong throughout northern New England, and the temptation existed in both parties to escape embarrassing local problems by emphasizing the foreign ones. Twisting the lion's tail was a national sport, played not only in northern New England, but elsewhere in the nation. Expansionism was pressed increasingly by the Democrats in other states, and in Maine any yielding to the grasping tactics of hated Albion [England] was considered proof of lack of spirit. (Merk, 1971: 58)

In the final analysis, the only real casualty of the Aroostook War appears to have been a cow, not a "lion," and the result was a dispute mediation process leading to the Webster-Ashburton Treaty of 1842, which set the terms for the present-day land boundary between the United States and Canada in the Maine–New Brunswick region.

Figure 1.8 is a well-known 1839 lithograph showing the conflict between the Maine and New Brunswick loggers in terms of the broader geopolitical contours of American-Anglo hostilities. Figure 1.9, drawn from information published in the American newspaper the *Columbia Democrat* of 30 March 1839, relates the boundary dispute to past settlements and claims. This newspaper, like others of the time, cast the dispute in nation-building terms, resorting to geopolitical rhetoric that aggrandized the rather petty dispute and declared Britain's position to be "unfounded."

The resolution of the Maine border dispute, as negotiated in the Webster-Ashburton Treaty of 1842, was hardly a "hegemonic win" for the United States, which did not acquire all of the territory it had hoped to gain. But it does point to the increasingly constitutive role that borders and border representations played in the United States in terms of mediating foreign relations and

Figure 1.8 "The Main Question," ca. 1839. Artist Henry Dacre ridicules the bellicose elements on both sides of the Maine–New Brunswick conflict. US President Martin Van Buren sits astride an ox with the head of Maine Governor John Fairfield. The ox confronts a dog with the head of the Duke of Wellington, ridden by Queen Victoria. In the background British and US troops face each other while men fell timber in between. *Source:* Courtesy of the Library of Congress, Washington, DC.

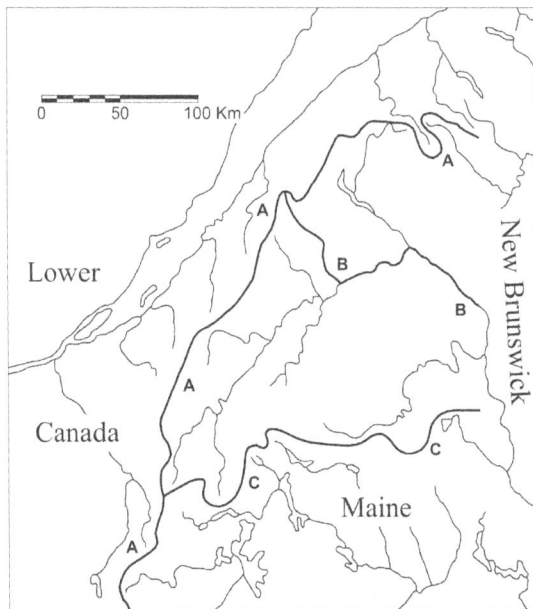

Figure 1.9 Map of the boundary dispute drawn from information in the *Columbia Democrat*, 30 March 1839. Line A represents the boundary line according to the 1783 treaty, Line B the recommendation of the King of Holland, and Line C the British claim. *Source*: Stephen Gardiner.

fuelling a sense of divine right to continental control. If beyond triggering a new round of agreements, the Aroostook War was of little significance in the overall scheme of Canada–US border development, it demonstrated how borderlands that had long functioned well enough without being precisely defined could become flashpoints for conflict and negotiation.

Borders were the testing ground for hegemonic discourses that legitimized American empire. Manifest Destiny provided the syntax for border building and for cross-border relations, even where smooth relations had prevailed. According to Merk (1971), acrimony in the Maine borderlands and the rise of anti-British sentiment were very much products of the War of 1812 and did not predate the conflict. So, informed by a popularized geopolitics that drew upon post-Revolutionary anti-British sentiment, the Aroostook War discourse referenced and reified a simulated collective, and constructed memory about the US–British relationship, and further developed it in the context of a specific situation and site. That narrative relied on specific understandings of the past, even where they failed to apply, as the "Aroostook War Fighting Song" of 1839 reminds us. Glossing the outcome of the War of 1812 in a way that has contributed to very different understandings of the "winners" even in contemporary times, the Americans sang proudly: "They need not think to have our land; / We Yankees can fight well; / We've whipped them twice most manfully, / As every child can tell."

Much more contentious than the Aroostook War, and equally steeped in the geopolitics of empire and Manifest Destiny, however, was the Oregon Boundary Dispute. The shared Oregon Territory had been a testament to cooperation between Britain and the United States—in their 2002 study, Findlay and Coates (2002) refer to it as a permeable border—yet it was here in the mid-nineteenth century that borders once again assumed a geopolitical meaning that went to the heart of US expansionism in North America. The dispute arose because the Convention of 1818 had left undefined the border between what is now British Columbia and Washington State. The resulting Oregon Territory had been jointly occupied by the United States and Britain. Under President James Polk, however, the United States rejected Britain's claim to much of the region north of the 49th Parallel. In 1849, "54-40 or Fight!" became the slogan of US President Polk's administration, which clearly intended to absorb a larger share of the territory into the United States. After considerable disagreement—indeed, rabble-rousing—on both sides, the dispute was resolved by the Oregon Treaty of 1846, which divided the disputed region along the 49th Parallel. The American position could be seen as a concerted attempt to apply Manifest Destiny with respect to the Canadian border from the point of view of the British, although clearly justifications were proffered for the legitimacy of their claim to what today remains much of British Columbia (Reimer, 2002). In fact, it was in context of that dispute, in 1845, that John O'Sullivan, whose definition of Manifest Destiny we have already encountered, commented: "Our manifest destiny [is] to overspread the continent allotted by Providence for the free development of our yearly multiplying millions" (see http://en.wikipedia.org/wiki/John_L._O'Sullivan).

O'Sullivan here was authorizing US hegemony in a way that cast its control of Oregon as "providential," that is, as a fulfillment of divine destiny. This was, of course, not the rationale that Polk gave to Britain in the diplomatic negotiations that led to resolution of the border conflict and its situating along the 49th Parallel. According to Reimer (2002), on both sides there was much in the way of "constructing competing narratives to uphold their nation's claim to the region based on historical events and evidence" (223). While the United States pitched Manifest Destiny, Britain developed its own narratives to substantiate their territorial claim.

The Oregon dispute has often been presented as the poster child of Manifest Destiny discourses in US history (see, for example, Wikipedia, "Oregon Dispute"). In fact, British claims to Oregon reflected a version of Manifest Destiny as well: "British leaders and writers accepted the global colonial regime and used its rules to assert their nation's claim. Britain had a right to the Northwest, they argued, based upon the same 'law of nations' that upheld the legitimacy of possessions held by European powers" (235). As the dispute drifted towards conflict, the Canadas looked to Britain for protection. War was looming, and it was the potential for that, along with political machinations within the Polk administration, that led to the 1846 treaty negotiations. The resulting agreement extended the boundary between Canada and the United States along the 49th Parallel "from the summit of the Rockies westward to the Pacific" (International Boundary Commission, 2011). There is every indication that, had the disagreement not been settled in this way, Britain would have been willing to wage war over the disputed territory (which it would not have done in Maine). Many American presses opposed to conflict over Oregon reminded their readers that in the mid-1840s, the very idea of border wars was becoming preposterous. Indeed, as it turned out, the Polk administration's attempt to acquire all of the Oregon Territory was arguably one of the last gasps in US efforts to build a continental empire by force. After the Civil War, most records indicate that artfully exerted economic or political pressures would be the tools of choice in efforts to take Canada. (We return to this point later.)

Aroostook and Oregon essentially brought an end to US militarism directed north. But lesser forms of sabre-rattling persisted: in the 1860s, the United States lent "apparent" moral support to the Fenian Raids on Canada, and during the

Civil War, Canadians offered "apparent" support to Confederate raids on the northern states.

Sometimes the resulting raids generated real concern—especially the now infamous St. Alban's Raid, in the course of which American "Confederates" based in Canada robbed banks along the US side of the border, killing one northerner in the process. They were pursued by Union forces across the Canadian border, which resulted in a full-blown diplomatic incident. The Canadians complied with American demands and arrested the criminals, but because they were deemed to be operating as part of an authorized Confederate government operation, their actions were not considered a felony. As a result, they were not extradited. Similarly, Fenian Raids of the 1860s and early 1870s, which were attempts by Irish Nationalists to drive the British from Canada (and from Ireland after that), were facilitated by their foothold in the northern American states. The US government did not support the Fenians, but a number of northern border states did not discourage them. The raids ended in 1871, although the Fenian legend lived on. These border skirmishes did not provoke full-out war but did affect how the United States and Canada positioned themselves as "mutual existential threats" and—more importantly for our purposes—how the border between the two nations was now perceived. We see this in cartoons and commentaries of the day. Figure 1.10, for example, an American cartoon from *Frank Leslie's Illustrated Newspaper* (New York), dating to 1870, shows the US border as a rather thin line between "Kanucks" and Fenians. The portrayal of Canadians and British is unflattering, suggesting chaos, disorder, and military weakness. Similarly, in 1864, an American publication *The Soldiers' Journal* reported that "we need have no apprehension for the future, and intimate no desire for any change, save in revising the treaty with Great Britain relative to our naval armament on the lakes bordering Canada, in order that our border may be more effectually guarded from the incursions of those rebels who have made these Provinces a place of temporary refuge, more with the design of annoying our government and people than becoming useful citizens of the Canadas" (http://chroniclingamerica.loc.gov/lccn/sn89038091/1864-12-14/ed-1/seq-4).

Beginning in the late nineteenth century, there seems to have been a change in American views about Canada. Over time, Americans seemed to show less enthusiasm for conflict and more interest in aligning Canadian and US interests in new and creative ways. As a result of all of these events (as we shall see in Chapter 2) there was a change in American perspectives. Naturalized geopolitical discourses were developing that would soon come to replace the existing civilizational mantra of Manifest Destiny (Nugent, 2009).

Figure 1.10 Bird's-eye view of the late sanguinary struggle on the Canadian border. *Source: Frank Leslie's Illustrated Newspaper* (New York), 18 June 1870. Library of Congress, Washington, DC.

RESISTING "DESTINY," MAKING IDENTITY

In 1845, the *Toronto Globe* closely examined the content of US geopolitical discourses regarding the Oregon Boundary Dispute. It found them rife with civilizational narratives:

> We know not what the President means by his declaration that the American continents are not to be any longer subject to colonization by any European power. We believe that, with very few exceptions, the whole territory of the two continents is claimed by powers which are more or less civilized: but if the United States watch over their own territory, they may leave other powers to do the same.
>
> The States object to a "balance of power." No wonder, they seem to cast the weight of all on one side, and that is their own. The States are not free from

blame in encouraging dissatisfaction in other countries, but they have never yet struck one blow for liberty (except on selfish grounds), although it is ever on their tongues. (9 December 1845: 2)

The historical irony of Manifest Destiny was that the civilizational discourses and the borders it produced ultimately reified and differentiated the territorial space in which the young country of Canada was constructed, long after the threat of American invasion and credible fears of forceful annexation had dissipated. The reaction to these annexation discourses proved to be fodder for the Confederation mills and were used artfully by John A. Macdonald and others in support of a Canadian federation. Indeed, as most Canadian history books remind us, north of the border the answer to Manifest Destiny was Canadian Confederation and the consolidation of British colonies under a single nation.

So if the border with Britain was seen as a security (or existential) threat by Americans, the same fear held on the other side of the line. The US sense of vulnerability to Britain was matched in Canada by an enduring fear of being conquered or annexed by the US. To this day, Canadian nation-building narratives see Confederation in 1867 as motivated by "defensive expansion" (Aitken, 1959), a theme we will expand upon shortly. This theory posits that US continental ambitions generated a reflexive resistance among those north of the border. By uniting under the government of the Dominion of Canada, a new Canadian nation gave coherence to what had been individual British colonies in North America, and ultimately offered greater collective security. Confederation created the territorial basis of Canada, and the border redefined Canada's territory in new ways. Nationalism came to be constructed in ways in which it had previously been ambivalent or uncertain.

In the process, the US boundary with Canada took on a new meaning (Wynn, 1987). It did more than just mark the fact of two empires (American and British) facing each other in a struggle for space—that had really been decided by the outcome of the American Revolution and War of 1812; rather, it reflected a power struggle in which the smaller British North American population resisted absorption. The border was iconic to this process. But bear in mind throughout this discussion that we mean British North America in a geopolitical rather than an ethnic or linguistic sense, as there were considerable numbers of those of non-British origins who occupied what was then Canada. Indeed, there were numerous identities and nationalities—French and Indigenous among them—that resisted being British and staked their own claims to alternate identity, even where attempts to impose British hegemony were made, as they were in Quebec (Nichols, 2010). But powerful geopolitical rationalities of that time period pushed to simplify allegiance, in order to create two singular nations, one that represented the "other" (American), and one that created British North Americans. Geopolitical discourse thus reflected a desire to construct British North America as synonymous with "Canada"—that is, to merge competing subjectivities and identities on a grand scale. For this project, a firm border was a necessity. Such a line would need to reject sharing a common territory with the United States (like the Oregon Territory), or any transnational spaces, uncertain boundaries, and national allegiance to countries other than Britain.

As Canadian historian George Woodcock (1989) reminds us, what most inhabitants of Canada in the early nineteenth century "shared, in greater or lesser degree, was the common enemy, and history has shown that a shared danger is much more effective in creating an awareness of common interest than any constructive incentive" (5). The Canada–US border became much more geopolitically significant after the War of 1812 than before, but it would be wrong to suggest that it inspired nationalistic sentiments of the sort it holds for Canadians today. It was defensive, to be sure. Unlike today, its existence did not create a distinct awareness of being "Canadian." Rather, Woodcock suggests that the establishment and reinforcement of a tentative frontier between Canada and the United States in 1812 reinforced Canada's *Britishness:*

> Fear and resentment of—and shared action against—a common enemy did not amount to even the beginnings of a Canadian nation or national sentiment … As for General Brock and his regiments … they were all officially British troops paid by Britain. They were waging a war to hold on to the remaining North American colonies. The aim was to sustain the continental balance of power and to provide space for Britain's superfluous men and women to find homes … The eventual emergence of a Canadian nation was far from General Brock's thought. (6–7)

All of this has prompted Woodcock to suggest that while there might have been support initially for the American "dream" of one nation in North America, in the years after the War of 1812, the acts of war committed by Americans in Upper Canada "turned their [Canadians'] collective image into that of the Enemy; the various populations of the Canadas were united in hating and fearing them" (5). Laxer (2003) too contends that the War of 1812 shaped Upper Canada's political culture by reifying loyalty to the British Crown as the highest political virtue.

Thus, for Canadians, the War of 1812 did a great deal to frame Canada as a territory *and* an imagined nation—albeit in a narrow sense as a "British" one. This narrative developed despite the existence of strong alternative national identities. In this sense, while the War of 1812 did not immediately reinforce a sense of reflexivity, or a sense of Canada being a different entity than Britain, it

did generate a hegemonic societal discourse whereby the inhabitants of the colonies identified themselves as non-Americans on "Dominion" soil. This reflexive discourse, constructed by Britain and those of British origins in Canada, held
sway for decades: as late as 1871, it was also advanced by the Americans themselves in a discourse that constructed Canadians as "British." By this time, of
course, the same border had been transformed. It has become the foundation for
an expanded national Canadian Confederation project. But in 1812, the idea of a
Britain settled and invested in North America was the metaphor that dominated,
and the border, with its line of forts and fortifications, was beginning to adjust.

Indeed, Berland (2009) suggests that the border has always been central to
the formation of Canadian identity. It has helped create a Canadian self-image,
one that tightly binds identity to territory, and it serves as a marker for the limits
of this identity, one that involves the creation of boundaries to separate self from
other (Wylie, 2010). In this sense, the boundary with the United States is the
most important border for Canadians (Berland, 2009), and Berland reminds us
that for Canadians, *border* is itself a metonym for *strong state,* and the creation
of the border is at the core of Canadians' historical understandings of their
nationhood.

Here we return to the idea that constructing that border was a project of
"defensive expansionism" (Aitken, 1959). As we have seen, Canadians believe
that the consolidation and confederation of Canadian territorial boundaries, in
1867, was undertaken mainly to protect Canada from US expansionist activities and to assert control over unsettled British territories—before the Americans did. Berland (2009) observes that the border narrates different stories and
uneven meanings: it "produces radically different meanings to the territories
it divides" (32). "On the northern side, scholarship has tended to understand
culture in terms of a longstanding struggle around sovereignty and space, while
to the south a growing literature on culture and globalization holds the very
premise of borders open to question" (3).

Before turning to explore the strong border metaphor Berland references,
however, we need to acknowledge that many historical scholars believe we
focus too much on borders and not enough on borderlands. Their interest
is in the borderlands that gave structure to points of connectivity across the
continent, and that in turn helped structure Canada–US relations, especially
through commercial exchanges (Hornsby, Konrad, and Herlan, 1989; Findlay
and Coates, 2002; Widdis, 1998). Widdis (1998), for example, discusses this
concept of borderlands and their heuristic importance as a foil to an overdetermined understanding of the evolution of "national borders" in North America.

For Widdis, an understanding of continental relations in the context of
borderlands returns what he calls the "symbol" of border to the "fact" of place.
Discussing the borderlands commonly referenced by historians and historical

geographers, he suggests that the configuration of borderland regions can be fully comprehended only with reference to particular historical and geographical contexts. This means, for example, that in northeastern North America (i.e., New England and the Maritime provinces), the fact of the existence of a broad cross-border economic community has a time and place. Murray makes this same point with regard to what borderland scholars have called the Great Lakes Borderland Region (see Bukowczyk et al., 2005), where, he suggests, many other things besides trade are responsible for joining people together. Borderlanders' ties grew increasingly closer in mid-century, when Britain and the United States replaced their bitterness over the War of 1812 with new and accommodative measures. These ranged from the Webster-Ashburton Treaty of 1842 to the Reciprocity Treaty of 1854. Nonetheless,

> however much the notion of a common North American individualism, lying just underneath the surface on both sides of the border, may prove to be a more seductive interpretive framework for early nineteenth-century Canadian-American relations, it should not be given a completely free rein. True borderlanders certainly existed, but even by 1840 they were far from a majority. Cross-border contacts became both broader and deeper, but the border itself never disappeared. In Upper Canada, British law, British institutions, and British concepts of justice had sunk deep roots, giving the border both a political and cultural configuration. Philip Buckner argues that in this period people on both sides of the political border "knew on which side they belonged and, equally importantly, who belonged on the other side." (Murray, 1996: 360)

More recently Wood (2002) has suggested that in the past, there were very different socio-cultural and ethnic ways of understanding the border—especially from the West's perspective—and that those on the margins of state and power did not by any means share one particular nationalist solidarity. This is undoubtedly true, as is her conclusion that the 49th Parallel was not a meaningful line for many immigrants. But the fact of this ambivalence did not prevent the border from assuming geopolitical significance for those who were more removed from the hardships of a prairie borderlands life or who constructed identity from a larger geographical vantage point. For them, border metaphors assumed gendered, racial, and national significance in ways that reinforced their geopolitical significance: "British Canadians who viewed Canada as a British dependency, even after Confederation, were more inclined to feel anti-American because strong ties to the United States seemed to parallel weaker ties with Britain ... The image of the United States was thus always central to British Canadians' image of themselves" (117). For Widdis, the issue is even more complex, when high levels of immigration that characterized borderlands regions are considered. The border created a series of opportunities that encouraged the development of local, regional, and national "associations that transcended differences and strengthened ties even in the face of developing north–south integration" (43).

PICTURE THIS

With regard to tensions between regional and national identities, Canadians (or at least Anglo-Canadians) held "manifest destiny" points of view of their own. But they understood that destiny in terms of British rather than American empire. This point is worth emphasizing. As Katenberg (2003) observes, there was indeed a counter-narrative:

> To be sure, Anglo-Canadian dreams of the Dominion as an equal partner with Britain differed from American notions of manifest destiny, but they did so in the details more than in scope. Some Canadian imperialists believed that the moral and the spiritual vitality of the British Empire depended on its new world frontiers. This "Turnerian" environmentalism, of sorts, was distinctively Canadian in its notion that the Dominion would help to fulfill a destiny that God had first given to Britain. Especially hopeful Canadian imperialists might even have fancied that the center of the Empire would move west to Canada. Such visions emphasized both the promise of material progress in the Canadian West and the conviction that Canada had treated its Indians with more Christian justice and British fair play than had the U.S. (547)

During the nineteenth century, then, as Manifest Destiny played out in geopolitical discourses, many Canadians resisted the call of "America"—quite actively, in fact. It is here that popular media, steeped in the geopolitical narratives of the day, are enlightening. Expressions of the Canada–US border relationship in the media indicate that Canadians viewed and represented borders variously as walls, fences, or gates, but rarely as borderlands or borderlines. Instead, lines signified the artificiality of the Americans' vision of the continent. Canadian public discourse was strongly focused on developing the idea that Canada was a "British" nation whose principal existential threat came from Americans and that it depended on Britain for its defence. Efforts by the United States to change this relationship by force and coercion were rebuffed. This is depicted time and again, for example, in cartoons and other popular media, which are excellent sources for the geopolitical codes of the time. Hou's (1997) commentary on Canadian political cartoons highlights how, in the mid- to late nineteenth century, the Canadian public imaginary resorted to the metaphors of "border fence" and "border wall" to represent the Canada–US border and Canada–US relations. Hou draws our attention to several cartoons that clearly render the border as a wall or (non-)security fence dividing Canada and the United States, reflecting Canadians' worries about US aggression and state-sponsored terrorism.

Figure 1.11, for example, published in Montreal in 1865, represents these perceptions during the American Civil War. Most interesting here for our purposes is that instead of a border there is a strong, militarized, and relatively thick imaginary boundary wall between Canada and the United States. As Hou (http://www.collectionscanada.gc.ca/education/008-3050-e.html) points out, the view is between Ottawa and Washington. Jean-Baptiste sits on the Canadian Parliament Buildings then located in Quebec, Lincoln on the White House. "Viewers at the time would have no trouble identifying the smaller, toque-wearing figure in the upper right hand corner of [the] cartoon ... the stereotypical French Canadian Jean-Baptiste ... Lincoln (sitting on the American White House) and Jean-Baptiste (sitting on the Canadian Parliament Buildings) appear to be engaged in the childhood game 'king of the castle' while Canadian soldiers stand guard on a wall separating the two countries" (http://www.collectionscanada.gc.ca/education/008-3050-e.html).

Figure 1.12, from the same collection, "deals with the threat of cross-border raids by the Fenians, a group of radical Irish Americans who sought to harm Great Britain by attacking Canada from bases in the United States" (Hou, 2008). As we have seen, the United States was ambivalent about these attacks: the US government did not condone them and viewed them as violations of their agreements with Canada and Britain; but at the same time, there was much anti-British feeling in the northern United States, and these attacks often enjoyed popular support there. American border states, remembering that Canadians had harboured Confederate cross-border raiders during the Civil War, often offered tit-for-tat support to the Fenians. In Figure 1.13, the border is imagined as a farmer's fence. From the perspective of present-day immigration practices, it is easy to pass through; it does, though, indicate a symbolic barrier between the two nations in terms of political processes and rule of law. "The cartoonist labels the two countries and the border between them, and the title and caption point out Uncle Sam's problem in controlling his 'boys'" (http://www.collectionscanada.gc.ca/education/008-3050-e.html).

These representations, drawn by Canadian cartoonists in the mid- to late nineteenth century and published in regional and local newspapers and magazines, all suggest that the Canada–US border was not simply the result of state-centred political processes, a response to North American geopolitical realities. It was also, increasingly, a border of *choice* and was understood by national narratives in ways that challenged both British colonial and American understandings. But by the 1860s, the North American world was changing, and the Canadians and Americans were considering a trade reciprocity agreement.

Figure 1.11 "Çe bon Mr. Lincoln," published in Montreal in 1865, during the American Civil War. *Source: Le Perroquet*, 15 avril 1865, 59. LAC, ref. no. C-112901.

Figure 1.12 "Uncle Sam and His Boys." *Source: Canadian Illustrated News*, 11 June 1870. LAC, ref. no. C-048854.

Figure 1.13 In this image referencing the Fenian threat, the Canada–US border is drawn as a farmer's gate or fence. First published in *Canadian Illustrated News*. *Source*: LAC, https://www.collectionscanada.gc.ca/obj/023001/f1/nlc009757-v6.jpg.

Canadian media and political cartoons of the day (besides Hou and Hou, 1997, 1998 and 2002, see *Canadian Illustrated News, The Grip,* and other daily newspapers of the day) indicate that Canadians now sometimes saw the border as a "doorway" or portal to US markets. The latter metaphor arose in the nineteenth century, when a partisan (liberal) political discourse sought to establish reciprocal trade with the United States. We will return to this economic aspect in later chapters.

WALLS, FORTS, AND FORTIFICATIONS

Outright hostilities ended with the War of 1812. The American and British empires no longer fought over North America. Throughout the nineteenth century, the sabre-rattling would be much more muted. American expansionism became more closely associated with peaceful annexation than with armed force. By the mid-nineteenth century, the survival of the United States as an independent nation was no longer in question and war with Britain seemed unlikely. Still, perhaps as a consequence of the Americans' constant rhetoric that they intended to absorb their neighbours, the British strengthened strategic land and maritime points. Thus, after the War of 1812, Old Fort Henry and other military outposts around Kingston, Ontario, were fortified to protect British naval yards (see Figure 1.14). Those installations stand to this day as monuments to an uneasy border. So do four anachronistic Martello towers whose collapsible roofs were to facilitate cannon fire against American ships and border posts.

Concern that hostilities might be rekindled also led the British to construct the Rideau Canal in the mid-nineteenth century. Its purpose was to transport British and Canadian forces between Ottawa and the US border without exposing them to attack along the Great Lakes and St. Lawrence River. After 1809, the United States stationed a permanent force along Lake Ontario. This was initially to enforce the Embargo Act and to combat smuggling, and only later to protect the northern border itself. Later, Fort Drum would become the centre of US naval and military activity for Lake Ontario, especially at the time of the Upper and Lower Canada Rebellions. By 1908, thousands of US troops were stationed at Fort Drum (see Rudmin, 1993).

These above-mentioned fortifications reflected and indeed defined a geopolitical agenda for both the Americans and the British for much of the early to mid-nineteenth century. The Canada–US border was not simply a cartographic line or an institutionalized space between nations: it had been the site of considerable chaos and bloodshed at the beginning of the nineteenth century, and the locations of the many skirmishes that were fought along the line are today the sites of monuments and historic battlefields. Yet it is striking just

Figure 1.14 Military establishments in Kingston. This view captures the prominent landscape of Martello towers, Fort Frontenac (British), the Royal Military College, and Old Fort Henry in the distance, all of which were built in Kingston because of its important location vis-à-vis the American military threat. *Source:* James Dobbin.

how "clinical" representations of the Canada–US border were throughout the nineteenth century, along the Canadian side. Battle illustrations by eyewitnesses (Figure 1.15) suggest military precision; the battles are presented as orderly skirmishes carried out across green fields. No "savages" are terrorizing the Americans—indeed, Indigenous peoples are barely represented. All of this has helped normalize and naturalize the border's function for Canadians and reinforce its role as a zone of "protection."

These orderly battle scenes, which have inscribed the War of 1812 on Canadians' collective memory, constitute of course a constructed reality. They are belied by accounts in non-Canadian newspapers. The *Times* (London), when reporting on the death of General Isaac Brock at the Battle of Queenston Heights, remarked in December 1812 on the disorderly and inferior state of the militia he led. This suggests that Canadian paintings of battle scenes showed what people expected rather the reality. For Canadians, the result of these representations was a collective metaphor: the border as site of fortifications and soldiers, of security and order, rather than a dark and frightening landscape of savagery of the sort portrayed in American representations of the Canadian frontier. Yet, as the Oregon Dispute and the construction of the Rideau Canal suggest, fear of contestation did not end in 1815. British soldiers and fortifications defined and protected the border well into the 1840s. Thus, the metaphor of the protective wall lingered among Canadians.

Figure 1.15 *The Battle of Queenston Heights*, by James B. Dennis, who witnessed the conflict. The painting depicts the American landing on 13 October 1812, which ultimately failed. *Source*: LAC, ref. no. C-014614.

The view that security meant military security, and that military security either countered or exacerbated violence along the frontier (depending on whose narrative), was a powerful factor on both sides of the border when nationhood was being negotiated, and it would remain so long after the threat of conflict had passed. That view generated narratives of difference rooted in methodological nationalisms that privileged the state as well as state territory. It also relied on metaphors of fortifications and walls, which were the military technologies of the day.

But there were other sets of metaphors that complemented the military border in that they visualized Canada and the United States as "singular" entities. In the mid-nineteenth century, for example, the press often depicted the Canada–US relationship as a personal relationship between two individuals. In Figure 1.16, Mother Britain and Brother Jonathan/Uncle Sam have a progeny, who is depicted as a toddler just beginning to stand on her own two feet. Like other political cartoons of the day, Canada, Britain, and the United States are personified in highly gendered ways, and the relationship is cast in a pejorative tone intended to convey a sense of inequality (a point which we will follow up in Chapter 2).

All of this suggests that nineteenth-century Canada–US boundary determinations were negotiated in context of a strong geopolitical framework that reflected specific assessments: American and British. Manifest Destiny continued to animate foreign and defence policies, meaning that, unlike the current situation, nineteenth-century America distained the concept of border walls and embraced expansionism. Under Manifest Destiny, all lands proximate to the United States were fair game for conquest. Americans used the term "line" rather than wall—in other words, when they called the border anything but the "Canada border," they called it a line. Cartographic renderings of border—that is to say, as lines on a map—were the preferred pictorial device, and American newspapers and speeches reflected the idea that Canada was on the other side of a tenuous obstacle—a mere line on the map that meant little and that offered little protection to those to its north.

Indeed, Americans consistently failed to grasp that the majority of politically influential Canadians wanted to remain British. Fulford (1998) notes that "in the War of 1812 between Britain and the United States, Americans thought that taking Canada would be simple. In President Jefferson's oft-repeated and ill-informed words, 'The acquisition of Canada this year [1812] as far as the neighbourhood of Quebec, will be a mere matter of marching, and will give us experience for the attack on Halifax next, and the final expulsion of England from the American continent'" (see also Condon and Sinha, 2003: 4). It was supposed that Canada would welcome Americans with open arms or at least see the wisdom of a Canadian–American union if it were allowed to proceed

MOTHER BRITANNIA.—" *Take care, my child !* "
UNCLE SAM.—" *Oh ! never mind, if she falls I'll catch her !* "

Figure 1.16 Canada portrayed as a baby with Uncle Sam and Britannia as proud parents. *Source: Canadian Illustrated News*, 23 July 1870. LAC, ref. no. C-050366.

(Nugent, 2009). Americans did not understand how different Canadians really were; Felix Grundy, an early-nineteenth-century Republican from Tennessee, posited that Canadians only wanted an opportunity to "throw off the yoke of their [British] taskmasters" (81). Even after the War of 1812, after "mere ... marching" failed to acquire central Canada, Americans viewed the border as both politically "dangerous" and artificial and weak.

Not surprisingly, given this situation, American images and editorial cartoons from the nineteenth century that visualize the relationship are rarer than their equivalents in Canada. Those that exist speak to the border's discursive and ideological rather than cartographical importance. Again, in the American media, a thin black line was the American metaphorical device of choice, symbolizing border's lack of substance. It represented the line between a weak neighbour and a strengthening empire bent on territorial conquest.

This thin black line reflected the context for changes in how the United States would work to achieve hegemony in North America: force was now out, and political processes, economic forces, and perhaps even popular consensus were in. By the 1860s, the land border between Canada and the United States had largely been resolved. Military discourses, like the ones that fuelled

the Aroostook War and the Oregon Boundary Dispute, had faded as negotiated boundaries gained favour. This did not mean that Manifest Destiny had
lost strength as a justification for gaining control of Canadian territory or that
Americans had stopped embracing that destiny. It merely meant that the US
approach to achieving territorial hegemony had changed.

CONCLUSIONS

Today, the markers along the Canada–US border reflect the work of surveyors
rather than generals. Those markers have inscribed the state on the landscape in
ways that are reinforced by domestic capacity—militaries, policing authorities,
politicians. Such landscapes of control are relatively new. Initially the Canada–
US boundary was more discursive than real, more a cartographic rendering that
was highly symbolic and that offered little physical resistance to armed force. It
was geopolitical, and as Laxer (2003) tells us, it was also relatively fluid, in that
it reflected the playing out of European power arrangements in North America. These arrangements were inscribed in relations between Europeans and
Indigenous groups, and they pitted European nation against European nation,
but they were not inscribed on the land. Except that they symbolized potential
territorial claims, borders played no material role in continental conquest. The
actual inscription of the Canada–US boundary on the landscape, once it was
completed, was an anti-climax.

At the same time, events in the nineteenth century had sharpened differences between Britain and the United States in North America. This was the
real legacy of the War of 1812 and a multitude of border disputes that followed.
As the following chapters will show, Confederation consolidated a Canadian
nation independent from Britain at the same time that the United States, in the
aftermath of the Civil War, turned its attention to settlement in the Canadian
"northwest." These events generated a new understanding of how borders functioned. The border became more than a territorial line; it "secured" national
populations, inspired national affiliations, and contested a mobile peoples' allegiance. The new border that resulted was seen to offer economic opportunity
as well as protection for the markets of farmers and manufacturers for the new
Canadian state. Needless to say, mobility, transnationalism, and the immigration
discourses they produced created the context for a new understanding of the
meaning of border for generations of Canadians and Americans to come.

Chapter 2

ALL TOGETHER NOW!
ANNEXATION, IMMIGRATION, AND NATURALIZED GEOPOLITICS

Throughout the nineteenth and twentieth centuries, the spectre of annexation was highly useful for creating a series of "identity crises" in Canada (Ince, 2011; Mackey, 1999). As we shall see throughout this chapter, as naturalized geopolitics and immigration processes are explored, what is relevant is that these "crises" were inherently reflexive. They created a Canadian nation-building project as well as a nation-building narrative through which Canadians distinguished themselves from Americans, not on the basis of racial differences but on the basis of their distinctive efforts to create a racial tolerant and multicultural society (Mackey, 1999). For this purpose, the border was essential. But it also required the understanding that state control could be brought about *through* the control of population processes. As Foucault (2008) reminds us, liberal states govern by "securing the population." This is a governance technology in which human life is increasingly the object of state regulation. So if the United States failed to achieve its goal of absorbing Canada by the early twentieth century, it is clear that immigration controls between Canada and the United States during this era of high mobility constituted what Foucault might consider a budding biopolitical governance strategy on *both* sides of the line. It promoted the racial affinity of white Canadian and American populations, while sorting out those of different racial stock. This raises the important question of how immigration practices were embedded in geopolitical discourses in favour of state and nation-building agendas. To better appreciate the process, we need to examine the story of the early and tentative application of biopolitics developed along the Canada–US borderline. We begin by defining "biopolitics" and by considering how race was constructed as an immigration category. How did immigration discourses construct a "common" racial stock from Americans and Canadians? And what sorts of border technologies supported these practices?

For academics who study borders, Foucault's work is always enlightening. While Foucault wrote on many topics and issues, his main interest was in how we create knowledge, that is, "how we know" and in how that knowledge creates discourses and subjectivities. His approach emphasized how powerful discourses developed historically to create comprehensive framings of knowledge, through which specific understandings or discourses were then mobilized. One of Foucault's important contributions to the study of borders was that he founded a scholarship concerned with how governments use discourses and technologies to control borders by controlling populations. He reminds us that, in earlier times, sovereigns exercised their power through total control over the body itself, through death (punishment); in the present-day liberal state, by contrast, this control is exerted on life itself—by defining legitimate protocols for "living." This constitutes a biopolitical technology (Foucault, 2008)—a "securing of the population" as living beings by developing state controls or governance exercised *through* rather than *over* the body.

Clearly, such theories have implications for how Canada and the United States approached immigration in the late nineteenth century as they too developed border technologies to "secure" populations. While some scholars argue that the Canada–US border was at this time meaningless in terms of its interest in controlling population movement, others argue that selective practices of control had already begun well before the turn of the twentieth century. It is enough now that we simply establish that this was an era in which biopolitical technologies first began, however incipient—one that saw to building links between population and its characteristics (such as race or national origins), the territorial container (state), and nation-building discourses. That is to say, by the late nineteenth century in North America, borderlines and immigration controls spoke to the need for territorial and population controls, and these then worked together to further the state's power. The result was a crude biopolitics, one that sought to control life itself in order to further state power and exercise state hegemony (see Foucault, 2008). The question was, of course, *whose* life, *whose* hegemony, and *what* geopolitical agendas would be advanced by biopolitical controls implemented on either side of the line?

As is always the case when constructing narratives of transnational mobility and border control, the answer to that question is rather complex. Americans and Canadians would not have recognized the concept of biopolitics and would not have explained developments as they unfolded at the end of the nineteenth and early twentieth century in such theoretical terms, of course. During that period, political power was understood in relatively straightforward ways. In the mid-nineteenth century, geopolitical discourses defined "population" and "citizen" in terms of national or ethnic origins as well as civilizational attributes. That is to say, nationalities were not equal—some were seen as more desirable than others, and this desirability was determined by civilizational discourses of the day. For a reminder of what this might imply, let us think back to how civilizational and naturalized geopolitical discourses were defined earlier in this book. Setting aside African Americans, Indigenous people, and other who were clearly non-Westerners, racial distinctions between "white" Canadians and Americans were seen, in the late nineteenth century, as increasingly impossible to make. That is, Canadians and Americans had common Western European origins, were "Anglo-Saxon," and thus were "kith and kin." As organic analogies concerning societies developed from pseudo-science and the misapplication of evolutionary theory, race increasingly meant "other than" Anglo-Saxon (see Mackey, 1999). In other words, Anglo-Saxons were not a race, but non-Anglo-Saxons all belonged to one race or another. Anglo-Saxonism became a catch-all category that also created the other—that is, non-white North Americans—thereby excluding them from Anglo-Saxon ranks. White North Americans, by contrast, were constructed as Anglo-Saxon, whatever their specific racial or ethnic origins. This meant they did not encounter the same obstacles to immigration—obstacles that had been placed there for non-Anglo-Saxons. The immigration border "wasn't"—at least for those who were considered "Anglo-Saxon." The values that supported racism were deeply embedded in an understanding of the natural world, which developed from a social Darwinist perspective concerning the "survival of the fittest" (Kohn, 2000). The implications for border control were profound.

The remainder of this chapter shows how this type of naturalized geopolitics played out in the relationship between Canada and the United States along the border, thus creating differential categories of population that could be "secured" by various national and geopolitical discourses.

ANNEXATION, AGAIN?

In the late nineteenth century, movements of settlers and high levels of mobility resulted in the ongoing development of a borderland between Canada and the United States. In many respects, this borderland facilitated transnational forces and transnational identities (Widdis, 1998; Bukowczyk et al., 2005; Konrad and Nicol, 2008). But it would be wrong to suggest that this historical process was free of tensions. Cross-border mobility contributed to the narrative of "one people" as it was pitched by the American press; but as we will see, it also set in place a reflexive understanding of the border—one that embodied resistance to potential US hegemony and a spirit of common cause in Canada. Indeed, by the late nineteenth century, the civilizational discourses of both US Manifest Destiny and British Empire were rapidly transforming.

In the mid- to late nineteenth century, many American newspapers expressed the belief that Canadians would inevitably choose to become part of the United States. As we have already seen, annexation discourses had originally been tied to military conquest, but by mid-century, forceful coercion was increasingly rejected. Other ways of convincing were tried instead. For example, on 29 September 1871, despite the failure of the 1866 Annexation Bill, the *New York Tribune* argued that the Dominion of Canada was artificial and that the Maritime provinces would surely be annexed by the United States in a relationship that would ally them to their "natural trading partners." But unlike earlier in the century, when the conquest of Canada was seen simply as "a day's march," the new discourse suggested that the United States should not "bully" the young nation's provinces into a union but rather wait for the inevitable to occur: "In short, let us act towards them in a frank, manly, honourable way, with no bullying and no wheedling. If we do this those of us who live ten or fifteen years longer will see half a dozen new States added to our Union from this British American territory."

We will return to the gendered implications of this statement later in the chapter. For now, it is important to understand why so many Americans believed that Canada's "voluntary erasure" would proceed regardless of the failed Annexation Bill of 1866—a bill that represented the last gasp of the militant and openly aggressive version of Manifest Destiny, at least towards British North America. A special report in the *New York Sun* on 21 April 1889 identified American perceptions of Canada's relationship to Britain and the popularized geopolitical discourses that framed the discussion. In reporting the results of a fact-finding mission to Britain, one *Sun* reporter described the substance of his interviews with roughly one thousand British individuals of "influence" and "substance." The question he posed was, How would Britain respond to the American annexation of Canada? While the respondents' comments were mixed, the notion of a shared frontier with Canada, which Americans considered so problematic, puzzled the Earl of Derby, who rejected the logic of Manifest Destiny by any means: "You say many Americans and some Canadians think it is in the destiny of Canada to become absorbed in the American Union? Well, I don't see why that should be so. Other countries manage to get along without wishing to annex the other. And surely in Canada there are more people who believe in the great future of their country and would prefer to see it as an independent state than there are those who desire to join the United States" (visit http://chronicling america.loc.gov/newspapers/).

The Earl was ultimately correct in his assessment. Still, as reports of Canada's resources grew ever rosier, so did US interest in some kind of union, propelled by the metaphor of the border as a mere thin black line on the map. These aspirations were supported by articles in American newspapers that reported on various groups or organizations in Canada voting in favour of annexation or lending their support to the cause. But stories like these clearly exaggerated the numbers and influence of Canadians who seriously entertained the idea.

Among them was a transplanted British journalist, Goldwin Smith, who, writing from Canada, strongly campaigned for annexation. His ideas, however far off the Canadian mainstream, found traction in the United States. Smith contended that Canada lacked the political will to sustain its east–west orientation in the face of the pull exerted by the "natural" north–south axis of the North American continent. Canada would become American, he warned, and it was only a matter of time: "Settlers from the United States are pouring into the North-Western Territories, which they were sure to do when in Minnesota and Dakota land became dear. The North-West will be American" (Sharp, 1947: 74).

Smith and his ilk were a minority in Canada, but in its ignorance of Canadian politics, the American press continued to discuss and reflect on the potential union, almost elevating the status of this annexation discourse to that of US foreign policy. Thompson and Randall (1994) write that although by this time Manifest Destiny was no longer being promoted as a call to arms, American politicians and policy-makers showed a calculated disregard of the validity of the Canadian state, thereby continuing the geopolitical tradition of advocating US control of Canadian territory. "As Representative William Munger of Ohio told the House in 1870, now that 'England's star has passed its zenith … Canada will fall into our lap like a ripe apple.' To help shake that tree, throughout the late nineteenth century the United States tested Canadian national sovereignty in boundary, fisheries and sealing disputes" (42).

It should not be surprising that the threat of Canadian absorption into the United States was met by resistance from Canadians. That resistance took the form of a political agenda that promoted the unification of the Canadian colonies and a burgeoning sense of Canadian identity. Between 1873 and 1892, notably in a Toronto publication, *The Grip*, Canadian cartoonist John Wilson Bengough pictured Canada–US relations in such terms for the Canadian public. In his 1886 collection of political cartoons, he published one (Figure 2.1) in which he explained: "This cartoon faithfully reflected the sentiments of the Canadian people on the subject of annexation. While it is still true that there is no general feeling in favour of the change indicated, there is an appreciable absence of the unfriendly feeling toward the United States" (100). But as Ince (2011) reminds us, the threat of annexation or absorption was indeed perceived by many as threatening to Canada, and that perception was incorporated into very public discussions much less benign than Bengough described: "Confederation needed to be strengthened and expanded if it was to survive, and what better tool to lay the foundations of nationhood than one which all peoples of British North America could relate to. Anti-Americanism was to be the principle policy of nation building as the infant Dominion sought to survive and grow in the shadow of America" (9). According to Ince, "Yankees were seen as aggressive, forward, and money-driven. In the minds of the new Canadians, all Americans

A PERTINENT QUESTION.

MRS. BRITANNIA.—"IS IT POSSIBLE, MY DEAR, THAT YOU HAVE EVER GIVEN YOUR COUSIN JONATHAN ANY ENCOURAGEMENT?"

MISS CANADA.—"ENCOURAGEMENT! CERTAINLY NOT, MAMMA. I HAVE TOLD HIM WE CAN *NEVER* BE UNITED."

Figure 2.1 "A Pertinent Question," published in *Diogenes* (Montreal) in June 1869. This cartoon depicts Canada as a young lady and America's misconstrued "intended," sitting with her "mamma," Britannia. Republished in J.W.A. Bengough, *A Caricature History of Canadian Politics*, Vols. 1 & 2 (Toronto: Grip Printing & Publishing Co.), 1886. *Source*: McCord Museum, M994X.5.273.42; print; used with permission. Anonymous © McCord Museum.

spoke in an inelegant, ungrammatical style, and their habit of chewing tobacco was reviled ... And all the while, fear of an American invasion remained" (9).

"Every American Statesman covets Canada," wrote John A. Macdonald, expressing a view held by much of the population. "The greed for its acquisition is still on the increase, and God knows where it will end" (9).

BORDERS, MOBILITY AND HEGEMONY

How do the issues of immigration, border management, and late-nine-teenth-century North American population mobility relate to the perception and the assertions of US hegemony described by Smith, Macdonald, and the *New York Sun* reporter? In the late nineteenth and early twentieth centuries, Canadians and Americans were on the move (Bukowczyk et al., 2005; Widdis, 1998). They were swarming to the Canadian "North-West," and from the American vantage point, the idea that Canada would not want to join the union seemed extremely implausible, given how more and more American "patriots" were making their home there. As this settlement wave continued, the belief that it was in Canada's interest to join the United States was promulgated by the Americans to the point that it was represented as "common knowledge": the Canadian North-West would simply become American, because Americans were positioning themselves to be the dominant nationality there. In the US political imagination, the Canadian "North-West" had achieved the status of a metaphor for Canada as a whole; what happened in the former would inevitably happen in the latter.

American media and public sentiment reinforced the popular sentiment that land and labour were intertwined and that if labour were applied judiciously, land would be secured. It would even be fair to say that belief has become part of US historical wisdom. Land and labour were, through American know-how, transformed into capital (Sharp, 1947: 67). The influx of American "ready cash, agricultural equipment and 'know-how' meant that the long and arduous years necessary on most frontiers to create a comfortable living were potentially bypassed on the Canadian frontier, in a process of leapfrog development": "it was up to Europe to supply the raw labour, but only the American west could provide men who were at once capitalists and experienced farmers" (67). This narrative reinforced an imperialism of sorts, for it treated "capital" as an American "quality." It authorized US "ownership" of land beyond the border and transcended the territorial limitations imposed by national identities. On 6 August 1904, in an article typical of the era, the *Daily Capital Journal* of Salem, Oregon, explained that Canada was not competent to stand as a nation independent of the United States, that it owed its existence to the United States and was thus rightfully American:

> Canada today owes its national existence to the forbearance and to the pacific policy of the United States. Canada neglects even such military preparation as would enable her to defend herself successfully against the United States ... The vacant lands in Canada, therefore, will be tilled up by men and women of other races, many of whom will maintain ties of affection and interest, not

with England, but with the United States. (http://chroniclingamerica.loc.gov/newspapers)

This belief concerning the inequality of the Canada–US relationship reverberated throughout the American popular press, reinforcing the idea that the American takeover of Canada was imminent. These same sentiments were reflected over and over again in other American journals of the day. On 18 October 1903, for example, the *Salt Lake City Herald* argued that the Canadian West would be the next area in which American farmers would settle, and as they did so, this newly opened territory would succumb to the pull of the American empire to the south. Even though the region had already been incorporated into Confederation, and even though the Manitoba had already been made a province, Americans still believed this was a virgin land waiting for their ploughshares.

Other American newspapers in the late nineteenth and early twentieth centuries proclaimed in headlines that "the Northwest is American," the suggestion being that the US was again turning its attention to the possible annexation of Canadian territory, as it had earlier in the century.

In sum, Americans viewed the country north of the border through a lens that was distinctly American, as well as geopolitical and nationalistic. By their calculus, Canada was a weak power that Britain would willingly abandon, and these perceptions merged into a discourse that encouraged American immigration. And as Canadians welcomed Americans (and, indeed as massive numbers of Canadians went south and were similarly welcomed), this great transnational moment was seized upon by some American publications as yet another rhetorical opportunity to promote a new type of union.

Knowles (2007) writes that "with typical American spirit they launched a vigorous counter-attack in an effort to halt or curtail the northern flow. Often this took the form of a virulent newspaper war against Canada" (90). But it was more often the case by the late nineteenth century that the idea was not to halt the flow but to use the flow—to secure the territory by securing the population. Examples of this abound. For example, on 15 April 1902, the *Minneapolis Journal* (Figure 2.2) depicted the flight of the American "farmer bird" across a boundary line of little substance. The thin black line represented in this image is not merely a cartographic convention: it embedded a common American perception of the western Canada–US border. Americans began to openly identify this area of Canada as "American." The result was the continued representation of the Canadian border as a "thin black line," much as we saw in earlier periods. It was not military dreams but land hunger that drove them to this imagery. Canada had been a nation for almost half a century by this time, but for Americans this was a "sleeping empire" only now awakening to the influx of those northward bound: "The Land is Found to Be Good and the Americans Are Bound To Have Their Full Share," trumpeted the headlines of American newspapers.

If Americans saw the long border as a potential source of geopolitical friction at the beginning of the nineteenth century, by the end they saw it as a golden opportunity for peaceful expansion. This fuelled a renewed interest in absorbing Canada long after the American Revolution, the War of 1812, the Civil War, and even the Annexation Bill of 1866. But unlike in earlier years, the belief in annexation was now being pitched in terms of a "naturalized" geopolitical discourse rather than a "civilizational" one. The continental mission of divine destiny maintained traction among most Americans, but continentalization no longer relied on strident or militaristic discourses. It was no longer angels but "farmer birds" which hovered over the new frontier (Figure 2.2). Americanization was to be ensured simply by "being there." The stream of Americans

Figure 2.2 "The American Invasion of Western Canada." *Minneapolis Journal*, 15 April 1902. *Source: Chronicling America*, Library of Congress; Minneapolis Historical Society.

northward heralded the extension of the American nation, or so Americans believed. The task now was to create a suitable space for a relatively benign and perhaps even friendly annexation: an annexation that nature clearly intended and that immigration and mobility appeared to facilitate. The annexation of Canada, at least in the North-West, was to occur through the "Americanization" of its population. As people and capital flooded north to the Canadian prairies (and south, to become *de facto* Americans), dreams of a "single race" under the American flag grew. The goal, then, was not to prevent the movement of people across the border so much as to define and protect territorial interests by moving the line apace with the people, effecting a "biopolitical" coup. The idea, at least in the minds of Americans, was essentially to adjust the line to accommodate America's spillover. Viewed in this way, the North-West border was a metaphor for Americanization, one that "naturalized" their hegemonic relationship with Canada.

NATURALIZED GEOPOLITICS: BUILDING A DISCOURSE OF OPEN BORDERS

As we have seen, the strengthening annexation efforts of the late nineteenth century were rooted in a movement that sought to absorb, through suasion and common interest, people of a common (albeit socially constructed) kind. This new project replaced a civilizational discourse that advocated aggressive conquest of "others" and was driven by a naturalized geopolitical discourse.

What is meant by a "naturalized" geopolitical discourse? What technologies of state control and expansion did it support? Essentially, this discourse embeds geopolitical aspirations and understandings in the natural world. Specific geopolitical agendas and perceptions are made to seem inevitable, "commonsense," and "natural" (see Agnew, 2003). Recall that in the introduction to this book and at the beginning of this chapter, civilizational and naturalized geopolitical discourses were explained as the "big ideas" that underpinned understandings of the world. In the eighteenth and early nineteenth centuries, the world was understood as a field on which to imprint empire and the political map as an outcome of power justified by religion, race, and superior military force. By the late nineteenth century, however, power relations among states (and the resulting territorial justifications) were based on understandings of how the natural order conditioned human existence in ways that demanded "survival of the fittest." Like civilizational discourses, the United States used these naturalized assessments in ways that also supported American hegemony, expansion, and empire, although the rationales and means for securing extraterritorial influence were somewhat different than civilizational logic had prescribed.

If civilizational geopolitics had been rooted in beliefs about civilization and empire (Agnew, 2003), naturalized geopolitics was "a view of the world which could claim grounding in the natural features of the Earth" (29). In other words, naturalized geopolitics marshalled enduring, natural, and even scientific laws in support of specific geopolitical understandings and outcomes. Pre–Second World War Germany provides the most obvious example of how scientific assessments fostered a naturalized geopolitical discourse. Social Darwinism and *realpolitik* increasingly informed the geopolitical agenda of the Third Reich, in this way fuelling the narrative of the "organic state." The Nazi state believed in *Lebensraum* (living space)—that is, that it had the right to expand aggressively, even to the point of invading neighbouring states and removing the "unwanted" or threatening peoples and races. Similarly, in late-nineteenth-century America, social developments and scientific theory juxtaposed to create a narrative that supported North American continentalism. The entire continent was increasingly presented as a natural container for a single society or people, all of whom would be American. This continentalist reading was rooted in North America's physical geography, which was strongly north–south in orientation—the Rocky Mountains, the Appalachians, the Great Plains. Accordingly, it was inevitable that settlement patterns would reflect that geography. Continentalism encouraged populations to spill across artificial borders in pursuit of land and resources.

Why? Because continentalism acted as a naturalized geopolitical discourse, at least from the point of view of the southern half of the continent. Indeed, from the perspective of the United States, it authorized American expansion. This reading of the physical landscape and natural world referenced "natural" regions and landscapes, which in turn became part of a normative geopolitical and territorial discourse. After all, there were no natural barriers between the two national territories of Canada and the United States; nature had provided seamless physiographic regions consistent with a seamless nation. Where these were favourable to settlement—for example, on the Great Plains—naturalized geopolitics demanded that the line between the nations be repositioned to ensure that the end of "good land" in North America conformed to the Canada–US border. From the point of view of this discursive narrative, God had granted Americans a unique territory for the use of the American people. By right, it followed, the edge of US territory should coincide with the edge of the "natural bounty." All of this reinforced the common belief that America was exceptional and destined for greatness (see Horsman, 1987).

Much as before, this sort of common belief about borders and bounty was often reflected in newspapers. On 3 July 1904, the *Saint Paul Globe* editorialized along just these lines:

> It used to be thought that nature, always so kind to the American nation, had carried her bounty to the limit and capped the climax by making the northern boundary of good agricultural land on this continent coincide with the northern

boundary of the United States. An American in search of a new home ...
would never dream of crossing over to the southernmost tier of sections in
Manitoba. A great change has been wrought. Now it is well understood that
the wheat belt crosses the international line in a northwesterly direction and
extends much farther west in Canada than it does in the United States. Now
it is generally understood that the virgin prairies of Western Canada are soon
to become the greatest spring wheat producing region in the world, and that
in many other forms of agriculture that part of Canada is to take a prominent
place.

This passage underscores that in the late nineteenth century, the impetus
for an American "invasion" of Canada was driven by economics as much as
by politics. The Americans, having pushed all European powers but Britain
from the North American continent, had now turned their sights on the rich
agricultural potential of the Canadian prairies and on Canada's resources more
generally (Bukowczyk et al., 2005).

Indeed, the movement of Americans into the Canadian West was "pushed"
by a number of economic factors, such as the vanishing of the American frontier, the demand for American capital, and growing American land hunger; but
it was also "pulled" by the opening of the West by the Canadian government,
which actively encouraged western immigration (Sharp, 1947: 70). Many Americans viewed the combination of available land and ease of immigration as the
perfect formula for expanding American society, economy, and politics. The
question was how that expansion was to be carried out, and there seemed to
be two choices: first, outright annexation of Canadian territory and the obliteration of what popular texts referred to as a "meaningless" border—an option
increasingly perceived as out of the question; or second, the institutionalization
of American hegemony by "securing the population" and making it "American." It was this second option that gained traction. As the *Seattle Republican*
pointed out on 17 July 1903, Manifest Destiny was achievable, but it would be
through a "naturalized" process, a joining of hands rather than a geopolitical
confrontation:

> Herein lies the national motive for the invasion of Canada; but there is an
> individual motive which promises to send two Yankees to one from all other
> countries, and when these shall have arrived in sufficient numbers that the
> country begins to have the appearance of being settled, then of their own
> motion, without solicitation from this side of the border, will they ask for the
> protecting arm of Uncle Sam to be placed around them.

The same editorial added that "England will protest; it will take time and
considerable diplomacy, but without the use of arms or the shedding of blood,

British America on the north will join hands with Mexico on the south, as together they plight [*sic*] their allegiance to that flag—the Stars and Stripes— whose banner over them means peace, prosperity and righteousness" (http:// chroniclingamerica.loc.gov/lccn/sn84025811/1903-07-17/ed-1/seq-5).

True, this expansionist ambition was hegemonic, and in the end, it remained unfulfilled; but in terms of American intentions, it was strong enough to change how the border was discursively imagined. As we have already seen, throughout the nineteenth and early twentieth centuries, Americans continued to represent the border as a thin black line that was increasingly under threat of erasure. At the beginning of the twentieth century, this idea held its ground, so that it was common for American editorial cartoons to deploy various border devices to suggest that this weak border could no longer hold back Americans following their territorial birthright. Americans had, after all, erased the borders of the

Figure 2.3 Many cartoonists were amused by the inbound movement of Americans. *Source: Vancouver Daily Province*, August 1911. Queen's University, Stauffer Library, Microfilm Collections.

former Spanish and French territories in North America, and by the late nineteenth century they wanted the same for the Canadian border. Figure 2.3 shows how Canadians parodied this weak border imagery, to their advantage.

REVISING THE AGENDA: SECURING THE AMERICAN POPULATION IN CANADA

The late nineteenth century witnessed a growing transnational relationship based on the mobility of citizens (Bukowczyk et al., 2005). Popular images that naturalized and extended US authority to the Canadian "North-West," and perhaps to Canada as a whole, illustrate that the Americans hoped more and more to gain territory from Canada. Those same motifs suggested that the border between the two nations was "thin" or non-existent. As they fostered the illusion (if not the fact) of ease of movement, Americans and Canadians, in different ways, attempted to "attach" state sovereignty to population. They did so not by controlling immigration but rather by "claiming" the populations within the new territories opened up by immigration and even by encouraging the flows. Population movements across the line were largely unregulated so that "migration criss-crossed the Canada–U.S. border with little oversight" (Bukowczyk et al., 81). There is little evidence that Canadians viewed Americans as a problem population or resented their presence (Sharp, 1947). They felt "the great majority of those American settlers are good citizens, but they have great powers of assimilation, and are first, last and always, Americans" (74). Widdis (1998) writes, for example, that in Saskatchewan in the late nineteenth century, the locals held mixed views of American immigrants. Preferred over more racialized groups, Americans remained relatively inconspicuous in the West. At the same time local newspapers and other texts acknowledged their contribution to development.

On the whole, then, Canadians generally welcomed Americans, although they did not support their "natural absorption" rhetoric. In the post-Confederation years, anti-American discourses expressed the power of rhetorical resistance to Americanization even while distancing themselves from any type of American immigration control. Canadians were more concerned with losing Canadians to the US than they were with Americans entering Canada (Bukowcyzk et al., 2008). The Canadian government resorted to naturalized framings of national territory in order to attract new immigrants, and not just Americans. Motifs about progress and the taming of the wilderness, about bountiful nature and prosperous farmers, were often deployed within and on behalf of the Canadian state (Figure 2.4). So was the motif of harmony and peace between races (Figure 2.5).

If Americans were generally understood as "not Canadians," and their continental ambitions were unwelcome in the West, at the same time, in their strong presence, many Canadians saw an opportunity to build a nation. In the late 1890s, under Immigration Minister Sir Clifford Sifton, Canada launched a massive recruitment campaign in both Europe and the United States that would continue until the First World War. Its purpose was to encourage immigration to western Canada. Americans benefited from the fact that when immigrants who entered Canada at any of its ports of entry were white (i.e., British, Western European, or American), little was done except to collect basic demographic information and shepherd the arrivals to distribution centres. As we will see shortly, the story was often different when immigrants were not white.

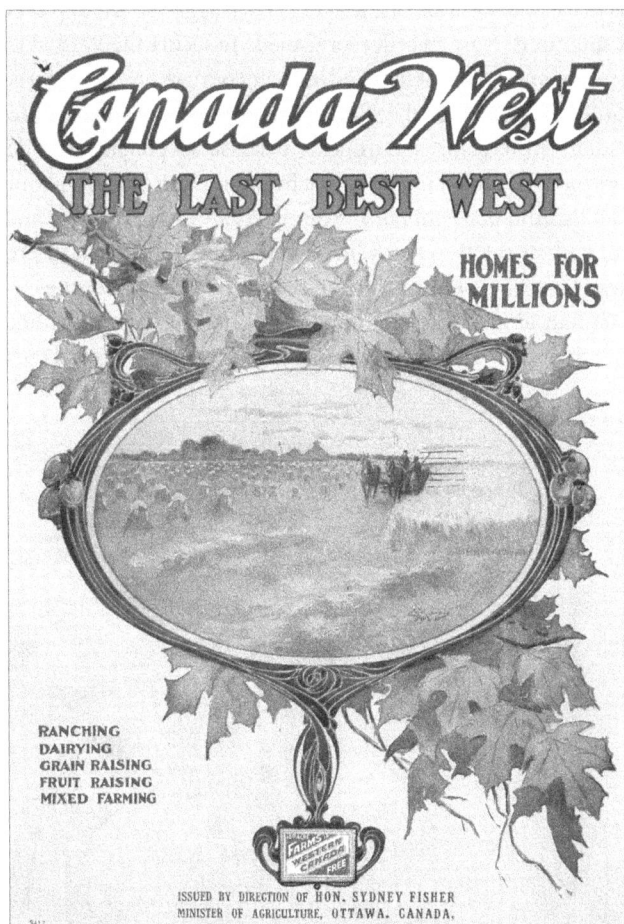

Figure 2.4 "Canada West: The Last Best West." Poster published by the Department of Agriculture, 1910. Original held in Canadian Pamphlet Collection, W.D. Jordan Special Collections and Music Library, Queen's University. *Source:* LAC, acc. no. C-030620.

The Canadian West, the nation's new "frontier," was to be the natural extension of the east and the hope of a fledgling Canadian nation intent on solidifying "Confederation." Zeller (1987) writes that in the post-Confederation years in Canada, the physical sciences contributed to a nation-building discourse, that is, to the idea of a transcontinental nation in Victorian Canada that would be separate from the United States. In the United States, inventory scientists and those interpreting the results of eighteenth- and nineteenth-century inventory sciences constructed their own naturalized discourses.

In this world, the metaphors for nation and border proved important. As we saw in the previous chapter, the Canada–US border had often been pictured by Canadians as a defensive wall, one that held back aggressors and pre-empted US territorial ambitions. Now, in order for Canada to secure the West, it would have to exert its sovereignty, the state needed to encourage people to settle the land *for Canada*. At the end of the day, Canadians did not care whether these settlers were Canadian, American, or European, because sovereignty was determined by state control of occupied territory, not by population origins. Required, then, was a border that did not symbolically or materially erect "walls"; something less substantial, such as the thin black line favoured by the American press, would do the trick. That line would delineate the space to be filled, the container in which Canadian identity and nationalism was to be fomented, but it would invite rather than turn away immigration. This metaphor allowed the Canadian

Figure 2.5 "Canada the Granary of the World" (1903). *Source:* LAC, acc. no. C-081314 .

government, as well as land agents like the British firm of Thomas Cook and Sons, to recruit aggressively in the United States, Great Britain, and Europe. The challenge was not to prevent Americans from coming north but to encourage them to do so. It was also to discourage Canadians from moving south (see Bukowczyk et al., 2005).

Representations of US hegemony along the Canada–US border now followed two distinct threads. Each took its cue from the rhetorical devices, texts, and representations of the border found in the Canadian and American press. First, Anglo-Saxonism was constructed in the United States as a racial category whose logic contributed to an inclusive Canada–US racial identity. Americans were able to imagine Canadians as extensions of themselves even while the same logic enabled Canadians to see themselves as "distinct" from Americans. Second, metaphorical understandings of the border referenced a naturalized geopolitics framework. How did images and texts change as a result of this

Figure 2.6 The welcome masses ushered through the immigration gate by Miss Canada. *Canadian Illustrated News*, 14 August 1880. *Source*: LAC, acc. no. C-075551.

naturalized geopolitical discourse? And how did these representations reflect a degree of reflexivity that generated resistance to Americanization? These are important questions.

ANGLO-SAXONISM AND A COMMON PEOPLE? US NARRATIVES

Late-nineteenth-century racial categories did not "naturally" divide Canadians from Americans, most of whom were of Western European stock. From this, it was easy for people at the time to contemplate that integration of the two populations in a shared "white" North America was scientifically inevitable. At the same time, this shared "whiteness," or so-called Anglo-Saxonism was exclusionary. The United States, for example, very much viewed itself as a "gate-keeping nation," one in which "immigration and its restriction, largely based on race and nationality, came to determine the very make-up of the nation and American national identity" (Lee, 2002). Moreover, US restrictions on Chinese immigration meant that many Chinese entered the country "through the back door." This effectively "transformed the northern and southern borders into sites of contest over illegal immigration, race, citizenship, immigration policy and international immigration" (55).

The American press reinforced this perspective and indeed encouraged the racialization of immigration. It idealized white Americans, counterposing them against Chinese men, who were often illustrated in derogatory ways—for example, eating rats and living in crowded "narcotic dens" (see *Puck Magazine*, 1868). Race was also perceived as a "border problem." Figure 2.7, published in *The Wasp* in December 1880 (see also Lee, 2002: 64), recasts the border as under assault from non–Anglo-Saxon immigrants, with the American eagle hiding behind a defensive gate. This discourse in relation to overseas populations (Kramer, 2002) created an exclusionary space, with racial exclusion being an important border management technology. The American press went along with this perspective, picturing, for example, "Chinamen" hiding in bales to cross the Mexican border, caught by diligent US customs agents.

In contrast to these "Orientalist" perspectives, Anglo-Saxonism as it was promoted in the late nineteenth century saw Americans and Canadians as a people of common ancestry and therefore of common destiny—as a single racial stock that should celebrate and promote its unity. Kramer writes that even the publishing industry was complicit in this and that Anglo-Saxonism was promulgated through "the *Atlantic Monthly*, the *North American Review*, the *Fortnightly Review*, *Scribner's*, *Century Magazine*, *Nineteenth Century* ... [which] burdened late-Victorian tabletops on both sides of the Atlantic." This "helped create an 'imagined community' of literate, English-speaking Americans and Britons with common affiliations and reference points, even among the less traveled" (Kramer, 2002: 1326).

Figure 2.7 "And still they come ..." The US border as an immigration wall. *Source: WASP,* 4 December 1880.

In this way, the Anglo-Saxon narrative came to be about a linear, heroic past and the possibility of a glorious future. It stressed the inevitable integration of the two populations within a progressive and ostensibly white North America. Gone was the "mongrel population" of Canada, as it had been called by Americans in 1867 (*Evening Telegraph,* Philadelphia, 18 March 1867: 4). So if (as we have already seen) the "civilizational line" of the early nineteenth century made much of the distinction between American and British/European worlds, the late-nineteenth-century United States saw "Anglo-Saxonism" develop as a totalizing yet integrating racial discourse. It amounted to a naturalized geopolitical discourse about the Canada–US border, and it worked to create a new, imagined, transnational space and community within which inclusion was predicated on racial commonality. This is not to suggest that "Anglophobia" among Americans, or anti-Americanism among Canadians, had disappeared (Kohn, 2000). Neither had done so (see, for example, Moser, 1998, or Mackey, 1999). It does, though, suggest, that Anglo-Saxonism emerged as a hegemonic and compelling American narrative regarding the relationship between the two nations—a narrative, moreover, that conveniently reinforced naturalized geopolitical discourses and realist geopolitical ambitions and displaced the argument that Canada was to be taken because it was "different." Instead, it was to be integrated because it was "the same." This racial discourse, thus combined with the continental vision of shared geography, contributed strongly to the foundations for open immigration, which would remain between the two nations long after the border was drawn.

But there was a subtext to this development. Americans reserved a spe-cial "brand" of Anglo-Saxon racial stock for themselves, and they used it to set themselves apart from their overseas ancestors (Horsman, 1987). This special Anglo-Saxon status probably had its roots in the larger project of building of an "American" republican state and an American national identity. It positioned Americans as a special and privileged branch—more advanced, if you will—of the larger Anglo-Saxon racial stock whose origins were in Britain and Western Europe (Horsman, 1987). Kramer writes that by the time American Anglo-Saxonism was well developed in the early and mid-nineteenth centuries, it was justified and was reflected in an unshakable belief in American exceptionalism, which was now combined with the force of a crude biopolitics. In effect, this was a political discourse that positioned Americans more favourably in relation to other North Americans and Europeans. This American racial discourse, when it was openly applied to North American immigration, privileged "Anglo-Saxons" and afforded them a mobility that other "races" could not hope to achieve.

But despite the now unshakable belief that it was a scientific fact, race was an imprecise term, one that was socially constructed and enforced. Grounded in political ideology, as well as an early version of what was to become known later as "social Darwinism" in its incorrect reading of biological evolution, Anglo-Saxonism was actually a ranked-race system that demanded an unachiev-able racial purity: "Anglo-Saxonism represented ... superior, but distinct, racial elements," which could also be constructed from combinations of other racial categories. Indeed, "while sharply delimited, that hybridity—and the possible theoretical possibility of future assimilations—lent porousness to Anglo-Sax-onism's boundaries in race, culture and destiny" (Kramer, 2002: 1322). Since it was predicated on a naturalizing ideological assessment of human origins, and since it reified certain categories of racial or ethnic stock as "Anglo-Saxon," it also created a collectively agreed upon racial threshold for excluding those who were not. These exclusions diminished the humanity of those who did not "fit," as we will see when we examine nineteenth-century "Oriental" immigration.

So by the late nineteenth century, Anglo-Saxonism in America was both a racial discourse and a naturalizing geopolitical narrative. While it created the argument for commonality among those of white European descent, it also char-acterized those of non-Anglo-Saxon origins in terms and images that were quite the "opposite" of Anglo-Saxon "qualities" (Kohn, 2000). But Figure 2.8 suggests that this "common people" found itself pushed to its limits when dealing with French Canadians. This image, taken from Grover Cleveland's "The President's Message" (1887), contrasts a dark and swarthy French Canadian, dressed more as *voyageur* (with furs, sash, and moccasins) than as mill worker, with a US cus-toms officer in his clean-cut and well-appointed uniform. The picture's imagery

Figure 2.8 From "The President's Message," 1887, by Grover Cleveland. The cartoon depicts a US border guard telling a French Canadian migrant that he "can pass free into the United States, but his Goods must Be Taxed." *Source*: Putnam and Sons, 1887, 35.

highlights that the border was open to "free and cheap labour," suggesting that contrary to the tenets of racial stock discourse, French Canadians were indeed of lower rank than Americans and that they were "free and cheap." Haglund (2007) suggests that there was a nativist reaction to French Canadian immigration in the United States. He notes that Anglo-Saxonism was at its peak of popularity in the late nineteenth and early twentieth centuries and that this ideology held that all the worthwhile political values and institutions—especially those that gave substance to America's identity—"could be traced back to the 'Teutonic' forests of antiquity, in which were to be encountered the first stirrings of democracy." French Canadian racism was embedded in this context, in the sense that a great many believed that "the Teutonic virtues carried in the genes of freedom-loving Yankees would not be able to withstand the onslaught from what was being styled by some the 'Chinese of the East,' teeming masses of French Canadians steeped in medieval religious mumbo-jumbo, speaking a different language, and willing to work at any wage, thereby throwing virtuous and proud Anglo labourers out of their jobs" (85).

The racial underpinnings of this naturalized discourse, which focused on constructing and securing populations of suitable stock for nation-building purposes, are obvious to us a century or so later; the gendered quality of the discourse is more subtle but equally misguided. Gendered imagery was increasingly important in imagining the evolving Canada–US relationship in the late nineteenth and early twentieth centuries, in the sense that stronger powers like Britain and the United States consistently portrayed Canada as a young woman. This was not unintentional. Kramer (2002) notes that Anglo-Saxonism was a highly "masculine" discourse that coded gendered inequalities. At the beginning of this chapter, we saw how the United States wished to annex Canada in a "manly" way. Many of the "youthful and vigorous" images of the late nineteenth century, which portrayed Canada as female and the United States as male, referenced this masculine Anglo-Saxon discourse that did more than simply resonate with the gendered attitudes of the time (Kramer, 2002). They also wove them into a geopolitical narrative of race and nation. For example, the popular press on both sides of the border represented the United States as a male suitor wooing the young (female) Canada. Figure 2.9 portrays Canada as a young maid, unable to resist the pull of the United States. The Library of Congress describes this lithograph as showing "Uncle Sam offering a bouquet of flowers labeled 'Reciprocity' to a woman labeled 'Canada'; Uncle Sam is being held back by a businessman labeled 'Trusts' whose feet are planted against a rock labeled 'High Protection' and is pulling on Sam's coattails, while the woman is being held back by a military officer labeled 'Toryism' pulling on her fur wrap."

The marriage metaphor points to a supposed genealogical relationship between Canada, Britain, and the United States. In some political cartoons, Canada was portrayed as an offspring or child (Figure 1.16), suggesting that neither of these two great powers took Canada's independence seriously. The fact that Anglo-Saxonism touched on the relationship between the United States and Britain as kindred empires, and, in so doing, constructed the US as the more powerful male or father figure (often in the form of Uncle Sam or Brother Jonathan, or a male president), complicated the way in which Canada–US relations developed. This merging of Anglo-American identities in the late nineteenth century constituted a racialization of identity that saw "Anglo-Saxon" racism develop "as a self-conscious bond" connecting Britons and Americans (Kramer, 2002: 1318). In this way, Anglo-Saxonism linked the American and British empires; Canada was the intended target of *and* the "collateral damage" in this socially constructed relationship. (We will say more about this later in the chapter and when we explore the Alaska Panhandle dispute.) Naturalized devices and genealogical metaphors were markers or stand-ins for assumptions about important political relationships between "empires," or "big boys" (as they

Figure 2.9 "Flirtation under difficulties" by J.S. Pughe, in *Puck* 55, no. 1409 (2 March 1904), centrefold. Copyright 1904 by Keppler & Schwarzmann. *Source:* Library of Congress Prints and Photographs Division, Washington, DC. 20540, http://hdl.loc.gov/loc.pnp/pp .print.

were often shown in representations of the time). This is where the common motifs of courtship and marriage fit as border representational devices denoting US hegemonic designs on Canada (Figure 2.10).

In the actual flesh-and-blood world of the nineteenth and early twentieth centuries, Anglo-Saxonism encouraged intermarriage—or, rather, strategic British–American marriages. "Through the unions and their offspring, a language of Anglo-Saxon blood and cultural 'kinship' crystallized around actual genealogy ... as natural as marriage between man and woman [because it] consummates the purposes of the creation of the race" (Kramer, 2002: 1327).

In the world of imagery, the same rules applied. The marriage metaphor that was commonly utilized to describe Canada–US relations and the borderline itself was used to help construct the trope of Canada as female, child, or young woman, or as joint British–American offspring. The narratives of Anglo-Saxon popular representation and biopolitical geopolitics went so far as to promote this metaphor through poetry. The following poem was published on 3 July 1903 in the *Coalville Times,* a Utah newspaper, and was quickly reprinted in other papers across the United States. Playing on the theme of a young maid Canada, it describes a genealogical relationship between Canada and the United States, one that must be politically consummated and that calls upon nature itself (or rather uses natural imagery) to sanction the nuptials.

Figure 2.10 "Trying Her Constancy, or, a dangerous flirtation." Miss Canada is wooed by Uncle Sam as John Bull (Britain) sleeps. St. Stephen's Review Presentation Cartoon, 20 October 1888. *Source*: LAC, acc. no. R9266-3552. Peter Winkworth Collection of Canadiana.

When Eagle and Beaver Wed

There's a maiden who though grown to womanhood, Is a child among the
  nations,
She is one of Britain's fair and lively brood, Held in check by her relations.
Her near neighbor is a cousin big and smart, And it seems somehow or other,
That they cannot always live like now, apart—She will have to leave her
  mother!
Her big cousin's noble eagle proudly soars, While her beaver coyly eyes him,
And if he came, a lover, to her doors, She would surely not despise him.
In the starry sky she reads her destiny, "Tis a bright and wondrous story
Of what the maiden Canada will be, When she sits beneath old glory.
Britannia may a tear of sorrow shed, When her daughter wills to leave her;
But Columbia will pat the lion's head, When the eagle weds the beaver.
(see Library of Congress, Chronicling America archives)

In this poem, the border has become "doors" facilitative of courtship and clearly not sturdy enough to rebuff the eagle's charms. America's destiny is continental, and Canada is America's genealogical ally, symbolizing, perhaps, the "marriage" of Anglo-American concepts of empire itself. The poem's gendered—and highly patronizing—symbolism contains metaphors that assume that the union of the "beaver" and the "eagle" is natural, thus reinforcing a sense of inevitability. A "naturalized" discourse is being deployed here that is further mobilized by the apparent Anglo-Saxon bonds between empires (bonds of race, heritage, and belonging) and that insinuates that a relationship between Canada and the United States is possible, embedded as it is in a new type of geopolitical rationalization of empire. The metaphor of eagle and beaver, the marriage of "cousins," and the idea of borders as "doors" can thus be understood in the context of a time when naturalized discourses were attempting to situate American exceptionalism within the broader racial category of Anglo-Saxonism but in hegemonic fashion. As Kohn (2000) has observed, "English speaking North Americans utilized kinship language to discuss their common heritage. Canadians and Americans referred to each other as 'cousins' or 'brothers' who shared the common 'mother' of Great Britain" (3). Figure 2.11, published in the American satirical magazine *Puck* in 1888, recasts this relationship in comic form—as a parody that evokes the eagle in a futile courtship of the beaver.

Of course, Canadians saw this very differently, as we will soon discuss. Their use of marriage and gender metaphors played reflexively to embedded discourses of US hegemony. In the Canadian press, Miss Canada or Maid Canada was a familiar character (see "The Art of Resistance," later in this chapter). Especially in the Victorian era, she was pictured as constantly anxious about the unwanted attentions of her American male suitor, Brother Jonathan (later, Uncle Sam).

This brief overview of American newspapers and historical texts sheds light on a significant trend in nineteenth-century border assessment and management that up until now has been largely ignored—that is, the way in which border images, reified in the press and in public texts, provide us with insights into contemporary perceptions of international order and international relations, especially as these understandings foregrounded common beliefs about race, gender, and nation. These images contained the terms of common understanding as well as the seeds of mistrust and separation. And they presented their case in ways that played to very different national audiences. Yet even as it excluded some, this genealogical discourse of Anglo-Saxonism positioned others who were not deemed Anglo-Saxon within a hierarchy where "inclusion" was possible. It was a template for constructing a national population in that it set the permissible "racial perimeters" of that population and ascribed meaning to physical stock, even when that stock extended beyond the border. This was something that Manifest Destiny could not do.

Overall, from an American perspective, the rise of "Anglo-Saxonism" as a racial discourse in the late nineteenth and early twentieth centuries and the "annexation" rhetoric of the American press were co-constitutive: both were examples of how a new geopolitical discourse regarding the Canada–US border worked to diminish the importance of the "civilizational" line of the early nineteenth century and create a new transnational space predicated on racial and national commonalities. The lack of distinction between, and immigration

Figure 2.11 "The Eagle and the Beaver," from the cover of *Puck* magazine, 26 December 1888. *Source*: Library of Congress, Washington, DC.

control over, white American and Canadian populations contributed to the annexation project. In the imaginings of American territorial architects, this space was not to be transnational and hybridized, not was it to be shared by Canadians and Americans; it was simply to be "American." This sentiment was perhaps expressed best in the *Seattle Republican* on 17 July 1903:

> The American citizens who are … taking advantage of the opportunity afforded in the broad prairies and fertile valleys of Manitoba, Saskatchewan, Alberta and Assiniboia are not lost to this nation. They are but the leaven that shall set in motion the process that shall draw those provinces and eventually all the British possessions in North America under the broad folds of "Old Gloria," the banner of the free. (Library of Congress, Chronicling America archives, http://chroniclingamerica.loc.gov/lccn/sn84025811/1903-07-17/ed-1/seq-5)

One final integrating effect of the Anglo-Saxon discourse in the United States—and it was highly significant—was that Canada, the United States, and

Britain were geopolitically positioned of as a trio, with Canada as the "junior partner." The "patriarchy" established by gendered metaphors also contributed to the understanding—among American and Canadian media, for example— that North American relations represented in effect a ménage à trois, that the United States and Britain were both keenly invested in borders and relations, and that Canada should position itself between. The result, for Canadians, was delegation to the status of junior partner. Figure 2.12, a Canadian cartoon protesting British support for the American position during the Alaska Panhandle dispute, reflects this understanding. In 1903, the United States and Britain established a commission to determine the border there, and in 1906 a survey was undertaken demarcating the 141st Meridian as the Yukon–Alaska boundary. An Alaskan Boundary Commission was founded under the terms of the 1903 treaty with Britain related to the disputed Panhandle line. Canadians believed that the boundary decision was not consistent with earlier treaties between Britain and Russia, and there was a sense that Britain had betrayed Canada in order to maintain friendly relations with the United States. The Boundary Convention, of course, was not signed by Canada, but by Britain and the United States.

CANADIANS DEFINE SELF AND OTHER

Shared racial discourses regarding immigration created an open but reflexive transnational border. It is important here to understand how shared racial

JOHN BULL: "Yes, 'e's makin' a lot of noise, Sam, but 'e'll get over it."—From the *North American* (Philadelphia).

Figure 2.12 A crying baby, "Canada," protests as Britain (John Bull) gives in to Uncle Sam's Alaska Boundary demands. John Bull tells Sam, "Yes, 'e's makin' a lot of noise, Sam, but 'e'll get over it." *Source*: Originally printed in the *North American* (Philadelphia); reproduced in the *American Monthly Review of Reviews*, October 1903, 668.

discourses produced exclusion—how the border was understood as a metaphorical barrier wall that had to remain porous—for it had to produce the category "Anglo-Saxon" from an extremely heterogeneous population (which, by the late nineteenth century, was increasingly not of Western European stock).

In Canada, race was used to construct Canadians as a distinct and special people, separate from Americans and Anglo-Saxon in only the broadest sense of the term (Mackey, 1999). Figures 2.5 and 2.6, are striking examples of how this narrative constructed the idea of a national population in the Canadian West. There, Anglo-Saxonism was an assimilating discourse that constructed the broadest category of "Canadian" possible rather than an exclusionary one based on narrow understandings of racial, linguistic, and ethnic origins. In effect, it reified an aspiration towards "multiculturalism" as a national project, essentially because Canadian immigration was increasingly multicultural. Mackey (1999) writes that in the late nineteenth century, "tolerance" was cultivated as a Canadian "identity marker" that distinguished Canadians from Americans. Rooted in the kind of "anti-Yankee" sentiments that were common at the time, the Canadians' belief was that Americans were deeply racist and intolerant. While Canadians were no less racist in their own way, they collectively believed otherwise and constructed the "myth of tolerance" as a Canadian attribute. This invention was oddly racist, in that "others" were defined by their difference and then included as "add-ons" to an Anglo-Saxon nation-building project.

In this sense, we can position Anglo-Saxonism as an important piece of the puzzle in a distinctively Canadian identity-building project, too. It played reflexively into an exclusionary, social construction of nationalism. As we have previously seen, the United States saw "Anglo-Saxon" racism develop as "a self-conscious bond" connecting Britons and Americans in the late nineteenth century. In Canada, Anglo-Saxonism did something else: it contributed to a nation-building device that created a singular population distinct from the United States, and in doing so, it eliminated as much as was possible the category of other, reducing "undesirables" to a small group of those who, by any stretch of the imagination, could not be seen as "Anglo-fiable," and justifying the work of bordering sites as exclusionary for "dangerous foreigners."

Still, while Canadian antipathy toward Chinese was perhaps not as open or as visceral as in the United States, it was undoubtedly constructed in similar ways and had similar effects (see Figures 2.13 and 2.14). Canada did not exclude the Chinese entirely, but it imposed a head tax that it hoped would deter Chinese immigration. Arguably then, as now, there was a high degree of "Orientalism" (as defined by Said, 1978) in the definition of unwanted foreign nationals, especially from one particular source of unwanted immigrants—China. The Chinese Immigration Act of 1885 imposed a $50 "head tax" on any Chinese immigrant who arrived in Canada. In 1990 a revised Act then increased this amount, as

Figure 2.13 The migration gate guarded by a vigilant Miss Canada. Printed in the *British Columbia Saturday Sunset*, Vancouver, 24 August 1907, 1. *Source*: Courtesy of Special Collections, Vancouver Public Library.

did an amended 1903 Immigration Act. Local newspapers were happy enough to see the construction of Canadian railways but were firmly against Chinese immigration. Figure 2.14 reflects the problematization of Chinese immigration in British Columbia.

As the century progressed, others came under increasing scrutiny. Specific immigrant groups were not explicitly banned; however, stringent requirements made immigration difficult for some groups. These categories are visible in the writings of immigration commentators and policy-makers in the late nineteenth and early twentieth centuries. W.D. Scott, Canada's Superintendent of the Immigration Branch between 1906 and 1925, categorized immigrant populations on the basis of their history and desirability and argued that certain races were not readily assimilable. In his classification scheme, the English, Americans, and Northern and Western Europeans were the most desirable immigrants; Hindus, Japanese, Chinese, and Southern or Eastern Europeans were unsuitable. According to Scott and those who crafted immigration policy at the time,

Figure 2.14 This illustration reveals the racist under-pinnings of Canadian immigration policies. *Source*: *Canadian Illustrated News*, 26 April 1879. LAC, acc. no. C-072064.

"a White Canada" was the most suitable outcome for the country (Thorner and Frohn-Nielsen, 1998: 82–97).

Still, it was the Chinese who faced "double jeopardy." Once they had reached North America, Chinese found it difficult to cross borders, and they often migrated from Canada to the United States without presenting the "proper" paperwork. In 1890, US officials claimed that Canada was responsible for the illegal entry of more than two hundred "Chinamen" through Toronto alone. Lee (2002) writes that between 1882 and 1920, more than 17,300 Chinese entered the United States from Canada (55). Journalists contended that "there is no part [of the northern border] over which a Chinaman may not pass into our country without fear of hindrance; there are scarcely any parts of it where he may not walk boldly across it at high noon" (54). By 1890, the Canada–US border was so open that Canada worried about *losing* people. The United States soon complained that Canada was too "lax" concerning immigration. But it was not Americans or Europeans that concerned them. It was the Chinese, whom American society had demonized by constructing racialized narratives.

PICTURING THE OTHER

This problematization of "Oriental" immigration justified formal screening measures at the Canada–US border. Border representations of the time map out a very racist picture. Illustrations from the late nineteenth and early twentieth centuries, for example, quaintly render Canada as a young woman, a mothering and virtuous protector of all that is good and at the same time a stern adversary of "immoral" non–Anglo Saxon immigration. While these types of racialized attitudes are often associated with British Columbia in particular, in Figure 2.15 an older, French Canadian Mademoiselle Canada guards the door to an influx of foreign and "threatening" immigrants, many of whom are "Oriental" (Lee, 2006). In Canada as in the United States, when it came to Oriental immigration, the border was often portrayed as a gate that non-Anglo-Saxons were "restrained" from entering by national icons such as Miss Canada, Britannia, or Uncle Sam. This gate was less a symbolic representation of the need to

L'IMMIGRATION

Sifton.—Voici un joli lot d'immigrants que j'ai eu pour presque rien.
Mlle Canada.—Mon Dieu ! combien va-t-il m'en coûter pour les renvoyer.

Figure 2.15   A French Canadian immigration cartoon. *Source*: LAC, http://www.collections canada.gc.ca/education/008-3050-e.html.

protect Canada from all immigration, or even immigration from the United States (since many Canadians were also Americans), and more a metaphor to depict the need to control the flow of "threatening" immigrants (i.e., those who could not be easily transformed into "Anglo-Saxons"). Before the First World War, this most often meant Chinese; after the war, this exclusion was more general and included unwanted foreigners including a growing roster of "others" like Japanese and Ukrainians.

In both Canada and the United States, many illustrations continued to depict borders as lines of defence, as gates and doors barring "Oriental hordes." By this symbolic device, those who were unlikely to achieve Anglo-Saxon racial purity were metaphorically excluded. In this we see the prototype of border as the site of security discourses of the sort that inform today's world. As Kuus (n.d.) reminds us: "international borders are best viewed not as lines representing already existing political entities called states or nations. Rather, these entities themselves are constituted through bordering practices" (8). This brings to mind an axiom about international borders: they "make the nation rather than the nation makes borders" (see also Agnew, 2007: 399). Perhaps we can best understand the historical Canada–US border in this way. The late nineteenth and early twentieth centuries saw the border remade into a biopolitical barrier that relied on deeply racist narratives to work. This discourse concerning Anglo-Saxon borders had real implications for how border perceptions and metaphors actually produced national identities—how they "secured the population" by their representations. Foucault might have said they constructed "biopolitical filters" that defined nation in terms of people as well as territory: that borders were embodied in people as well as inscribed on the land (see Propescu, 2012). Indeed, biopolitical border screening as we know it today first appears in these immigration discourses in the late nineteenth century, which positioned the intersection between mobility and otherness as a threat. The press on both sides of the border responded with representations that gave the border biopolitical substance. This generated an immigration metaphor that saw the border as a series of different tropes: wall, fence, or gate, depending on the origins of those who wished to cross. The border was starting to become "polysemic" (see Balibar, 2002)—that is to say, carried within the individual and experienced differently by different individuals.

This helps us understand the contradiction between Canadians' resistance to becoming American and their acceptance of American immigrants. Indeed, one might have expected Canadians to view this perception of the border—as a gate or portal limiting the inbound flow of some—as a golden opportunity to exclude Americans and their threatening "annexation" narratives. But they did not. Instead, they included Americans in their imagined Anglo-Saxon racial stock and hoped to make "Canadians" out of them, *in* Canada.

A 1911 advertisement published by the Canadian Department of the Interior informs Americans that "40,000 Men [Are] Needed in Western Canada to Harvest 100,000,000 Bushels of Grain" (see Figure 2.16). In this poster, the Canadian and American populations are represented by an American farmer and a Canadian colonial official (perhaps Clifford Sifton), separated only by a river. The body of water is clearly impeding the northward movement of the American farmer into the bountiful Canadian West, yet a similar physical landscape is found on either bank, referencing naturalized understandings of border and reducing its impact. Indeed, there is a bridge that promises to connect the two, facilitating the wishes of the beckoning official.

From a Canadian perspective, instead of maximizing differences, the bridge motif can be read as an attempt to minimize them: it pictures Canada and the

Figure 2.16 Immigration recruiting poster to encourage American settlement in the Canadian West. Department of the Interior, Government of Canada, 1911. *Source:* LAC, acc. no. C-056088.

United States as economically and socially distinct but also as easily linked by a mobile population (see Bukowczyk, 2005; Konrad and Nicol, 2008). Moreover, in this poster, the industrious American farmer whom the Canadian authorities are attempting to lure is racially white and is surrounded by American accoutrements that will surely contribute to the development of the Canadian Northwest. When we examine Anglo-Saxonism and similar racial constructs of the day, we find that part of the message of open border that Figure 2.16 references was authorized by highly racialized discourses that linked Canadians and Americans of Anglo-Saxon descent and that distinguished them from non–Anglo-Saxons. Such racializations facilitated mobility within economic borderlands while excluding non–Anglo-Saxons from similar rights of ownership. This is a very different representation of mobility than the immigration gate and portal.

So when historians speak of an open border between Canada and the United States in the nineteenth century, they are referring to the lack of effective enforcement of (and interest in) immigration policy vis-à-vis "desirable" or "Anglo" populations. There were already immigration policies and technologies of control that focused on populations considered "undesirable," with desirability determined by categories such as health, income, and race. Indeed, in 1869, Canada implemented an Immigration Act whose main focus was on preventing diseases from entering Canada, especially from ship's passengers, and on ensuring the safety of passengers on board immigrant ships. It also included provisions to ensure that the infirm did not regularly immigrate from abroad. But it was not until 1906 that the Immigration Act was revised. The new version was intended to instrumentalize what discourse and practice had already begun: to block immigrants who belonged to dangerous or undesirable categories. These included the insane, those with criminal records, those whose condition or special needs might strain the resources of the federal government, and those of suspect races.

THE ART OF RESISTANCE

If Canadians dealt with race and bordering metaphor and practice in similar ways to Americans, they also utilized a similar and gendered symbolism to reflect the relationship. For Bengough, a prominent Canadian political cartoonist of the nineteenth century, the Canada–US relationship was a vehicle for parodying metaphorical understandings of the country as "the weaker sex"—a metaphor consistent with Canadian middle- and upper-class Victorian gender constructions and Protestantism (see Kutcher, 1975). It was also consistent with political understandings of Canada as the weaker nation (or as a "not quite" nation). Both Canadian and American political cartoons pictured the United States as a suitor to Miss Canada. Figures 2.10 and 2.11 are more than representations of Canada as a young woman; they are part of a genealogy of images depicting Canada from infant through to young woman and on to matron. Such representations were common throughout the late nineteenth and early twentieth centuries. By the early twentieth century, Canada was often depicted as a mature woman well able to meet and rebuff American advances. There were by this time, of course, other popular metaphorical renderings of resistance, which created new subjectivities for the construction of Canadian identity. After Confederation, for example, Canada was personified not just as a young woman, or man, but by the "Fathers of Confederation" and other venerable politicians. Sir John A. Macdonald embodied the spirit of the new nation, and besides being a target for partisan cartoons, he was an iconic figure for illustrations of the Canada–US relationship. Figure 2.17, an electoral cartoon from 1891, combines Miss Canada with Sir John A. Macdonald. Here, Miss Canada is being rescued by Macdonald from Uncle Sam's clutches as she runs through the gates that divide the two nations. This symbolic rendering of the relationship clearly reverberated with Canadians.

But there was another Canadian cartoon hero: Jack Canuck, Johnny Canada, or Johnny Canauk (more recently, "Captain Canuck" or "Captain Canada"), who was first introduced as a young man around the time of Confederation. He is often represented as a British Canadian, or an "Anglo-Saxon" in the broadest sense of the word. Bengough pictured Young Canada as a male "giving the boot" to Uncle Sam (see Figure 2.18). This male figure subsequently appeared earlier in several roles—as lumberjack (see Figure 3.8), man of the woods, officer, or "ordinary Canadian" (visit http://punchincanada.blogspot .ca/2011_04_01_archive.html). As we will soon see, this male character became known alternatively as Jack or Johnny Canuck and was a representational character for discourses that pictured, in more "manly" ways, the Canada–US relationship. This was particularly true in the early twentieth century, with reference to land settlement and natural resources, where Canuck was often pictured as an outdoorsman or a foreman overseeing cross-border economic activity. As the twentieth century progressed, he came to be the protector of Canada's natural resources—but that is a story for the next chapter.

Some of the most popular "art of resistance" with reference to bordering practices took the form of renderings of the Macdonald government's protective National Policy, which resorted to tariffs to restrict the movement of various categories of goods across the Canada–US border. In perhaps the ultimate act of resistance, Bengough, borrowing from Republican images of the time, recast the Republican "elephant" as a marker of Canadian identity (Figure 2.19). This elephant is talented and can do a variety of tricks for then Prime Minister Macdonald. In Figure 2.19, the elephant is a beast that Macdonald is able to ride deftly.

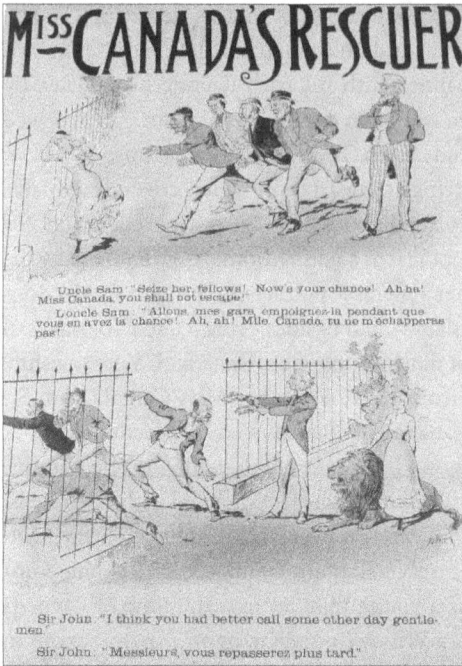

Figure 2.17 "Miss Canada's Rescuer." Electoral campaign poster from 1891. *Source*: LAC, acc. no. 1983-33-1096.

Figure 2.18 "Uncle Sam Kicked Out!" A young Canada kicks Uncle Sam down the steps of "Dominion House" while John Bull (England) watches. *Source*: M994X.5.273.46. © McCord Museum.

Figure 2.19 The "National Policy" is a talented elephant in this Bengough political cartoon. *Source*: M994X.5.273.201. © McCord Museum.

CONCLUSIONS

For much of the nineteenth century, in the American press, the Canada–US border was often depicted as a thin and relatively weak line that was unable to stem the tide of migration. Similar natural landscapes were divided by the line, and ways of overcoming this artificial division were constantly imagined. That border metaphor remained stable throughout the late nineteenth century. But in the Canadian imaginary, the border was initially seen as a metaphorical "wall" with America—a wall that had been raised by military conflict and aggressive military discourses. By the late nineteenth century, it too had been "downgraded" to a line or even the equivalent of a joining bridge, sustaining a rural imagery of two nations "sutured" together. Sometimes it was represented as a signpost directing flows of peoples, or as a wooden wall dividing different races even as economic policies attempted to join them together. Still, Canadians did not accept Americanization as inevitable. Strong US overtures to acquire Canadian territory were rebuffed during this era; even so, linkages between the two national populations were beginning to develop (Konrad and Nicol, 2008).

No actual immigration policies were crafted with the intent of preventing population movements across the line, except when those populations were obviously
"foreign." Anglo-Saxonism became a convenient nineteenth-century category
for racial inclusiveness in much the same way that "multicultural" became an
iconic term for Canadian citizenship in the late twentieth century. At the same
time, however, the late nineteenth century saw the first stirrings of a "border as
security" discourse, in this case as a means to keep out undesirables.

These developments, we must remember, accessed specific intellectual
foundations and authorized very difference discourses. Manifest Destiny and
Anglo-Saxonism were not mutually exclusive, but neither were they one and
the same. They authorized different understandings of power and were based
on very different perceptions about civilization and the natural world. Manifest Destiny was embedded in a civilizational geopolitical discourse that saw
America as heir to the classical civilizations of Greece and Rome and as a torch
bearer for humanity's survival. This civilizational rationale was very much a
nineteenth-century discourse, whose compelling narratives ended around the
1870s. Naturalized geopolitics, on the other hand, encouraged the resort to biological or scientific categories and meanings even if the science was "dubious"
(as in the case of social Darwinism and Ratzel's "organic model" of the state;
see Agnew, 2003). Naturalized geopolitics, which arose in the late nineteenth
century, was seen as an authoritative discourse that supposedly lent rigour and
predictability to political geographies. It also led to a conflation of biology and
politics—a crude and early "biopolitical discourse" in Foucauldian terms, one
that reified the concept that state and society were coterminous—a situation
that saw social difference as a product of boundary lines, of state territory. We
return to this point in the next chapter.

Chapter 3

THE UNCROWNING OF CANADA?

A Campaign Poem—"The Uncrowning of Canada"

Lord God of our fathers be with us, rise up at Thy people's cry,
For blindness has stricken our rulers, and the fate of our land draws nigh.
Rise up, lest we falter, and save us; they have put a strange song in our mouth
For our rulers would barter our birthright for the gold of the Kings of the
    South.
Thou hast given us long, deep forests to guard with their music and dreams.
The milk-white snows of the winter, which water our land with their streams;
Thou hast given us prairie empires whose boundaries pillow the stars,
Thou hast given us mountain ranges with our hands we have broken their
    bars.
Thou hast crowned us with wealth and dominion; we have girded the sea to
    the sea
As a potter would fashion a vessel we are molding the nation to be.
The centuries open before us, East and West are the doors for our feet,
And the smile of Thy favour is on us, the name of our country is sweet.
Begotten of free-born peoples, lords of the land and the flood,
We have mingled our blood in battles and sealed our charter with blood;
Who are we then, to squander our kingship for the lure of an alien land?
To bring them our loaves and our fishes, and to bow ourselves under their
    hand?
Lord God of our fathers be with us, rise up at Thy people's cry.
For blindness has stricken our rulers, the fate of our land draws nigh.
Rise up lest we falter, and save us, and blast with the lire of Thy mouth
The treason that offers our birthright for the gold of the Kings of the South.

—Frederick George Scott

(Reproduced in *The Commoner,* in Lincoln, Nebraska, 29 September 1911.
Scott was a Canadian poet, and this work reflects Canadian nationalist
sentiments simmering around the issue of reciprocity.)

INTRODUCTION

The late nineteenth century saw the construction of the Canada–US border not just as a line on a map but as an exclusive economic boundary that served nation-building discourses and protected national marketplaces. Masonry walls, increasingly a popular metaphor for the Canada–US border in the popular media, embodied this border relationship quite well. True, the Canada–US relationship was not as separate as the masonry metaphor suggested—a great deal of American capital flowed across the line, contributing to the establishment of many US branch plants—but none of this really compromised the strength of the tariff wall that Canada had erected for nation-building purposes. Even while Canadians developed resources and products for US markets (some 40 percent of Canadian production flowed to US markets by the mid-nineteenth century), they were raising further obstacles to US control of Canadian economic policy.

But despite all of this—and this will be the present chapter's main point— economic hegemony remained a deliberate and even self-consciously imperialistic US strategy throughout the late nineteenth and early twentieth centuries. Canadians responded by developing highly nationalistic discourses that relied on the general understanding of border as "tariff wall." Mouat (2002) reminds us, however, that such discourses often amounted to little more than a nationalistic gloss over disparate processes of regional economic development, and that the reality was often quite distinct from the nation-building story. Not everything happened as a result of national policies and nationalism. Similarly, Gwyn's (2005) analysis of economic relations between Nova Scotia and New England to the 1860s suggests that more equitable regional economies did develop across the Canada–US border that played to comparative advantages on both sides of the line. So did railway projects and regional boosterism in the eastern provinces—exercises in which international boundaries and nationalist discourses were often less important than divisions between central Canada and the Maritimes (Sutherland, 2005). Such is the story of the complex evolution of Canadian regional economies and the political economy project.

Canadian nationalism and regional complexity notwithstanding, there was a real belief on the part of Americans that economic hegemony was to be realized through capital investment and expansion (N. Smith, 2003) rather than through trade in goods. This constituted a US foreign policy of sorts. So the tariff wall suited American goals. Indeed, as Smith reminds us, the late nineteenth and early twentieth centuries saw expansionist, hemispheric ambitions emerge in the United States as its economy grew: "The dilemma facing the U.S. ruling classes in the 1890s was not primarily one of space, however, for all that it came to be expressed that way. The real dilemma lay in the overaccumulation of capital and surplus value by a rapidly industrializing national economy and the shrinking opportunities for reinvestment domestically" (15). Economic protectionism helped to further the development of discrete national economies for the United States and Canada; it also provided the outlet for US capital investment. Moreover, the economic protectionism expressed in policies and articulated through public debates on both sides of the border created its own imagery, and this imagery "did work" in translating geo-economic strategies and choices into geopolitical ones. These strategies, choices, images, and discourses were neither monolithic nor carved in stone; overall, however, they sustained normative and generally state-centred understandings of the meaning of border as a container for the development of a national economy in Canada, while increasingly encouraging the US capital classes to extend their economic influence beyond the border. Cross-border localities and regions continued their informal trade and interactions, but by the early twentieth century, regional experiences had been subsumed by a discourse that understood trade and industrial production, and even clashes over resources (Taylor, 2002), in more state-centred and ultimately nationalistic ways. This did not mean that regional economies and cross-border relations were unimportant; it did mean that even these could also be understood as pieces of larger nation-building discourses.

As a result of all this, there was a real duality in the logic governing the cross-border movement of capital, people, and goods during the late nineteenth and early twentieth centuries. In this era of the "tariff wall," the capital classes developed new investment opportunities of exactly the sort to be protected and nourished by Canada's national policies, with their emphasis on manufacturing protectionism. Much of this investment, however, was American. While farmers and American immigrants who wished to farm in the Canadian West were on the move, the numbers of mobile wealthy American investors and financiers were fewer. They need not be as mobile precisely because their capital was. The twentieth-century tariff wall and the immigration gate it relied on were complementary bordering technologies, albeit unequal in terms of the targets of their affective strategies and the nature of the mobility they encouraged. Indeed, if Sparke (2006) reminds us today that the mobility of non-business classes in North America are disadvantaged by border management, this was not so true in the past.

BUILDING THE WALL

The Canada–US border never had actual agency. It was never animated; it could not, and did not, take action. Rather, as we have seen, it was a symbol whose meaning was appropriated for different purposes, and on both sides of the line, those purposes were construed and increasing positioned as in the interests of nation-building. As was hinted in Chapter 2, "nation" increasingly became the dominant motif for organizing life and living within North America political territories—or more aptly, for the marshalling of national sentiment via geography, race, and ethnicity, so as to create strong territorial states. One new role assumed by the Canada–US border over time, as part of its state-building project, was to regulate capital investment and economic relations. Bukowczyk and colleagues (2005) suggest that it was in the nineteenth century that North American capital markets first differentiated between the American and British North American societies. This was at least partly due to how geopolitical discourses encouraged nation-building through the application of state power "pumped up" the border on both sides of the line. Thompson and Randall (1994), in their account of the historical events that created the contemporary Canada–US relationship, write that "the border has also been a principal mechanism for articulating and implementing immigration, economic development, and nation building policies which it has become on a symbolic level, the embodiment of national identity and sovereignty" (3).

In this regard, the border's role became highly symbolic as well as materially effective. As we have seen, by the early twentieth century, one hegemonic narrative developed in the United States towards Canada was pitched in terms of promoting American influence and absorbing Canada through the portal provided by agricultural settlement of the Canadian North-West, rather than through any kind of territorial annexation rooted in conquest or unilateral legislation (such as the Annexation Bill of the previous century). This created a specific type of racialized discourse concerning immigration and the development of clearly defined but still tentative biopolitical bordering discourses. But it also facilitated a type of economic imperialism—or perhaps, more accurately, such economic imperialism evolved hand in glove with this biopolitical motif. As noted earlier, that land and labour were intertwined, and that by exercising judicious use of labour, land would be secured, amounted to a truism, one that has reverberated in American historiography and that has become part of American historical wisdom. As Sharp (1947) reminds, and as we have already discussed in Chapter 2, this truism applied to the invasion of Western Canada's farmland. It was predicated on the belief that through American know-how, land, and labour were transformed into capital. This narrative reinforced an imperialism of sorts, for it insinuated that "capital" was in effect an "American quality" that authorized Americans' "ownership" of land north of the official US–Canada border, and that investment transcended the narrow territorial limitations imposed by national identities. In effect, so this discourse went, Canada was "up for grabs."

Today, of course, immigration mobility in North America is restricted while goods move freely. As Sparke (2006) suggests, this is the result of a neoliberal program that has attempted to facilitate business and to further the North American economy's integration with a highly globalized world. In this understanding of border management, it is keeping people in place, rather than making them mobile, that contributes to a division of labour that in turn heightens the neoliberal state's productive force. In some ways, the process today is a reversal of that of centuries past: goods travel easily, people, not so much. But if we understand both outcomes as part of a process whereby the state uses borders to further its economic ends, and if these ends at the larger scale play into hegemonic continental relations, the results are not so dissimilar. From the second half of the nineteenth century through to the mid-twentieth century, an important "end" that monopolized state power was to strengthen the position of national economies. For Canadians, protectionism offered breathing space for manufacturers. For Americans, protectionism created room for American capital by extending capital investment across the border while raising high tariff walls to Canadian goods. This relationship was to sustain the border between Canada and the United States for more than a century after Canadian Confederation.

CUSTOMS, TRADE, AND SECURITY: A BUDDING RELATIONSHIP

To understand how economic relations sustained a different kind of border relationship between Canada and the United States than did immigration, we need to look briefly at the history of cross-border trade. The first problem raised is how to position this border in time and space. The idea that borders could be, or even should be, an impediment to continental economic activity was not well developed in North America before the nineteenth century, except perhaps in the general sense that they were an obstacle to acquiring the resources of neighbouring nations and empires. As we have seen, the Canada–US border in early-nineteenth-century North America functioned as a marker of national space—one side was an imperial space of British monarchs, the other a space of republican governance.

The first customs house in Canada was established in 1796, in Annapolis Royal, long before there was a nation of Canada carved from British North America before US independence was a *fait accompli* (Winterdyk and Sundberg, 2010: 2). The ensuing economic relations among the Americans, Canadians, British, and Europeans were complex, based partly on geopolitical developments, and changed greatly after the American Revolution, when the United States disentangled itself from Britain. After that time, cross-border trade in commodities, both industrial and agricultural, was taxed, for reasons that both sides justified in terms of different national strategies. Around this time, a customs house was founded in St-Jean, Quebec, in the Canada–US borderlands, which regulated duties on the trade between the countries (Winterdyk and Sundberg, 2010). In this rather inauspicious way, a long-term economic relationship between two nations was formally established, one that in the late twentieth century would see the development of the world's largest two-way trade relationship and provide the impetus for North American economic integration. The British Parliament enacted the Customs Consolidation Act only in 1841, in this way "empower[ing] the Canadian Government to regulate trade with the United States and establish[ing] a Canada Customs as Canada's first law enforcement agency ... By 1845 some 63 customs ports were opened along the Canada-United States border, with the Port of Quebec City being the largest" (Winterdyk and Sundberg, 2010: 2; see also Figure 3.1).

Although customs houses were erected at a more rapid pace after 1845, the customs house did not serve the same array of functions that a border post or port of entry does today. The customs house was not there to facilitate North American "free trade" but to capture the profits of trade. The difference is significant. Smuggling, for example, was a widespread activity that was difficult to control prior to the establishment of customs houses and customs agents. For some, smuggling was simply criminal activity, but for Joshua Smith (2005), who traces smuggling activities in the Bay of Fundy, smuggling activities in the late eighteenth century should be understood as representing "the struggle between those who favoured a free-trade system relatively unencumbered by regulation and those who clung to an ideal of trading privileges generally

Figure 3.1   A border of sorts—the Quebec City Custom house. Photographed by Alexander Henderson between 1865 and 1875. *Source*: MP-0000.1452.51. Montreal harbour near Custom House, QC, 1865-75. © McCord Museum.

labelled as mercantilism" (109). But smuggling was also a statement about the degree to which residents on both sides of the international boundary, and the communities that predated the division, saw the line as an artificial construct to be resisted (117). Smuggling was a widespread activity that was difficult to control prior to the establishment of customs houses and customs agents. In Bay of Fundy, for example, it was not until after the American Revolution and the War of 1812 that smuggling came to be viewed as an undesirable activity, one to be halted through the deployment of governmental forces. Not until the nineteenth century was the customs house, however limited its range of duties, more centrally positioned in defining the border within national narratives through accounts of criminal transgressions, including the smuggling of people and liquor.

This publicity is highlighted in an article in the *Dodge City Globe-Republican* of 20 June 1892, which reported on how illegal trade was an idea constructed in light of the border's economic function in the Pacific Northwest. It described a smuggling case in 1882 in which

> treasury agents here have just finished an unsuccessful search for a gang of smugglers who have been bringing many fine blooded Canadian horses across the border without the formality of consulting the custom house authorities. It is said the smugglers are six in number and have been operating successfully for over a year. Many fine animals, brought in without paying duty, it is charged, were disposed of at the stock yards. The information that smugglers were at work came from the collection of customs at Pembina near the Canadian border.

Similarly, on 9 October 1910 the *Los Angeles Herald* reported a story it had picked up from the New York newspapers, that smuggling in general had been a problem in the United States, with contraband travelling through the mails and by ship:

> Nowadays ... we who serve at the port of New York don't see the great smuggling. That goes on along the Canadian border. Think of that long, long line from the St. Croix River to the Straits of Juan de Fuca, and no patrol—3000 miles and customs stations a day's journey apart. Canada's border indeed is the last remaining smugglers' paradise.

Reports like this are among the earliest social constructions of what was being seen as the "dangerous Canadian border," and a common motif in contemporary border discourses. Indeed, according to the same *Herald* article, a man may be out shooting prairie chickens, yet have in his game bag several pounds of opium which he can leave on the American side of the line at an inn where he stops for a drink. Many inns straddle the line. If an inspector appears he has simply to hand the contraband to a confederate over the threshold of the next room, and instantly it is not contraband, for the holder of it is in Canada.

Perhaps even more brazen and outlandish were the lengths some went to in order to smuggle liquor:

You have perhaps heard of the woman who went back and forth between Buffalo and Montreal so frequently that she was thought to be subject to some mania for motion? She was a motherly sort—always carried, in fact, an infant. A model babe! Never hungry, never felt pains, never cried. Its invariable stillness and quiet induced suspicion. Examination revealed it was made of tin and filled with—whisky! Quiet, indeed, yet full of spirit.

Then there was the man fishing in the St. Lawrence one summer's day, who broke two lines on some unknown obstacles off Prescott, Ont. Diving down, he discovered his hooks fast to a barnacle on a slim lead tube. That tube had been conveying contraband liquors under the river from a Canadian distillery to the American side during eighteen months.

Such stories give local flavour to how the border was understood and enforced by the state on both sides. The collection of customs duties, the imposition of law and order, and the policing of criminal activities prevailed. Those same stories speak to the unruly side of border life and add substance to an image of "frontier." But in holding up the images and stories of an unruly border, they stress the degree to which border transgressions were evaluated in terms of "customs offences," while today illegal immigration and counter-terrorist narratives now take precedence. Policy-makers on both sides are concerned about how to maintain economic flows while addressing "security" concerns. In the late nineteenth and early twentieth centuries, by contrast, constructing obstacles to the free flow of trade, rather than people, *was* security.

While the metaphor of tariff wall or economic border was regionally specific, overall it fed into a larger narrative of protectionism as a nation-building tool. Thus the customs border did not meet the interests of all regions—Canadian or American—outside of the industrial heartland of central Canada and the US Northeast. In some places a considerable degree of cross-border trade went on through unofficial venues, as was the case along the "frontier" in the Pacific Northwest, where there were concerted regional efforts to construct railways linking Washington and Oregon to British Columbia (Mouat, 2002). The same is true of the Maritimes and New England (Smith, 2005). Nonetheless, our focus is on the dominant discourses and metaphors that won the day and that

informed decisions at the highest levels. Those discourses became the "authorizing codes" for action and management along the border. And they largely
resisted free trade or reciprocity, belying the notion that Canada and the United
States had any "natural" and historical interest in economic "partnership."

What we are striving for here, though, is not in an inventory of the localized, regionalized transnationalism and hybridization of Canadian and American national identities across the line, although this undoubtedly occurred in
many borderland places (as Dimmel [2011], Smith [2005]; Lutz [2002], Widdis
[1998], Wood [2002], and others demonstrate). Such discourses abound, and
they provide insight on how unregulated borders might be. But our interest is in
the national narratives that were constructed, often in contradistinction to "reality," in numerous borderlands regions, especially where American and Canadian
neighbours shared cultural, social, and economic resources and where national
legislation and narratives of "firm" borders and nation-building often seemed
irrelevant (Dimmel, 2011; Konrad and Nicol, 2008). Increasingly, unregulated
cross-border trade between Canadians and Americans, although frequent and
common, was frowned upon. Such trade transgressed the ideal: a border built
to make the state strong, to define and contain its people and power.

If, by the first decade of the twentieth century, customs enforcement officers
clandestinely patrolled parts of the frontier to prevent such transgressions, their
intent was to collect their dues and (in the language of contemporary theorists)
to "discipline" the spaces of enclosure (see Deleuze, 1990). By defining what was
not legal activity, the economic border prioritized and criminalized certain types
of cross-border flows. Beer, kerosene, diamonds, and hard liquor crossed the
line under cover of darkness or without reporting to customs agents, and these
were illicit activities. American capital and people could enter freely and was
welcomed; American goods could not. Clearly, the border established a line not
only between what were then distinctively different economic systems but also
between categories of legal and illicit cross-border activities from the purview
of economic protectionism. Yet it was not possible to police the border in its
entirety, as is the ambition today. Customs houses were few and far between,
often at major ports of call rather than positioned along land boundaries. Today,
customs and border agencies at border posts define the land-crossing experience
between Canada and the United States, and there is no avoiding them, especially
for immigration purposes. But in the eighteenth and nineteenth centuries, they
had little to do with regulating border-crossing processes beyond those associated with smuggling. They were concerned, instead, with collecting tariffs.

This story has another interesting and important sidebar, however.
Although customs duties were collected throughout much of the early history of the border, there were also moments of unrestricted trade. In 1854, for
example, Canada and the United States negotiated a Reciprocity Treaty. It was

in effect for only a dozen years, but it served what Berland (2009) might call a metonymic purpose. The 1850s "golden age" of free trade created a context that Americans and some Canadians desired to re-create well into the late nineteenth century. Still, for most Americans in the mid-nineteenth century, reciprocity was not a compelling issue unless Canada was prepared to extend its ready access to the British market, which it was not. Moreover, the 1854 round of reciprocity was short-lived. In 1866, the United States abrogated the Reciprocity Treaty, ostensibly as a response to British aid to Confederate states during the American Civil War. Canadian governments sought a reciprocity treaty with the United States between 1867 and 1878 but failed to "persuad[e] Washington that renewed reciprocity held any advantages for the United States" (Thompson and Randall, 1994: 56).

Was this sudden termination of reciprocity the harbinger of today's border dilemma, where "security trumps trade" (see Konrad and Nicol, 2008)? Wilkinson suggests that it was not: it was instead attributable to the hope that "the resulting dislocation of Canadian commerce might quicken natural impulses for voluntary annexation" at a time when Canadian exports to the United States constituted about forty per cent of total exports" (Merze Tate, cited in Wilkinson, 1986: 97). From that year forward, throughout the late nineteenth and early twentieth centuries—indeed, all the way to the 1980s, when the Canada–US Free Trade Agreement (FTA) was negotiated—free trade remained unrealized. Neither Americans nor Canadians seemed wholeheartedly in support, or rather in support both at the same time. Post-1866, the United States rejected reciprocity proposals from Canada and continued to advocate protectionist, high-tariff policies until 1911, when reciprocity seemed to be on the horizon again. This deal fell through, however, after Canadians rejected the Liberal government precisely because of its free trade platform. The reciprocity debacle also contributed to the political vulnerability of the Taft government in the United States, which not only pushed free trade but let it slip that this was a means of annexing Canada through the back door. This will be touched upon later in this chapter.

Why was free trade so problematic? Although it is now taken for granted in the Canada–US relationship, it was anathema in nineteenth- and even twentieth-century Canada. The dilemma was, however, that while it was believed by most Canadians that the country could develop only through protectionism and strong linkages to Great Britain, the "mother country," capital for economic development increasingly came from the United States. Meanwhile, US policy-makers believed and promoted the idea that Canada's economic weakness would serve US interests, and they hoped to encourage that weakness by investing while raising high tariff walls against Canadian goods.

Americans, in other words, saw tariff walls as a means to hurry annexation; indeed, this subtext is embedded in texts and newspaper accounts of the time.

Furthermore, the United States saw reciprocity with Canada as equivalent to free trade with Britain, and since many Americans still wanted to "twist the lion's tail," this too raised problems. As early as 1851, the *Boston Morning Journal* reminded its readers that "reciprocity was not merely an issue between Massachusetts and Canada, but between the United States and British North America" (Longley, 1981: 262).

METAPHORS MADE TO MEASURE: CANADA AND THE TARIFF WALL

As we have seen, the Canada–US border functioned quite effectively over the historical period as a series of gates, doors, and portals; it sifted through the "hordes" beyond North America, identifying desirable citizens. This immigration discourse was sustained by racialized and gendered motifs of Canada–US/UK relations in ways that reified nationalistic goals. In this state-centred universe, however, walls were more suitable symbols for the border's economic function. Canada developed its National Policies, which imposed regulatory tariffs on US manufactured goods and certain commodities. These tariffs were referred to, aptly, as a "Chinese Wall" by some (see Thompson and Randall, 1994: 57) and as a "tariff" wall by others. The wall imagery was reflected in the press on both sides of the border. Thus, in the late nineteenth century, tariffs became a prominent feature of the border and the wall a symbol for independent economic policies. By the early twentieth century, a metaphorical "border of substance" appeared in both the Canadian and the American press—or, more precisely, the older image of the border reappeared. The "wall" had been a popular metaphor in the Canadian press earlier in the nineteenth century, when potential conflict and invasion characterized border relations (see Chapter 1); this same symbol now reappeared as representative of the economic border. But there were no armed soldiers, fortifications, artillery, or the like. Their places had been taken by the customs house door and similar technologies.

Hou and Hou (2002) show how this change was illustrated in Canadian political cartoons of the day. In editorial cartoons from the first half of the twentieth century, the Canada–US border is often represented as a "customs wall," a tariff wall, or similar; metaphorical devices render the border as significant mainly in economic terms. But note that this wall, or barrier, is depicted as a trade and customs, but not a military, enclosure—and it does not yet concern itself with the movement of people; its focus is on the movement of goods, specifically manufactured goods.

Indeed, the customs wall (especially in Canada) was often drawn as a brick or masonry barrier, sometimes punctured by a hole or culvert, sometimes supporting a teeter-totter or bridge (see Figure 3.2). This was a highly stylized metaphorical representation, but everyone knew what was meant: the nation's economic space had to be protected. The rendering of the border as solid provided both hope and reassurance that it would withstand those who would tear it down by negotiating reciprocity treaties. Figure 3.3 suggests that, through capital investment and the creation of American subsidiary companies in Canada, Americans still saw protectionism as a means to further US interests and to pull Canada closer to economic dependency and eventual annexation; conversely, Canada's National Policies called for protectionism as a means to build a nation (even though Canada's survival depended on trade). The height of this metaphorical rendering's popularity occurred in the late nineteenth century and the first decades of the twentieth. While Confederation was concerned with railways, other policies were enacted to promote Canadian economic development. These also became National Policies and were part of a political platform created by John A. Macdonald, whose Conservative Party soundly defeated the Liberal Party in 1878. The new policy platform was implemented that same year. Among other things, it called for high tariffs on imported manufactured items in order to protect young and relatively fragile Canadian manufacturers. Not everyone agreed on the wisdom of this course, however, and support was sharply divided by partisan politics and economic interests. The prominent Canadian cartoonist J.W.A. Bengough, for example, gleefully pictured Macdonald's protectionist National Policies as an "elephant" in his drawings.

Figure 3.2 The border as a tariff wall. *Source: Vancouver Daily Province*, 12 September 1911. Stauffer Library, Microfilm Collections, Queen's University.

Figure 3.3 Cartoon depicting Canada (King) and the United States (Roosevelt) breaking the tariff wall. *Source: Hamilton Spectator*, 16 November 1935. Courtesy of Stauffer Library, Microfilm Collections, Queen's University.

With respect to this metaphor, and specifically the cartoon found in Figure 2.19, Bengough (1886) wrote: "In anticipation of the difficulty that the new Ministry would meet in reconciling the various conflicting trade interests in the promised tariff changes, the N.P. was referred to as a White Elephant—a beast proverbially awkward to have on hand" (418). Without referencing the border directly, this cartoon acknowledged both the protectionist orientation of the National Policy and the fact that some but not all Canadians viewed the tariff wall as politically expedient (Bengough, 1886).

Both economic and immigration borders were fodder for the popular press, and Canadians felt passionately about both. Free trade would have gone against the interests of Canadian manufacturers, who were concentrated in central Canada. It would have been a boon to western farmers, who would have been able to sell to American markets and purchase manufactured goods more cheaply from the United States, so it was often constructed as a "Western" issue. Nonetheless, there were powerful central Canadians who believed that free trade would stimulate the Canadian economy. Indeed, George Brown and the Liberal Party championed free trade, and Brown used his newspaper, the *Globe,* to promote it.

NATIONALISTS AND CONTINENTALISTS

Thus we see at this time tensions developing over border technologies. Competing "nationalist" and "continentalist" visions of Canada emerged as a series of metaphors about tariff walls and borders. These metaphors referenced different understandings of space and international affairs between the two countries, reflecting a "popular geopolitics." By the early twentieth century, it was well understood that nationalists enjoyed more clout than annexationists. But there remained another round of acrimonious reciprocity debate on the table. By 1911, the argument was increasingly being made by Prime Minister Wilfrid Laurier that lower tariffs with the United States need not mean looming annexation. This key point continued to be made by the Liberal Party and the American press: reciprocity could be decoupled from Manifest Destiny, thereby creating a "border-flattening" trade relationship while protecting Canada's territorial sovereignty. But voters rejected the idea when Wilfrid Laurier lost the 1911 federal election largely because he called for reciprocity with Americans in his election campaign. This also constituted a debacle for the Taft administration in the United States, which had promoted reciprocity. With Laurier's defeat, the reciprocity issue died, at least until the late twentieth century, when the Canada–US Free Trade Agreement was negotiated.

These events did not go uncontested in the popular press and in political discussions. A broader spatial logic was at play among the many of the business class, one that promoted economic continentalism. But the anti-reciprocity discourse achieved and maintained its status as the dominant discourse in the early twentieth century. For Canadians at least, economic security meant defeating rather than implementing free trade. The dominant motifs of the border were nationalistic and strongly supported differentiation between Canadian and American political and economic systems. As such, continental integration was challenged by specific geo-economic and geopolitical interests—through the discourses of nation-building. These in turn were reflected in nationalistic representations. For much of the late nineteenth and early twentieth centuries, then, the image of the border as "wall" or high wooden fence referenced a geo-economic barrier as well as geopolitical one. Indeed, geopolitical rationales for strong borders took the back seat to geo-economic ones.

There was yet another mapping of the border in the popular imaginary—one that referenced how Canadian society would be threatened by greater cross-border trade and investment. In this mapping, the evils of reciprocity and unfettered trade were foregrounded and the border was depicted as a thin black line easily transgressed by American (and sometimes British) interests, as represented by Uncle Sam and John Bull. These colonial and imperial understandings of the border generally appeared in the context of greater US investment in the resource industries, and we will return to this issue later in this chapter. For now, it is enough to understand that those investments were generally seen to fly in the face of Canadian resistance and national self-interest (Figure 3.4).

True, the alternative vision—support for free trade and greater cross-border investment—was also represented as a metaphor in some of the media. Reciprocity and closer economic relations with the United States were illustrated in the popular press as a hole in a wall, or a fence, or a door creating an opening for cross-border interaction (see Figure 3.3). But these counter-representations were less common. Nonetheless, all of these border images and representations, like the immigration border described in the last chapter, reflect that by the early twentieth century, the main concerns along the Canada–US border had become economic rather than geopolitical, with the key issues being natural resources and competition between Canadian and US manufacturers. In immigration discourses, the border had usually been a gate or door guarded by a feminine figure; here it was a wall, and the guardians were male, be they politicians or other. Immigration borders levelled or sorted on the basis of race; the tariff wall, by contrast, was impenetrable. The end result was that the Canada–US border was levelled with respect to immigration flows as both countries used population mobility for nation-building purposes; but it was raised higher in terms of economic exchanges. Political cartoons now began to represent "protectionism" as

Figure 3.4 The border as a thin black line fought over in the reciprocity debates. *Source*: *The News* (Toronto), September 1911. Courtesy of Stauffer Library, Microfilm Collections, Queen's University.

the bricks that built the wall between the two nations. But here the point should not be missed that these bricks were also sutures linking the two economies even as they divided—they helped establish the perceptions that in turn created the "branch plant" or dependent economy of early twentieth century Canada. Indeed, they were highly reflexive in this respect.

HEGEMONY, RECIPROCITY AND ANNEXATION

In the late nineteenth century, the fear surfaced that reciprocity would benefit the US project of annexing Canada by fostering the latter's economic dependency. Canadian policies advocating protectionism were seen as a defence against this (Eden and Molot, 1993; Wilkinson, 1986; Thompson and Randall, 1994). Increasingly, the tensions created by Canada's east–west national policies, counterpoised by the north–south ambitions of the United States, challenged the territorial imperative represented by the Canada–US border.

We have seen how reciprocity led to an impenetrable border trope in Canada. Americans also had their perspective. Many Americans at the time saw reciprocity as a new means for securing Canada, as buttressing "a new American continentalism … distinct from the annexationist variant prominent during the nation's first century" (Thompson and Randall, 1994: 88). The Americans' goal was to secure Canadian natural resources at favourable rates while preventing Canadians with access to those resources from competing with US manufacturers.

In the early twentieth century, considerable pressure for reciprocity was therefore mounted by US political interests. This reflected a new American national project that was decidedly outward looking. Smith writes that a "new geography" was emerging in the early twentieth century: America stood poised at the edge of its "century," and it understood that it required "the repackaging of the most cherished myths of national superiority addressed to global claims" (Smith, 2003: 17). This was not simply a revisioning of geography to suit American global ambitions. The American historian Thomas Bender (2006) writes that in the early twentieth century, when US President Woodrow Wilson

> spoke in universalist terms, he presumed, as Americans always had, that global commodity, goods and financial markets should always be at the disposal of the United States. Conservatives agreed, but somehow thought that an American protective tariff was compatible with this idea. The natural resources, commerce and investment opportunities of other nations ought to be available whenever and wherever Americans desired and on the terms they preferred.
> (59)

This passage summarizes how partisan politics positioned itself in the United States as a hegemonic discourse concerning the world in general but Canadian resources in particular. Canada and the United States, headed by the Laurier and Taft governments respectively, had almost succeeded in negotiating a reciprocity agreement in 1911. This would have heralded a new era in relations between the two countries. The *New York Times* reported around this time that reciprocity was "backed by such a force of public sentiment [in the U.S.] as we do not recall behind any measure in our political history" and that America's business leaders were eager for Canadian reciprocity (Thompson and Randall, 1994: 89). But American opinion was informed, much as in the past, by a misreading of Canadian nationalism.

After reciprocity was defeated in Canada, "the wall" came to be a border trope in the United States as well as Canada. Figure 3.5, drawn by Rogers of the *New York Herald* after the defeat of the Laurier government, depicts Canada as walled, with the United States (personified as corporate interests) standing

Figure 3.5 Canada, represented by a female figure wearing a British Crown, is shown building a masonary wall around itself as a result of the defeat of the Laurier government. *Source: Meaford Mail Tribune* (Oregon), 22 September 1911. Chronicling America, Library of Congress.

outside. A crowned figure represents Canada, and her distress is obvious. A headline accompanying this cartoon reads "Trade Under the Flag is New Policy." The article goes on to suggest that Champ Clark's comments in the presidential race, during which he was said to have claimed that nine tenths of Americans wanted to annex Canada, had significantly affected the Canadian results. (Clark was speaker of the US House of Representatives who was heavily invested in the reciprocity debates.) Articles and cartoons depicting the event could be found in newspapers in major cities; smaller American newspapers then picked them up. Figure 3.5, for example, was reprinted in the *Medford Mail Tribune* (Oregon).

The strength of American opinion on reciprocity as a means to secure Canadian markets and facilitate capital expansion must be understood as related to broader economic and societal forces, especially to the naturalized geopolitical discourses circulating at the time. We saw in the previous chapter that those who supported the Americanization of the Canadian West referenced land and settlement as well as the common racial stock created by Anglo-Saxonism. Similar societal assessments informed the discourses of reciprocity. Canada was "kith and kin," no longer a "foreign" European nation. On 17 February 1911, the *Seattle Republican* argued that "the interests of the two countries are almost identical and at the present time more persons go to Canada from the United States than from England or Europe combined, and it is not right or just for us to impose a hardship upon our kith and kin."

This imagined genealogical link was useful for the era. On 10 November 1909, the *Los Angeles Herald* decried that "it has been too much the fashion to look across the border only with the glint of Anglo Saxon land greed in the eye." Indeed, this was an era when, as Thompson and Randall (1994) write, the amount of US investment in Canada nearly doubled, with most of that investment going to resource extraction and related industrial activities. The tariff walls raised against the movement of goods did not prevent US capital from crossing, and those who had argued that protectionism was a way to exert greater control over Canada and its resources were now proved right. Americans had invested heavily in Canadian enterprises throughout the nineteenth century, and between 1900 and 1920 that investment doubled.

Two important consequences of this investment were increased pressure for American exploitation of Canadian resources and the establishment of US "branch plants" on Canadian territory. As many Canadian economic historians have pointed out, the branch plant was an ingenious and rather proactive way of skirting the tariff walls between the two countries, especially for American firms that wanted access to Canadian manufacturing plants and to raw materials like timber. These branch plants tended to employ American managers, but the goods they produced were sold in Canadian markets. Moreover, the capital for major Canadian endeavours, including railways, was often raised in US markets. The size of the investment can be appreciated with reference American journalist Gustav Meyers's account. Meyers, suggested that in 1911, of the $500,000,000 in US investment that had gone to Canada over the years, $180,000,000 had been placed "in over 300 factories which, to a great extent are branches of American Trusts" (see http://www.yamaguchy.com/library/myers/ can_wealth/c_wealth_00.html). With reference to these types of financial transactions, Thompson and Randall (1994) write that "most of the new investments went into resource extraction and into secondary manufacturing ... To avoid paying United States tariffs against manufactured products, the resource companies tried to do as little secondary processing in Canada as possible, and to ship their wood, ore or asbestos back to the United States in unrefined form" (81). This fact was reinforced once again through the artful use of "the thin black line" as a border trope by both Americans and Canadians.

THE "KINGS OF THE SOUTH," OR DRAWING THE THIN BLACK LINE

As the United States depleted its own natural resources, it looked north to Canada. Canadian newspaper representations of cross-border trade from the 1930s and 1940s tell us that at the macro-level, the border's main function was economic; also, that the relationship between Canada and the United States was anything but convivial regarding the politics of trade. Hou and Hou (2002), exploring the contents of political cartoons at the time, suggest that Canadians were deeply afraid of becoming economically dependent on the United States. Representations from the early twentieth century demonstrate this (see Figures 3.6 and 3.7) and point to a common device—the border as a permeable line or even an open waterway (Figures 3.8) leaving Canada open to US interests. The thin black line that emerged in Canadian representations of the Canada–US border relationship stressed how the Americans (and also the British) viewed Canadian resources as a resource reservoir to be exploited. The line replaced the wall representation of the reciprocity debates as a device intended to provide a cautionary tale.

It was true that the US economy required large quantities of natural resources like timber, which Canada had in abundance. Despite the strong tariff wall, by 1930, many Canadian resources were being exported to the United States. Moves were made to counter this through specific controls. For example, rather than export unprocessed pulpwood to the United States, Americans were required to purchase the manufactured product. This resulted in strong US investment in the Canadian newsprint industry. The same with mineral and energy resources, although American capital and companies controlled much of Canada's mining industry in the nineteenth and early twentieth centuries. By the 1930s, around 40 percent of mineral production in Canada was being

Figure 3.6 "La Frontière de l'Alaska." *Source*: *La Canard*, Montreal, September 1903. *Source*: Stauffer Library, Microfilm Collections, Queen's University.

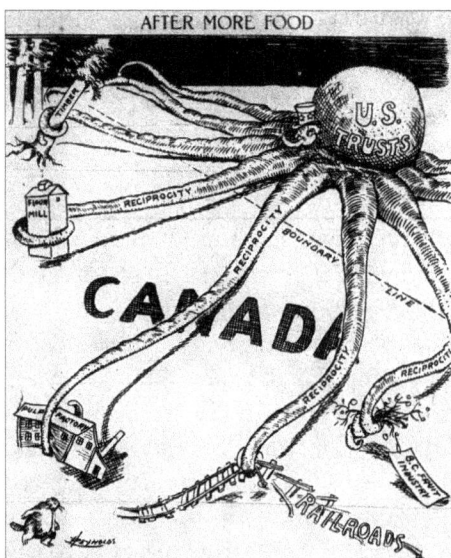

Figure 3.7 "After More Food." *Source*: *Vancouver Daily Province*, 3 April 1911. *Source*: Stauffer Library, Microfilm Collections, Queen's University.

undertaken by US companies, and by mid-century, "economists began to suggest that heavy reliance on U.S. direct investment had stunted the development of the Canadian economy" (Thompson and Randall, 1994: 110).

All of this led to several rather different understandings and symbolic depictions of the border based upon resource economics, and specific boundary metaphors were useful with respect to interpreting US capital investment: the weak border was one in particular that encouraged a reading of "seamless continental economy." The "resource bounty" metaphor was increasingly the way in which Canadians, very reflexively, believed Americans saw their nation, in that it reinforced the necessity of promoting the border wall image—the opposite of the message of the line. For the business classes that were more continentally connected through money markets, investment projects, and family ties; however, the thin black line metaphor represented opportunity rather than loss and risk.

The prospect of a relatively open resource border thus served as the representational device for depicting this relationship. Along with the thin black line, this early version of a "continental economy" was metaphorically supported by renderings of the border as obsolete, or as a facilitative enclosure fence on an otherwise seamless continent marked by continuous stretches of natural resources and agricultural land and a north–south orientation of the North American economy. Figure 3.8 underscores this relationship. Printed in the *Montreal Star* on 25 October 1927, it depicts the border as a wooden fence separating Canada from Britain but not the United States. The latter, personified by Uncle Sam, works with Jack Canuck to bring capital to the building of Canadian "enterprise." The snow, sled dogs, and sledge all point to a cold and wild Canada, consistent with the image of a natural resource bonanza. Figure 3.9, published in the *Halifax Herald* on 12 March 1926, speaks to the fear that Canada, country of bountiful natural resources, would see its forests stripped for newsprint by an industrialized and congested United States. No border exists to protect the province. The *Vancouver Daily Province* image (Figure 3.7) saw the United States as a giant octopus whose tentacles cross a thin, broken, boundary line to grasp resources and industries.

The early twentieth century thus saw the development of an extremely reflexive boundary between Canada and the United States, ostensibly as a result of its multiple roles in immigration, trade, and investment, all three of which linked the two nations. That border increasingly referenced activities and actions taking place across the boundary line. Tariff walls were meant to resist the tidal wave of US influence; immigration gates allowed Americans (those same people supposedly intent on Americanizing Canada) to enter by the thousands. Neither the border nor the discourses it consolidated did much

Figure 3.8 "John's making a mistake not going in with us, Jack," says Uncle Sam. *Source: Toronto Daily Star*, 19 February 1927. Courtesy of Stauffer Library, Microfilm Collections, Queen's University.

to stem American immigration to or investment in Canada—or indeed, American interest in resource industries. Viewed in this way, the border's function was not substantial. As a metaphor and a developmental discourse, however, it had an important legacy. It pictured both Canada as a whole and specific regions within the country with an abundance of natural resources as natural hinterlands for US manufacturing interests—and only to a lesser extent as British and Canadian ones. This contributed to a "heartland/hinterland" version of Canadian academic and regional geography, and the idea that the "main event" in North America was the US. The belief that Canada was an undeveloped British colonial dependency awaiting American control was in this way encouraged in the United States well after Confederation, even after the rise of an industrial Canadian heartland created its own national development logic.

Regardless of the specific metaphor used by the popular press—that is, whether line or wall—the economic border discourse bolstered a specific national and often reflexive understanding of the Canada–US relationship.

Figure 3.9 "Stripping Our Virgin Forests." *Source*: *Halifax Herald*, 12 March 1926. Courtesy of Stauffer Library, Microfilm Collections, Queen's University.

Through that discourse, Canada–US relations were forged and representations were made. The discourses that distinguished Canadians as a nation, and that distinguished Canadians from other peoples, were constructed as part of a larger project of building a national economy and a differentiated national identity. And for the most part, those interests resisted free trade or reciprocity, belying the notion that Canada and the United States had any "natural" interest in economic "partnership" (although "partnership" is currently the popular word that today describes the relationship in our post-9/11 world, as we shall see later in this volume).

On the other hand, although reflexive nationalism dominated the relationship at the time, there was a partnership of sorts, in the sense that the interests of the corporate and business classes dominated decision making along both sides of the line as national interests prevailed over regional ones. The "Kings of the South," as they were called in the George Frederick Scott poem of 1911 that opened this chapter, had their "Princes" in Canada, and it is to this relationship that we now turn, exploring the perspective of a contemporary critic, Isaiah Bowman.

Bowman (1928), one of the most influential American geographers in the early twentieth century (born in Canada), argued that "it is sometimes assumed that the thoroughgoing economic dependence of Canada upon the United States and the strong regional and racial differences from section to section tend to draw Canada to increasing degree within the political orbit of the United States. The intensity of the discussions on the reciprocity proposals of 1910 reflected this fear" (71). Bowman understood, however, that there were very dialectical boundary relationships and that there was a difference between nation-building narratives and regional cross-border relations. He observed that "the gravitative pull of the United States has been emphasized by the fact that it has always been natural for the separate units of Canada to trade region by region with the United States" (71). Recognizing the Canadian perspective, he added, "In fact, it was in part to offset such regional trading that confederation was put through and transcontinental railway systems were built" (71).

But Bowman went on to acknowledge an important division represented by the international border. Perhaps because he was born in Canada, or perhaps because he wished to offer greater insight to Americans, when reflecting on geo-economics as well as geopolitical issues in the early twentieth century, he pointed out

> to think of Canada as a part of the United States is sheer fancy. Something very little understood in the United States is the continuance and growth of loyalist sentiment in Canada. The whole of Canadian political life has been colored by persistent loyalty to the British Crown. There is also to be taken into account the activity of both British and Canadian imperialists themselves. The market aspect is still important to both ... Canadians as a whole look upon their place within the British Empire as a much more important asset than union with the United States could be. (71–72)

Bowman here was saying that the growing impact of US economic policies on Canada was not simply a prelude to Canada's absorption into an American territorial empire. Rather, it positioned Canada in an expansive American century (see Smith, 2003)—that is, in an empire of time rather than space. By the early twentieth century, the United States was less interested in making an empire of the western hemisphere than in establishing imperialistic policies that would make such an empire redundant. In Latin America, for example, an emerging imperial discourse that would invent the "Third World" was creating space for US economic and political hegemony that did not involve overt territorial control (Slater, 2008). Meanwhile, US companies were investing heavily in Canadian resources, and neither reciprocity nor tariff walls affected this. Political control was off the table, for Canada was protected by Britain, and

Americans understood this. But by manipulating Britain, Americans could gain access to Canadian resources. In the early twentieth century, America's star was rising, and its influence over Britain was growing. The Alaska Boundary Dispute provides ample evidence of this.

BREAKING WITH BRITISH: THE ALASKAN BOUNDARY DISPUTE

As we have already seen, for much of the nineteenth century, from their position as citizens of British colonies and then of an independent nation in the British "dominion," Canadians had resisted annexation and political absorption by the United States. There was a palpable sense among Canadians that their national project was distinct from the American one. Central to this geopolitical discourse was border imagery. Increasingly, the narrative of state was used to command control over the border, which separated American and Canadian spaces even while creating institutions of common interest.

But in the early twentieth century, Canada's relationship with Britain, so strong throughout the nineteenth century, began to weaken, exemplified by the Alaskan Boundary Dispute of 1903. Canada and the United States disagreed about the location of the Alaska–British Columbia boundary. After arbitration by a six-member tribunal (three Americans, two Canadians, one British), the US position prevailed. This outraged Canadians and contributed greatly to new rounds of anti-Americanism. It also spurred the Canadian government to take steps to control its own foreign policy.

Reactionary rhetoric about the 1903 boundary decision flooded the Canadian media. The Canadian view was that the tribunal's ruling was not consistent with past treaties between Britain and Russia regarding the same territory and boundary. Canadians sensed that the British had betrayed them in order to maintain friendly relations with the United States. The Americans were pleased with the result and saw it as a victory, mainly because it gave them control over the Alaskan coast; even so, the decision generated little fanfare in Congress or in the American press. Figure 3.10, from a Texas newspaper, reflects the sentiment of the era fairly accurately. It shows the British representative on the tribunal and one of the US representatives. The two Canadians are not depicted, wrongly suggesting that the negotiations were strictly between the British and the Americans. This was an intentional erasure of Canada, as reflected also in Figure 2.12, another American cartoon, in which John Bull and Uncle Sam are seen driving in a boundary stake along the contested border. The United States and England compare Canada's objections to the bawling of a baby.

Similarly, Figure 3.11, another American political cartoon about the outcome of the dispute depicts Canada as a roasted turkey to be carved up between US and British interests. Canada, for its part, saw the Alaska decision as a

Figure 3.10 *Palestine* (TX) *Daily Herald*, 7 November 1903. *Source*:
Library of Congress, *Chronicling America*. Image provided courtesy of
the University of North Texas, Denton.

monumental land grab intended to ensure American control over Canadian
resources. In that, they realized Britain was just as culpable as the United States.

The boundary agreement was signed for Canada by British representatives.
The result, the Herbert-Hay Treaty, amounted to a rapprochement of sorts
between the British and the Americans; Canada's wishes had been set aside in
the process. Because of this, historians Thomson and Randall (1994) see the
treaty as the last gasp of frictional border geopolitics and as the dawning of a
new era in bilateral relations. The first decade of the twentieth century would
see the establishment of the International Boundary Commission (IBC) and the
International Joint Commission (IJC). From now on, perhaps in some measure
due to the Alaskan dispute, border relations would become increasingly institutionalized (see Chapter 4).

Canada's increasing social, political, and economic commonalities with
the United States drew the two countries towards a new era of bilateralism
(see Chapter 4; see also Thompson and Randall, 1994). Meanwhile, though,
the United States continued its hegemonic ways, albeit through rhetoric and

A Canadian Cartoon on the Boundary Decision.
Toronto World.

HOW CANADA IS ALWAYS SERVED.

Waiter Alverstone (of the Fat-head Diplomacy Cafe) — 'Oping you'll pardon, sir, the mutilation of your h order, sir. I took the liberty of cutting hoff a wing for that colonial feller that's just gone hout.

Figure 3.11 "How Canada Is Always Served," a political cartoon originally in the *Toronto World*. The caption continues: "Waiter Alverstone (of the Fat-headed Diplomacy Cafe)—'Oping you'll pardon, sir, the mutilation of your order, sir. I took the liberty of cutting hoff a wing for that colonial feller that's just gone hout." *Source: Minneapolis Journal*, 23 October 1903. *Source*: Library of Congress, *Chronicling America*. Image provided by the Minneapolis Historical Society, Saint Paul.

international commissions rather than overt acts of aggression. By this time, Manifest Destiny and its annexation agenda had taken a more benign form: Canada was to be gradually erased and absorbed. US corporations saw Canada's industries and natural resources as important sites for capital investment (Thompson and Randall, 1994). Nationalism coloured how both Canada and the United States saw their national economies. Canada was clearly more protectionist, soundly rejecting free trade with its neighbour, which by 1911 most Americans did not. But rejecting reciprocity was not the same as discouraging US investment in Canada. In the early twenty-first century, much has been said about how Canadian access to US goods and markets has become the central factor in cross-border security cooperation. Much the opposite was being said in the early *twentieth* century, when access to *capital* was more important for nation building. The state's role in this was to enact policies that would allow corporations to achieve their ends. The two available options were reciprocity and tarrif walls. This process set the terms for the construction of a twentieth-century border that actually *over*determined North American market relations and capital formation at the same time that it *under*determined cross-border immigration. Later in the century, this economic relationship would be reassessed and identities in relation to economic integration would be retooled, but it is clear that in this earlier time, US hegemony entailed encouraging Canadian economic dependency. Canadians willingly participated in this, although they strongly resisted reciprocity. The tariff wall did not prevent US funds from being invested in Canada, especially in the resource and manufacturing industries. Instead, it paved the way for the creation of a border that would contribute to core–periphery relations between Washington and Ottawa and that would see Canadians represented as "hewers of wood and drawers of water."

By the 1930s, however, the metaphor of the wall was about to change, symbolically if not practically. What geo-economics had previously divided, in centuries past, continental investment was suturing back together. Bowman (1928), an astute observer, offered some prescient words. He said, as early as 1923, that "Between Canada and the United States, the relation of their boundary to trade is not nearly so important now [1923], with smooth-working agreements, as is the equitable use of common resources upon it" (72).

CONCLUSIONS

In the late nineteenth and early twentieth centuries, that reciprocal economic relations should prevail between Canada and the United States was a perennial notion, although from a political perspective, it was not particularly successful or expedient. The notion would rise again, strongly and successfully, in the late twentieth century, leading to the Canada–US Free Trade Agreement negotiations (see Chapter 4). Two main points need emphasizing as a prelude to that later discussion.

First, "economy" and "security" have been important border discourses for more than a century, and the tensions thereby produced maintain hegemony. "Economy" and "security" do not necessarily clash; indeed, many security specialists today argue that human security, military security (or traditional security), national security, economic security, food security, and other securities are all a single security. We cannot say that changes in economic flows in the Canada–US relationship over the past century (from closed to open trade borders) have changed the US's hegemonic intentions. The United States still applies geo-economic and geopolitical pressures to serve its own interests and further its political and economic dominance.

Second, in the late nineteenth and early twentieth centuries, natural resources pulled US capital and corporate investment to Canada. Indirectly, then, Canadian resource regions served as a front line for American security interests. The Americans' northern neighbour was "wild," and Canada was a less developed country and thus an insecure place. Such places could be positioned on the frontline of American geopolitical and geo-economic mappings, and indeed they were. A close relationship developed between spaces of security and spaces of development—a forerunner, perhaps, to the security development nexus that emerged between the two nations in the twenty-first century.

So if we look forward to the period that followed the reciprocity debates, the Alaskan Boundary Dispute, and the end of Macdonald's National Policies platform, it is clear that the twentieth-century interest in treaties and commissions did more than institutionalize the border. It also changed its functions and operations. Land borders, for example, were to be scientifically surveyed and legitimized by border management bureaucracies. The jointly maintained "neutral border" was to be depoliticized, and the International Boundary Commission (IBC) would further this. No longer would the border be a contested site, a site of "undesirable" immigration, constantly subject to erasure and redefinition; now it would be a series of markers and measurements underscoring cooperation between the two nations. The border was naturalized, neutralized, and depoliticized so as to create a discourse of cooperation. All the while, there was a seamless expansion of capital investment. Tariff walls continued to divide the two countries' trade in goods, but US territorial ambitions continued to affect Canada's economy, culture, and politics, and American corporations made significant headway in terms of their influence on the Canadian economy.

Up until the early twentieth century, this integration discourse was generated by both Canadians and Americans. But the bureaucratic cooperation signified by relationships across "the line" did not necessarily indicate partnership. In order to understand Canada–US relations today, it is important to appreciate the way in which unequal relations were always present. For example, it is often said in the twenty-first century that the United States, with its neurotic concern about terrorism, does not "*understand*" Canada's economic need for open borders. Yet our discussion suggests the opposite: the United States has always understood and manipulated this unevenness in its border policies with Canada. It has deliberately set out to foster economic dependency by political means. Economic policies were the leading edge of a new form of hegemony and were seen as such by American political and economic elites (Smith, 2003), who manipulated those policies for hegemonic ends. Indeed they understood very well the importance of economic dependency.

Chapter 4

SMOOTH-TALKING
COMMON BORDERS, COMMON SPACES

B order representations in the late nineteenth and early twentieth centuries strongly suggest that issues of sovereignty and territory were closely related to immigration, resource extraction, the acquisition of land, and economic tariffs. In this chapter we explore how those border representations and discourses developed into a more general metaphor of "partnership" in border management as the twentieth century progressed. This partnership metaphor and the narrative it created increasingly glossed over the asymmetrical outcomes of the resulting "cooperation," in order to further US extraterritorial interests and fuse them with those of a Canadian entrepreneurial class. This reflected a geopolitical logic and representation that made the United States a central power in world affairs and positioned Canada as its "dependent." It lead to a truism about the interconnected nature of these two North American nations. As Doran (1984, 139) reminds us, Americans see their relations with Canada through the prism of the relations with the rest of the world. Canadians tend to see their relations with the rest of the world through the prism of their relationship with the US.

The trigger for this new geopolitical understanding of "how the world worked" deployed a discourse that justified American hegemony. It also organized, along ideological lines, understandings of international relations. Moving away from the raw hegemonic and rather shrill texts of Manifest Destiny, and also away from the overt racializations deployed in Anglo-Saxonism and naturalized discourses of power (see Chapter 3), as the century advanced, so did a geopolitical discourse organized around a division between "free" and "communist" societies. The metaphor for global relations became "the bipolar world." This binary view of geopolitics and world affairs placed the United States at the centre of the "free world" (Agnew, 2003). Cold War discourse helped create a new rationale for security arrangements as well as a new imperative for cooperation along the Canada–US border (Coates et al., 2008; Farson, 2006). By the mid-twentieth century, "cooperation" was the buzzword in any discussion of Canada–US relations, even though that cooperation was often elusive and usually one-sided. The global division was so sharp that Canada could never be on any but the "American side" of the bipolar world. The Cold War border of significance in the mid-twentieth century, however, was not the line between Canada and the United States but the space between the United States and the Soviet Union that lay over the top of the globe. This space was Canada—more specifically, the Canadian Arctic.

A BUDDING "PARTNERSHIP"? CANADA AND THE UNITED STATES IN THE TWENTIETH CENTURY

> On both sides of the line, we are so accustomed to an undefended boundary three thousand miles long that we are inclined perhaps to minimize its vast importance, not only to our own continuing relations but also to the example which it sets to the other nations of the world.

US President Franklin Delano Roosevelt spoke these words in a speech in Quebec City on 31 July 1936. They suggest that many decades of cooperation and interconnectedness across the Canada–US border had by then fostered a common identity—a close and deep relationship that generated the political will to create common security policies (Konrad and Nicol, 2008). While this is not entirely untrue, remember that this reading of "common legacy" only developed in the early twentieth century and that it referred to a particular kind of identity and cooperation. It was increasingly directed for and by a political, military, and business class that hoped to generate wealth. This they helped to do by ensuring that US capital could invest with ease throughout North America (Thompson and Randall, 1994; Smith, 2003) and by creating a continental space that would protect US interests—mainly economic but also, by 1936, military and security as well.

The story of the shifting significance of the twentieth-century border, and the creation of a common border, really begins in 1908. After the reciprocity debacle and other events (see previous chapters), Canadians were to be pardoned for doubting that a formal partnership was possible with the United States—at least, a partnership that did not reduce Canada to "adjunct status" by fair means or foul. By the time the United States entered the Second World War, however, a new discourse envisioning a bilateral relationship was being developed, one that would position Canada as an American "partner" in continental defence.

The First World War had seen English Canada rush to the side of Mother Britain; but in the Second World War, the United States played a more prominent role in Canada's war effort. This was reflected in how military security developed as a North American project in the years leading up to the conflict. That partnership was directed by Americans but greatly facilitated by Canadians (Mahant and Mount, 1999), and advanced a US strategic view of global relations. The symbolism of the Canada–US border would be affected by the new continental security paradigm.

This chapter situates Canada–US border discourses and representations within broader geopolitical understandings of a new world order that would reinforce US hegemony in pre- and post–World War II years. It also critiques the notion that the discourses of partnership reflected equitable and cooperative relations. Current border slogans such as "Partnership and Prosperity" suggest happy cooperation, dating back a century or more, and political elites on both sides of the border tend to promote this perspective. History suggests that evoking a shorter timeline is more realistic. Still, by the early twenty-first century, the Canada–US "partnership" had already survived a number of landmark changes in goals, procedures, and governance methods. Canadian diplomats have even called the relationship "intermestic" (Canada, 2001), meaning that it is managed by a blending of domestic and international interests (see Mahant and Mount, 1999). Cooperation, broadly defined in terms of trade, defence, and other initiatives, has been perceived as a successful "strategy" practised by Canadian as well as US public policy-makers, and historical, cultural, and economic transnationalism has been depicted as a legacy fostered by this cooperation, especially under the NAFTA. Moreover, cooperation in national security since 9/11 seems to reflect mutual respect and common values (Canada, 2011). The initiative to develop a common security perimeter seems to illustrate that the Canada–US border works best when it is seamless, reflecting historical realities and current cultural and economic imperatives.

As Haglund (2007) reminds us, the world's longest "undefended border" is—and has been for some time—"the world's longest indefensible cliché." Indeed, he continues, in the aftermath of 9/11, there has been some question as to whether it will survive the securitization measures initiated by the "War on Terror."

Why this is the case requires us to look more closely at the story of the partnership cliché. This chapter begins by exploring how US hegemony evolved from developing "smooth" border agreements in early twentieth century to the point where it now has a powerful impact on Canadian national security discourses. It examines the idea that the twentieth century saw significant changes in perceptions of the border and in bordering practices. These changes affected how US hegemony was exercised across the line as well as how Canadians asserted their nationalism and responded to US pressure to create a common boundary landscape, security community, and economy. The first element of the relationship to examine is cooperation—how it was initiated and institutionalized. This process opened with foreign policies that "neutralized" the border in naturalized geopolitical discourses; then, in the era of Cold War geopolitics, those discourses were transformed so as to support globalization, neoliberalism, and "open borders."

We then pose a number of questions. How and when did a security community develop around the understanding of common interests? From where was this border imagery derived? How did it help create a seemingly "intermestic" border relationship? Could we evaluate the NAFTA more critically, as have some scholars (Sparke, 2006; Muller, 2010), at least with respect to its "openness"? And how did these cooperative discourses generate "reflexive" (reactive) as well as transnational or cooperative national rhetoric? Quite simply, we explore how perceptions of the border and of border management helped perpetuate Canadian dependency and US hegemony even while seeming to promote a common continental economy and a "borderless North America."

Our story begins with the "cooperative" inscription of the Canada–US border. In 1908, the International Boundary Commission (IBC) began carrying out common survey and maintenance projects. These would expand later into security cooperation under the Kingston Dispensation and NORAD. The story ends with the development of common Canada–US trade and security agreements on the eve of the NAFTA. These projects and others envisioned the border in different ways, but they all increasingly referenced a border metaphor that eschewed enclosures and walls.

COOPERATIVE INSCRIPTION

We have seen that borders mattered, economically, politically, and in terms of monitoring a biopolitical nation-building project, but a great deal of work in the early twentieth century went into making the border appear to be as seamless as possible. Building perhaps on nineteenth-century notions of reciprocity and Manifest Destiny, or reflecting the extraordinary mobility of borderland populations in the late nineteenth and early twentieth centuries, the metaphor after 1900 of a "smooth" border provided, by the early twentieth century, the normative framework for the Canada–US border. It was deliberately reinvented as a benign and peaceful site by federal governments on both sides of the line. No longer did the Canada–US border mark the edge of empire (British) or of bursting ambition (American). It was instead constructed as a benign space between two nations. Common border maintenance was institutionalized as a means to foster neighbourly cooperation. Of course, as always, the border metaphor contained within it multiple and reflexive meanings. Still, the new border management agreements of the time increasingly provided the backdrop against which Canada–US relations would be practised.

Arguably, these bilateral treaties were more important as foundations for the boundary-building process that followed than they were as capstones for what had gone before (although this relationship is generally understood in the opposite way; see Thompson and Randall, 1994; Konrad and Nicol, 2008). In other words, the creation of joint boundary commissions on land and sea was the opening rather than the closing act of a twentieth-century boundary discourse. They facilitated US hegemony and began to build a new type of geopolitical space. After the Alaska Boundary Dispute was resolved in the Americans' favour, the United States, Canada, and Britain negotiated a series of treaties to establish common border-management institutions. These included the International Boundary Commission (IBC) and the International Joint Commission (IJC). These bodies were to "co-manage" the Canada–US boundary on both land and water.

In the early twentieth century, then, instead of a "shared" or "smart" border, the metaphor in play was "smooth." This metaphor at least partly recognized the co-managed border established by the IBC and IJC. It was this that Bowman (1928) was referring to when he wrote that Canada and the United States had developed a new border arrangement, "with smooth-working agreements, as is the equitable use of common resources upon it" (72).

How did this smooth border develop? And why is it significant? Let us begin by looking at how the historical pieces fall into place.

THE INTERNATIONAL BOUNDARY COMMISSION

In 1908, Canada and the United States signed a treaty that established the International Boundary Commission (IBC), whose task would be to demarcate the entire international boundary from the Atlantic to the Pacific: "Although the land sections of the boundary had been marked by monuments, mounds or rock cairns … in the treaty of 1908 provision was made to suitably mark the water boundary by buoys, monuments, and ranges and in such other ways as the Commissioners judged desirable" (IBC, http://www.internationalboundary commission.org/centennialhist.html).

The boundary had long ago been defined by treaty (see Chapter 1), and most of it had been surveyed by 1874. By 1908, the "fires of national honor" that had flared up over the boundary's precise location, fires that had scorched Canada–US relations for 140 years, were past. It was left merely to inscribe the border on the landscape and then to maintain that physical presence. By 1908 this process was already completed. But the resulting physical boundary had become overgrown and its markers obliterated; it was necessary to rebuild these to avoid any uncertainties that might lead to disputes (IBC, http://www.international boundarycommission.org/boundary.html).

Boundary commissioners were now the overseers of a new transnational initiative. The treaty's terms were to be carried out jointly by Canada and the United States under the direction of two commissioners, one from each country. The commission did its work under the terms of the 1908 treaty until 1925, when permanent provision was made for maintaining the international boundary. This new agreement continued the task of the Canadian and US commissioners to inspect, repair, and rebuild the boundary, keep sight lines open, and situate new monuments. They would also report annually to their respective governments.

The IBC was not the only boundary institution organized jointly by Canada and the United States. A second set of negotiations followed to create a similar arrangement for water boundaries. Like the IBC, the International Joint Commission (IJC) was established in the first decade of the twentieth century, in this case, by the 1909 Boundary Waters Treaty. It established a joint commission to resolve disputes in waterways shared by Canada and the United States.

The development of institutions like these created what some have called a "cooperative," "institutional," or "bilateral" era in Canada–US relations (Thompson and Randall, 1994). For some, this cooperation testified to American political largesse coupled with the vision of "great men," like President Franklin Roosevelt, whose approach to North American politics and familiarity and friendly attachment to Canada were instrumental in achieving cooperative agreement (Thompson and Randall, 1994). As a result of benign foresight—so the story goes—an era of "partnership" had begun that was to join Canadians and Americans in a common North American project. This partnership was to be ensured by the cooperative work of the boundary-makers, whose mandate was entirely depoliticized.

Were the "fires of national honour" in fact "relegated to the history books," as the IBC's official history suggests? Did the IBC's founding in 1908 reflect a new spirit of cooperation between the two nations? Perhaps. For seven years early in its lifetime, "eight treaties and agreements were negotiated to manage a wide variety of contentious issues from cross-border water management to maintaining the boundary." These, the IBC suggests, "helped to define a relationship of respect and friendly co-existence for the next century." As McEwen (2001) reminds us, the IBC is still active today, and "given the boundary's geographical and political stability, and the harmonious trans-border relationships, a foreign observer might find it remarkable that there still exists a permanent international organization whose sole concern is the physical maintenance of a line that separates two national sovereignties" (1).

The IBC was designed to meet the practical problem that the border had become difficult to identify after years of neglect. It was difficult to manage a line that was unclear or indiscernible, although this is not to say that expansionism and "national honour" had vanished in the early twentieth century. What the IBC did—and this is not insignificant—was institutionalize boundary management by synchronizing the boundary-marking and groundskeeping bureaucracies on either side of the line.

So the IBC had a second sort of importance. Sullivan, Bernhardt, and Ballantyne (n.d.) contend that it helped prevent "histrionics" over the border so that future disagreements could be addressed without jingoism. The border was to be managed as a neutral zone, with the tools for this in the hands of scientists and surveyors. This would establish an orderly line through an unruly natural space.

Consistent with its founding in an era when "scientific management" was to be applied to conflict resolution, and border drawing was to be approached as a cartographic exercise (Thompson and Randall, 1994), the IBC turned the border into a series of numbers and markers. This was intended to banish politics from the equation. In retrospect, though, this approach did just the opposite by drawing it as a neutral and precise line that could not be challenged. In a self-referencing way, the map captured the line but the line was embedded in the map. This approach rendered the shared spaces of borderlands discrete and linear. Clearings were cut across the continent in a formally organized joint effort to divide national spaces. Even as President Taft talked of "adjunct status" for Canada, IBC personnel were busy embedding the border into the landscape, inscribing separate nationalities. While in today's world this is a normal exercise that addresses modern security needs (along with surveillance towers), in the context of 1908, carving such a line across the landscape was an exercise in taming and controlling the wilderness—and in proclaiming competency of the state itself to maintain its territory. It also created a landspace that could be read in a state-centred way and that was comprehensible as a state narrative: the territorial state and its sovereign control were to extend "here and no farther."

If the IBC's way of understanding border space deflected attention from other political aspects of bordering, the border was to be understood in terms of physical geography and what we would now call GPS coordinates. Once inscribed on the physical landscape, the border became part of the landscape itself, as a swath of cleared land. State and nature were thus fused. As such, as Walsh (2010) reminds us, the early twentieth century was a time when states "transformed borders into institutionalized zones of regulation defined by a matrix of surveillance" (113; see also Torpey, 2000: 5). That also describes the Canada–US border, whose unruliness was being tamed scientifically by surveyors and landscapers.

The IBC border, then, promoted neutrality and cooperation in ways that cloaked more contentious matters, such as racist immigration policies, trade reciprocity, territorial ambition, and indeed hopes for "annexation by other means," which, as we have seen, the United States entertained well into the twentieth century. It rendered border politics invisible. The IBC's scientific management of the border fostered perceptions of routinized daily cooperation; the border was seen as jointly acknowledged and respected. Perhaps this is what Bowman meant by the metaphor of the "smooth" border.

Although scientific border management did not actually end talk of annexation—which continued well into the 1930s, when the United States considered absorbing British Columbia in response to what it viewed as a growing security threat in the South Pacific—this form of management did entrench the view that territorial issues were "about" natural geography, that foreign policy might be crafted in a naturally justified way, and that everyone stood on common ground, even if that common ground was a 12-metre swath of cleared land across the continent. In those times, physical environments were considered by many as having "agency," as conditioning the affairs of nations and the character of peoples. Thus, the "smooth border"—especially one that had been drawn so scientifically—was an important metaphor for Canada–US relations.

THE "SMOOTH BORDER" AND SECURITY COOPERATION: BILATERAL BORDERS

An early indication that this institutionalized border trope might be little more than convenient fiction, however, emerged in the 1930s. On a visit to Canada in 1936, Roosevelt heard himself referred to as a foreign ruler, and remarked, "I am grateful for the honors; but something within me rebelled at that word 'foreign'" (US Embassy, http://canada.usembassy.gov). In his *magnus opus* on the US geographer Isaiah Bowman, whom we met earlier, Smith writes that during the Roosevelt administration, geography was a well-honed discipline applied to promote American interests. Americans' articulations of those interests were neither naive not accidental. So for those who question the transparency of the narrative of Canada–US cooperation, Roosevelt's statement about not being in a foreign country when in Canada repeated a contemporary if wishful American understanding of hemispheric geography, one that reinforced the US perspective on Canada that was emerging in the 1930s in the context of global geopolitics. If Canada was not foreign, would it be because it was a friend? Or something else?

Brister (2008) notes that only two years later "a series of articles appeared in the Ottawa and Toronto newspapers in early January 1938 that discussed the weaknesses of the Canadian defences on the Pacific coast and hinted that a Canada–United States security plan was in the offing." This did not bode well for an equal partnership. In a statement reminiscent of what followed from the 9/11 attacks, "the articles hinted that America might choose to fortify its border if Canada chose not to act (to carry out the security measures deemed necessary for American security)" (16). Beginning in 1939, Canadians were required to

A PEEP INTO THE FUTURE

Picture Of A Canadian Tourist Crossing The Border On A Pleasure Trip To The United States.

"It is proposed in Washington to man the border line that has not seen a gun for a hundred years, with ten thousand men armed with rifles and machine guns."

Figure 4.1 A Canadian tourist crossing the border on a pleasure trip to the United States. The caption reads: "It is proposed in Washington to man the border line that has not seen a gun for a hundred years, with ten thousand men armed with rifles and machine guns." *Source: Montreal Daily Star*, 11 January 1930. Courtesy of Stauffer Library, Microfilms Collection, Queen's University.

present passports for a brief time as part of a US crackdown on what it had been told were large-scale Nazi activities in Canada, which included Germans infiltrating the US from there. Figure 4.1 pictures the border as Canadians at the time imagined it might look should such changes occur. The machine guns, mortars, and tanks depicted in this cartoon might be absurd exaggerations, but they indicate that Americans understood the border as a specific security problem.

Roosevelt's sentiments demonstrate that if the Canada–US relationship was consistently glossed as "cooperative" and friendly, there was a darker side. The cooperative narrative belied the situation on the ground. Brister (2008) reminds us that Roosevelt and the then–Canadian prime minister Mackenzie King were both adept at manipulating the Canada–US relationship, despite being seemingly friendly allies. Indeed, for Brister, this was the era when the "security piece" of the economy/security dialectic that is now well-established in relation to the Canada–US border first fell into place. It supplemented and interacted with the economic and immigration relationships previously developed, because

Mackenzie King was forced to balance American security concerns with Canadian economic interests, all the while remaining mindful of an increasing sense of domestic sensitivity regarding national sovereignty. While King may be perceived by some as a bland politician either incapable or unwilling to make a decision unless absolutely forced to do so, the reality is that he was a calculating strategist who balanced the forces working for and against his country. (5)

It was around this time that the Canada–US security commitment, represented by the Kingston Dispensation of 1938, took shape. It too reflected this complex and evolving relationship, which we will discuss in greater detail in the following section. Here, however, we look generally at the context in which the Dispensation was developed, to understand that its "*mi casa es su casa*" tone belies the fact that of its negotiation "at the same moment the security community was forming, during the crisis atmosphere of the late 1930s, when a war in Europe was looming, and when it seemed that American security might be imperilled should Canadian involvement in the European war make the Monroe Doctrine untenable" (Haglund, 2007: 88). At one point, the US government even let it be known that it was prepared to occupy British Columbia if necessary (Brister, 2008). So despite the common border discourse established through cooperative border-making institutions in the first decade of the twentieth century, by the 1930s a new type of cooperation was needed that went beyond the scientific definition of the border and would accommodate the Americans' expanding international agenda.

Indeed, security continued to be a contentious issue for the Canada–US border relationship in the years that followed. Brégent-Heald (2012) writes that in 1939, a number of Hollywood movies represented the Canada–US border as both dangerous and a model of cooperation for the world. This double perception has considerable traction even today. After the Japanese attack on Pearl Harbor, Hollywood released two dozen feature films dealing with "Axis espionage" (8). The border with Canada was an important and iconic site in this "cycle of films: it was alternatively represented as dangerous and permeable, and as manned by staunch Canadians and Americans who defeated the Nazi threat."

These representations challenge the notion that border institutions such as the IBC and IJC fostered a peaceful, institutionalized, scientifically managed, cooperative border. There was more to the story than this. Even as old acrimonies and suspicions faded, new security threats were emerging.

For example, until the 1940s Canada had failed to gain Congress's cooperation for the building of the St. Lawrence Seaway. That project had been under discussion for more than forty years but found little traction in the United States. In 1929, the project had been represented as a mutual decision to exploit the continent's natural geography (see Figure 4.2); but that argument made few inroads among American policy-makers until it was recast as a security discourse in the 1940s. By that time, the Roosevelt administration had successfully framed the seaway as essential to the joint defence of the North American continent. As such, the discourse about the seaway was part of a broader one in which Canada's "adjunct status" was to be exploited, marking it as a security frontier for Americans. The seaway plan was approved in light of that argument, although the project would not be completed until long after the war, in 1959. But by that time the Kingston Dispensation had long been concluded, forever changing the nature of cross-border relations and the discourses that sustained them. It is to the Kingston Dispensation that we now turn.

OVERCOMING THE DANGEROUS BORDER

It is not hard to concur with Brégent-Heald (2012), who writes that during the early twentieth century, the so-called cooperative border metaphor was often challenged. To address these challenges and to alleviate US concerns about an "insecure Canada," military and security cooperation was negotiated in the late 1930s. Shortly before the Second World War, Roosevelt delivered a speech in

Figure 4.2 The St. Lawrence River, depicted in a 1928 cartoon. *Source: The Grain Growers Guide*, Montreal, 1 May 1928. Bata Library Microfilm Collections, Trent University.

Kingston that would serve as the foundation for the new security partnership. In that speech, he declared that America would not "stand idly by" if Canada's physical security were threatened (Clarkson and Fitzgerald, 2009: 4). Coates and his colleagues (2008: 55) suggest that today, such a comment would probably raise hackles; at the time, though, the news was "joyfully received." Just how joyfully remains a matter of debate, however. Brister (2008) writes that the news was received more phlegmatically by the Canadian government, which realized that sovereignty issues might well be generated down the line. Nonetheless, Mackenzie King responded to Roosevelt's "pledge" by himself pledging that "as a good and friendly neighbour, Canada has a responsibility to see that it did not become an avenue of attack against the United States" (Coates et al., 2008: 55). The result, in 1940, was the signing of the Ogdensburg Agreement, which provided for the shared protection of North America, and which established the Permanent Joint Board on Defence (PJBD). This agreement institutionalized the Canada–US military relationship in terms of defending the continent (Lagassé, 2003: 16).

With the Ogdensburg Agreement and then the Hyde Park Declaration of 20 April 1941, for perhaps the first time, Canadians and Americans had united diplomatically against a perceived existential threat using a bilateral defence agreement that divided defence responsibilities between the two North American nations (Brister, 2008). In Canada, this agreement, once concluded, generated both relief and trepidation; in the United States, it fed the controversy over possible US involvement in the war. Roosevelt and Mackenzie King, meanwhile, outwardly delighted to be consummate "good neighbours," celebrated the excellent relations between their countries. Still, the agreement was not unprecedented. Kilroy (2007) writes that "the two nations already had significant military ties, having fought together in World War I and having shared security cooperation from intelligence agreements" (3). He adds that "the United States and Canadian militaries shared similar doctrine and tactics, military equipment, and schooling, having both emerged from the British military-school model." It was only natural that security cooperation would follow: "Sharing a common language, as well as a common lexicon and cultural heritage, made the relationship between the two nations much more 'natural' than the often strained relationship between the United States and Mexico" (3).

This naturalized understanding of common values and friendship is tempting. But as Lagassé (2003) observes, when "faced with an implicit suggestion that America would be willing to protect the continent alone if necessary, Canadians—that is to say Canadian Prime Minister Mackenzie King—realized that Canada had to bolster its own defences to alleviate its neighbour's concerns" (16). Similarly, Brister (2008, 2012) emphasizes the tightrope walked by Mackenzie King with respect to Canadian public opinion and his own government in developing a defence agreement with the United States. Part of the problem was that some American political leaders were calling for the United States to annex Canada before the Germans did!

As in the days and months following 9/11, in the wartime United States there was palpable insecurity concerning the Canada–US border. That insecurity was not necessarily based on an assessment of facts; rather, it was being promoted by specific interests. Brégent-Heald (2012) writes that perceptions of the Canada–US border were manipulated to provoke mistrust and to draw the United States into the European conflict. In Hollywood movies, representations of the border cynically manipulated border imagery, buttressing the idea that security arrangements with Canada needed to be carefully monitored and controlled in order to protect Americans. This, too, played to long-standing American territorial ambitions.

Hollywood movies did much to provoke Americans and placate Canadians heavily involved in the war effort and were strategically deployed to that end.

REPRESENTING CANADA'S "JUNIOR" STATUS

The 1940s, then, saw a formal reorientation of North American geopolitics in the form of a mutual defence treaty and a joint defence planning board. While in the previous century it had been thought that if Canada were ever invaded it would be by the Americans, this was viewed as less and less likely by the mid-twentieth century. Still, if Canada and the United States were now committed to defending themselves jointly, the terms of the defence relationship were clearly American. Canada's "junior" role in security was also hinted at in other representations of the time. In Canada, military recruitment posters and cartoons recycled the eagle, lion, and beaver metaphors of the nineteenth century. These icons represented nations and national relationships, and they resonated within Canadian popular culture. Figure 4.3 shows the Canadian beaver accompanying the British lion to war—a metaphorical representation that could not possibly end as well for the beaver as for the lion. Moreover, if the logic of the food chain is evoked—the beaver being on a lower rung than the lion—this poster also referenced continuing colonial relations.

Canadians might have found Figure 4.3 comforting, in that it referenced a relationship with Britain that at the time was a source of national pride for many. Yet representations like these had for decades delegitimized Canada's status as an independent nation, at least from the US perspective. This meant that when, on 15 August 1940, the Germans launched the Battle of Britain, Canada had no choice but to consider the eventuality of having to defend itself. The subtext, however, was as both Canadians and Americans understood it, was that in the absence of British protection, the United States would have to safeguard the

Figure **4.3** The beaver and the lion in a Second World War recruiting poster. *Source*: LAC, acc. no. 1983-30-243.

Canadian nation. This was the context in which Roosevelt and Mackenzie King negotiated the Ogdensburg Agreement and established the PJBD. It relied upon a new border metaphor, and Figure 4.4 reflects this reassessment and the new cooperation arrangement. It was a wooden fence in which Canada was but one piece of board in a hemispheric plan.

A SEAMLESS ARCTIC

The integration of military activities in the 1940s continued after the Second World War and emerged forcefully as a new border issue when the North American Arctic became a Cold War buffer zone. During the Second World War, the Canadian government had established the Northwest Staging Route between Edmonton and Fairbanks, Alaska, to provide air support for the Soviets on the Eastern Front (Coates et al., 2008). Soon after, with the attack on Pearl Harbor and the US entry into the war, the North was reconceptualized as a soft spot for American security (Farish, 2010). At this time, the Alaska Highway was built to link the Northwest Staging Route to Alaska; the oil fields at Norman Wells were further developed for similar reasons. This led to the CANOIL project and the

Figure 4.4 John Collins, "Defence Mending Time," *The Gazette* (Montreal), 28 August 1940. *Source*: McCord Museum, Montreal, M965.199.1874.

construction of a large number of refineries to link the Norman Wells fields to Alaska and the continental United States. Similarly, a system of radar installations, known as the Distant Early Warning or DEW Line, was established by the United States with Canada's permission (Coates et al., 2008; Bone and Mahnic, 1984). All of this infrastructure was paid for by the United States and approved by the Canadian government, with the proviso that these facilities would be Canadian property after the war.

The war positioned the Canadian Arctic as a platform for US defence, and the Yukon–Alaska border as a frontier over which US forces spilled. At least initially, all of this raised questions about the status of the United States in the Canadian North. Coates and his colleagues argue that "the Americans ran northwest Canada from early 1942 until the end of the war as a kind of friendly army of occupation ... American military police enforced American law—sometimes on Canadian civilians." Meanwhile, Mackenzie King observed that "we are going to have a hard time after the war to prevent the U.S. attempting control of some Canadian situations" (Coates et al., 2008: 59).

After the war, the Americans would accept their diminished role in the Canadian northwest and acknowledge Canadian sovereignty over the vast landscape. But meanwhile, the Cold War was creating yet another context for security and repositioning Canada accordingly, as America's security frontier (Farish, 2010). It was not US territory but its buffer zone. Canada was now protecting the Americans from Soviet missiles, and this required a new type of "high-tech" (for the time) security infrastructure on Canadian territory. These new, radar-based military outposts were fanned out in lines at various latitudes.

It is worth looking more closely at these Northern installations and their geopolitical ramifications in order to make the point that in a "Bipolar World Order," Canada became a US Security frontier positioned between the Soviet Union and the United States, especially if one looked north and adopted a "Mackinderesque" view of international relations. Mackinder, a consummate geostrategist, argued that the heartland of the Eurasia and the pivot of history lay in the Soviet Union (Smith, 2003). His theories, now classics of geopolitical studies, informed Washington's assessment that the Soviet Union was dangerous because of its "strategic" location. This lent a messianic vigour to the Cold War geopolitics as practised by the United States (Smith, 2003). These geopolitical assessments assumed that Canada was a buffer zone and an American geostrategic frontier. Washington's Cold War discourses suggested that Canada would continue to exist as a nation at the discretion of the United States, provided that it served to defend the United States. Most Canadians found it difficult to disagree, so pervasive was the theme that the Soviets posed the ultimate existential challenge.

Mackinder argued that the Soviet Union needed to be "contained," and those arguments had a strong impact on geopolitics as practised by both Washington and Ottawa. The latter saw little hope that Canada would survive politically in a bipolar world without the United States to defend it. Notions of a "militarily weak" Canada, which had raised American hopes for annexation in the eighteenth and nineteenth centuries, were now recast as reasons for its political and military alliance with the United States. These assessments strongly influenced Canada's relationship with the United States during and after the Second World War and indeed well into the 1980s (Agnew, 2003). Indeed, Canadian and US interests in the Arctic during this period revealed many commonalities. Here, the "merger of science and strategy" smoothed the Canada–US border. It mitigated against "border thinking." Any number of contemporary representations, including Cold War maps and propaganda images, centralize Canada's position in continental defence. In Figure 4.5, for example, linear boundaries mark strategic defence areas of the North American continent protecting the

Figure 4.5 Cold War image from 1947 depicting the DEW Line. *Source*: Used with permission of the Porticus Centre, http://www.canadianmysteries.ca/sites/norman/coldwarhotwars/coldwarlaunched/5370 en.html.

American "bull's eye." Canada's General Letson, described the situation as one in which "Canada is interposed between the U.S. and the polar sea and is therefore the buffer state for any attack which might some across the polar cap" (Coates et al., 2008: 64). Pearson himself made precisely this point in *Foreign Affairs* in 1953, as Farish (2010: 177) reminds us:

> Canadian politician and [future prime minister] Lester B. Pearson heralded the achievements of the cartographers, policemen, missionaries, mechanics, and scientists who together had opened a new territory. He and others were waging a campaign to introduce what seemed at first glance to be a distant and forbidding landscape into the popular imaginations of North American citizens—a campaign, tinged with colonial and civilizational tones, which eyed the apparent successes of Soviet enterprise and settlements in Siberia with nervous envy ... The Arctic was, after all, only a few hours by plane from the North American heartland. (Farish, 2010: 177)

In Figure 4.6, the DEW Line installations are presented as a series of lines through a "no man's land" designed to protect the southern half of the continent—and particularly Americans. This imagery surely affected how the United States perceived Canada, especially northern Canada, especially where images from the region consistently pictured igloos and Inuit during the early twentieth century. Even today, many Americans view that region as a northern security frontier (see President George Bush's 2009 National Security Presidential Directive #66), manned only by Canadians in snow houses with dog teams. The legacy of the DEW Line also speaks to how frontiers of common interest were established through artful descriptions evoking powerful ideologies (Free World versus Communist threat), strategies (containment, radar, detection, surveillance) and assessments of nature (frozen wastelands, borderless and uninhabited). In the context of these existential threats, any questioning of the North's position as "frontier" was unimaginable. Farish (2010) argues that concepts of the natural world, and the relationship between the Arctic, strategy, and science, made the metaphor all the more powerful.

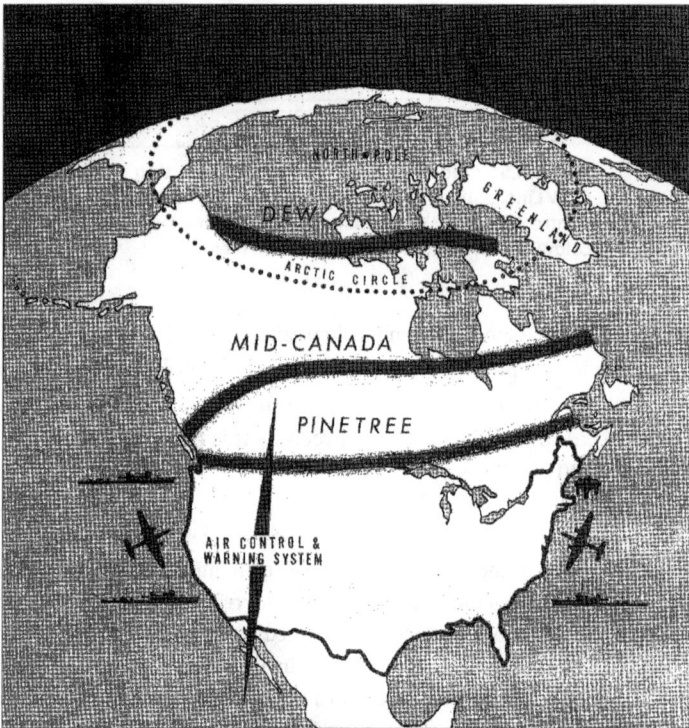

Figure 4.6 This 1961 graphic shows the position of the DEW Line in relation to North American defence and positions Canada as something like a security "glacis" for the United States. *Source*: Wikimedia.

There is much more to this story, of course; a longer account would reveal, for example, how Canada's recent "Arctic sovereignty in crisis" discourse actually first developed in the wake of the Second World War and the Cold War (for example, see Farish, 2010; Lackenbauer, 2011; Coates et al., 2008). But for our purposes, the main point is that these events contributed significantly to the metaphor of a Canada–US security partnership and its "smooth" border imagery. That is to say a border that is present and uncontested but that is seamless for the purposes of geopolitical interests. This discourse, contested as it might have been at times, was firmly in place as early as the Second World War.

EXPANDING COOPERATION: FROM NATURALIZED TO IDEOLOGICAL GEOPOLITICS

Other important developments in security cooperation in the 1940s and 1950s included the founding of NATO in 1949. Writing from a US perspective, Kilroy (2007) tells us that these developments further solidified a "mutual security relationship in light of the post–WWII threat of Soviet communism. Canada and the United States expanded security cooperation in 1958 through the formation of the North American Aerospace Command (which became NORAD), providing for the territorial defence of the Northern Hemisphere from ballistic missiles and other air-borne threats to both nations" (3–4; see also Figure 4.6).

Again, there are numerous important details about the development of these security arrangements that cannot be discussed adequately in this short history. The important point for our purposes is that common security was not a "natural outcome" of a singular destiny or continental geopolitics; rather, it emerged from a number of socially and politically constructed factors. These included the development of a single military culture in 1940; the common identification of an overseas existential threat in the wake of two twentieth-century world wars; a powerful US military presence in the Canadian Arctic (Coates et al., 2008); and Cold War geopolitics that compelled the two nations to cooperate at a time of highly exaggerated fear of nuclear holocaust. This cooperation, launched at a critical time, was continued after the war. Building on the creation of the PJBD, Canada and the United States formed a Military Cooperation Committee (MCC) in 1946 to manage joint military planning (Lagassé, 2003: 17). And there were the events of 1949, when Canada and the United States helped found NATO, and of 1958, when they founded NORAD. Lagassé (2003) notes that "geography and the nature of Canada–US relations were such that Canadian involvement in an improved continental air defence system was inevitable when requested by a resolute United States. Securing Canadian interests, therefore, was better achieved by negotiating a favourable regime structure" (17).

All of these agreements created the context for joint Canada–US security arrangements, which included military interoperability as well as common strategic mappings and security discourses. The result? "Today, Canada and the United States are party to more than 80 treaty level defence agreements and over 250 memoranda of understanding between the defence departments, and approximately 145 bilateral forums in which defence matters are mentioned" (Kilroy, 2007: 4).

While the Canadian and US militaries are mutually supportive and deeply embedded in NORAD, evoking the idea of a "natural" relationship is not part of the dominant Canadian discourse. There is instead a clear understanding of the deeply asymmetrical nature of the relationship and how it has positioned Canada as a junior partner in the North American security relationship. As President Taft once put it, Canada was an adjunct to America. Much of what is now considered to be "inevitable" in the modern Canada–US border relationship, however, was actually brokered or, more precisely, "socially constructed" by the ideological framing of Cold War politics, when not to cooperate with the Americans was to face potential extermination by the Soviets.

The "mocumentary" *Atomic Café* illustrates this sort of media-induced hysteria all too clearly. While it is amusing to watch in retrospect, fears of Soviet aggression and nuclear holocaust were very real for all who lived through that era. The Cuban Missile Crisis interacted with popular culture by a variety of means, including anti-communist sermons from the pulpit, Girl Guide meetings, news broadcasts, and "duck and cover" drills at Canadian and American elementary schools, strengthened US hegemony by reifying a common understanding of the threat the Soviets posed. This was no longer a naturalized geopolitics in the sense that we have previously defined it, but an ideological geopolitics grounded in an understanding that the world was inherently "bi-polar."

"The era of ideological geopolitics," as Agnew has labelled the postwar years (Agnew, 2003), indeed provided a strong framework for positioning the Canada–US border. It provided the rationale for interoperable militaries, common threat definition, and even the sharing of Canadian national territory in the High Arctic and elsewhere. As Mahant and Mount (1999) demonstrate, by the 1950s the United States was advocating standardization of equipment among its allies, particularly Canada and Great Britain, because "our commitments and risks are so extensive and important that Canada in a military sense must be considered as if it were an integral part of the United States" (31). A powerful geospatial logic turned all of North America into the "bull's eye" for a hostile Soviet Union. This Cold War framing fostered a multitude of binary geospatial codes such as Communism and Democracy, or the Free World and the Communist World. The bi-polar world created clear "with us or against us" boundaries that rendered the Canada–US border as a meta-narrative: one captured and managed militarily by the United States. This, in retrospect, reinforced the "smooth" border imperative.

REFLEXIVE NATIONALISM: UNDERMINING THE SECURITY COOPERATION

So far we have explored the historical sequence of events in the "real world" on which understandings of Canada–US security cooperation were based. Those events suggest that by mid-century, initiatives that involved new arrangements were creating and drawing upon new metaphors and stories of nationhood and thus reifying borders as symbolic sites anchoring the politics of cooperation. During the Second World War and the early years of the Cold War, these images contributed to a common North American security goal.

But popular assessments that reference collective understandings are not always uniform. Sometimes they may also help identify alternative readings. One such alternative reading was the one produced by the cartoonists who developed Captain Canuck/Canada as a wartime superhero. This trope is so well developed that Library and Archives Canada (LAC) has developed an archival site for Canadian superheroes and "defenders of the North." Captain Canada, a more recent superhero device than Captain Canuck, is one of a long line of "identity guardians" who began with "Young Canada" (depicted by Bengough as a male; see Figure 2.16) and Jack Canada, who represented the rugged out-doorsman (see Figure 3.10). Indeed, there have been at least nine Canadian superheroes since 1941, when they first began appearing in comic books. Iron Man was the first, followed by Furness, but

> the nine most significant costumed heroes to personify the Canadian spirit have been Nelvana of the Northern Lights, Johnny Canuck, Canada Jack, the Northern Light, Captain Canuck, Northguard, Capitaine Kébec, and two different Captain Canadas. "Together with intriguing associates like Kébec (an associate of Captain Canuck, not to be confused with Capitaine Kébec), Beaver Boy, and Fleur de Lys, these superheroes have steadfastly stood on guard for the "True North Strong and Free." (LAC, 2009, https://www.collectionscanada .gc.ca/comics/027002-3000-e.html)

Canada's first superheroes (Nelvana, Johnny Canuck, Canada Jack) emerged during the Second World War as the direct result of a ban on the importation of American comics like Superman and Batman. That ban served as an opportunity for a homegrown industry to reference a burgeoning Canadian pride in the context of the war: "In part an outgrowth of our national political-cartooning tradition, the early Canadian comic book superheroes threw themselves into the battle against the Axis Powers, both abroad and on the home front" (LAC, https://www.collectionscanada.gc.ca/comics/027002-3000-e.html).

Still, in the context of the Americans' "unequal assessment" of Canada's security competency, the "U.S. domination of the comics medium during the 1950s and 1960s meant that when Canadian superheroes did finally return during the

1969–74 period, they were initially buffoons" (LAC, 2009; https://www.collections canada.gc.ca/comics/027002-3000-e.html. By the time Captain Canuck (Figure 4.7a) was developed in the 1970s, by Richard Comely, however, the view reflected by the cartoonists was different: Canada was a hypothetical superpower whose hero was intent on saving the world, and especially Canada. His methods accessed Cold War discourses and anti-communist ideology. Canuck was followed by Scott Stirling's Captain Canada (Figure 4.7b). Reflecting a burgeoning Canadian nationalism in the 1970s (Dittmer and Larsen, 2007), Captain Canada parodied his American counterpart, Captain America, while constructing a global role for Canada. In doing so, he positioned Canada as an equal and opposite force. Such images, while compliant with American Cold War discourses and superpower ambitions, offer evidence of a reflexive discourse that positioned Canada as a global power in its own right. While they did not overtly challenge the "partnership arrangements" put in place by the various mutual aid and joint defence agreements developed earlier in the century, these very public and popular images reassessed them.

For Dittmer and Larsen (2007), Canada's superhero represented a late-twentieth-century, louder and more confident brand of Canadian nationalism. They suggest that Captain Canada can be read not only as a statement about Canadian identity but also by extension as a parody of the American comic book genre, which "satirizes the moral code that underpins the American superhero" (748). Captain Canada also draws attention through parody to the highly asymmetrical Canada–US "partnership." After all, Canada's superhero was a work of fiction—of science fiction at that—precisely because the very notion of Canada as an equal power during the Cold War "would not fly" (pun intended). This brings us to a point raised in Cavell's (2004) volume—that Canada's Cold War popular discourses, while outwardly conforming to the broader political meta-discourses of anti-communism, included culturally constructed and highly charged anti-American sentiments.

Comley's Captain Canuck and other popular culture understandings of the Canada–US relationship during the Cold War era, and even after, represented a reflexive and aesthetic rebuilding of border on the basis of national and cultural pride. In doing so they parodied the *realpolitik* and moral codes of Second World War and Cold War security described earlier in this chapter. Thus we need to examine another important piece of the puzzle: how the "smooth border" initiatives developed to generalize US interests at the end of the Cold War resulted in both more integrated border arrangements *and* nationalistic reflexivity. The North American Free Trade Agreement (NAFTA) is a case in point. The NAFTA agreement of the 1990s, and various other border agreements negotiated in the late twentieth century, saw the ongoing development of a continental approach to trade and security. The fact that a "smooth" free trade

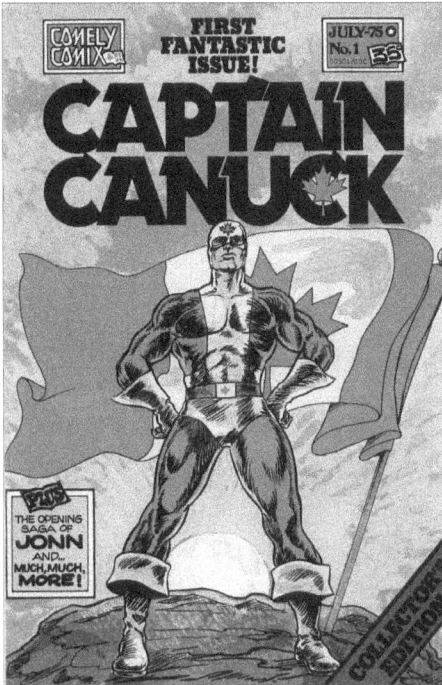

Figure 4.7a The debut of Canadian superhero Captain Canuck. *Source*: *Captain Canuck*, vol. 1, July 1975. Used with permission of Richard Comely.

Figure 4.7b Captain Canada. *Source*: *Atlantis 1*, no. 1 (1983). Used with permission of G. Scott Stirling.

vision for the border became dominant in the 1970s and 1980s is by no means unrelated to developments dating back to the Second World War and the Cold War that followed it.

SMOOTHING THE ECONOMIC BORDER

The perception that Canada was America's partner, and the related perception that Canada must respond against American dominance, did not end with the Cold War. Those perceptions continued to define security by contributing to a continental North American security map and the defence implications to be read on it. The new map paid little attention to international borders; instead, it reflected US-led continentalism and *realpolitik*. Cold War geopolitics had pushed Canada closer to the United States, if only because the discourses constructed by the latter to geospatially code "communism" and the threat of the Soviet Union were so ideologically totalizing as to be impossible to escape.

The two countries' experiences in security and military cooperation thus facilitated discussions about how to build better links between the Canadian and US economies in the late twentieth century. But to understand this, we need to review in more depth how Canadian and US interests had been jointly positioned during the Roosevelt–Mackenzie King years both in terms of their security *and* economic implications. Hart (1988), for example, contends that the modern trade relationship between the two countries began in the 1930s, when Canada took up the invitation of President Roosevelt "to negotiate a new kind of reciprocal trade agreement under the revolutionary new delegated mandate provided by the Congress in 1934" (208). This was not reciprocity, nor was it free trade. It was something in between. The hallmark of this relationship was Americans' willingness to exempt Canada from measures aimed at other trading partners. As we have already seen, if the warm friendship between Roosevelt and Mackenzie King had "created a special relationship between the two countries which lasted throughout the 1960s" (208), we should be careful not to exaggerate that special relationship. "When U.S. interests were clear, such as in efforts to shift on Western Canadian farmers the burden of U.S. concessional wheat sales to third markets, there was nothing special about the relationship" (209).

As important to fostering the warm relationships as the Roosevelt–MacKenzie King relationship was the fact that after 1939 the US's need for strategic resources (related in part to the Second World War) resulted in a more general "economic foreign policy" in which Canada's resource supplies were deemed "American" (as was the case with the Norman Wells project; see Mahant and Mount, 1999: 99–100; Bone and Mahnic, 1984). There was a sense that the western hemisphere's oil reserves were for American use only; indeed, around this time, the US government expressed its first interest in developing Alberta's

Oil Sands for its own use (Mahant and Mount, 1999). Similarly, the US government worked to control and regulate other strategic resources in order to prevent industrial and civilian shortages of war materials. Canada was viewed as a "domestic" provider of strategic materials to the United States. It was deemed a "secure" provider for many strategic minerals and metals, and also for oil. As US Secretary of the Interior Stewart Udall later observed, Canada and the United States together produced a "great vault of resources, a storehouse ... We should not allow national boundaries to inhibit our effort to achieve maximum economic strength" (qtd. in Mahant and Mount, 1999: 107). Figure 4.8, a photograph commemorating the laying of a pipeline from Montreal to Portland, Maine, reflects this symbolic energy and resource cooperation and how border metaphors were developed to express it.

After the war, pressure to maintain a smooth economic border continued, even when "capitalism was pitted against communism and trading blocks and a variety of international trade and development institutions evolved" (Farson, 2008: 25). With the end of the Cold War, "one dominant economic ideology remained" and all nations "began to move toward free-market capitalism" (25). Thus by the late twentieth century, trade agreements and security cooperation were increasingly being positioned at the heart of the transnational arrangements between Canada and the United States, notwithstanding the fact that, as Brister (2008) reminds us, defence cooperation and integration continued to develop in a variety of ways.

After the fall of the Berlin Wall, many in the highly industrialized nations generally concurred that the "end of history" (see Fukuyama, 1989) was at hand and that so was the power of the "old nation-states," which had long been steeped in parochialism and economic protectionism. The new discourse of globalization promised a Brave New World; it also suggested that borders had outgrown their usefulness. Disease, warfare, and other sources of international tension had all but disappeared, and their regulation by borders was increasingly seen as redundant, or so the story went. After negotiations that advanced a similar logic, Canada and the United States signed a free trade agreement in 1987. "It was often posited," writes Farson (2006), "that the U.S.–Canada border would become less significant as greater economic integration occurred ... It might vanish altogether" (31).

But it did not. After common economic and security interests were negotiated, the border remained. Nonetheless, the general point is that even in the mid- to late twentieth century, the border was understood as retaining its vital role in providing both Canada and the United States with security and economic growth.

Indeed, in the post–Cold War era, new agreements were forged to recast the Canada–US border in terms of trade and security imperatives, meaning that

Figure 4.8 Photograph taken in 1941 at Highwater, Quebec, where an oil pipeline crosses into the United States. *Source*: National Film Board. LAC, item # WRM 1057.

the current tensions between security and economy that characterize post-9/11 border discussions are not new. They are part of a longer tradition. An embedded security-economy dialectic is long-standing, according to Doran (1984), who argues that "from the American foreign policy perspective, nothing exceeds the importance of the political strategic dimension; from the Canadian foreign policy perspective, this dimension is secondary to the economic and commercial dimension" (189).

In order to better understand this development, in the pages to follow we examine the issue of free trade and then explore the relationship between free trade and security.

FTA TO NAFTA: THE FREE TRADE BORDER MODEL

During the 1980s, Canada and the United States negotiated the Free Trade Agreement (FTA). Within a few years, this was enlarged to encompass Mexico (NAFTA). Notwithstanding Canadian national narratives that had long emphasized British or Old World affiliations (see Nicol, 2005; Coates et al., 2008), North American regionalism—specifically in terms of market integration—was by this time much more palatable to Canadian policy-makers (although not initially the general public) than it had been in the past. But it was not simply the "pull of destiny" that created these agreements. In the wake of the Second World War, new possibilities for multilateralism had softened Canada's protectionist disposition:

> A less fearsome option to [a] bilateral trade agreement [with the U.S] presented itself. While Canadians might not have wanted to commit to a trade relationship framed solely on the basis of U.S. political interests and Congressional whims, the GATT [General Agreement on Tariffs and Trade] and the world system it references seemed more appropriately "multilateral." In 1947 Canada, the United States and twenty other countries had signed a "provisional" agreement to reduce tariffs on goods and to begin eliminating other barriers to trade in goods. (Condon and Sinha, 2003: 7)

GATT was an international agreement in favour of trade liberalization and was conceptually linked to postwar ideals of peace and prosperity (7). GATT was influential in North America; indeed, it was expressed primarily through specific trade relations with the United States, such as the Auto Pact between Canada and the US, which furthered trade liberalization. All of these pressures combined to push Canadian policy-makers to reassess free trade with their southern neighbour. They came to see it as a necessity. This was the context in which the FTA and the NAFTA can best be understood. Both were predicated on broader understandings of neoliberal economic imperatives, and both referenced multilateralism. Hale (2011) suggests that after the NAFTA, the Canada–US relationship was marked by a new permeability and integration, and that the border between the two assumed a more globalized function, in that it facilitated and indeed encouraged the free flow of trade. Farson (2008) observes, however, that after the NAFTA was implemented, Canada became more focused on US trade than at any other period in the recent past.

Still, the border did not "vanish," as pundits had suggested it would; indeed, under the FTA and then under the NAFTA, it *gained* functional prominence. Rather than signalling the end of North American borders, the NAFTA heightened political and cultural attention to them (Nicol, 2006). The Second World War era had been characterized by burgeoning military integration and mutual aid; the NAFTA demanded border infrastructures that would serve as portals for the entry of goods. Deregulated trucking saw the end of loading and unloading yards along the border; infrastructures were enhanced to fast-track international shipments. But since major highways on both sides of the border lacked "articulation" (see Turbeville and Bradbury, 2005), and as the volume of trade increased, truck queues lengthened, resulting in bottlenecks and slow clearances (Figure 4.9) (Konrad and Nicol, 2008).

So what was a well-developed security cooperation in the mid-twentieth century now found itself positioned within a growing continental economy, and

Figure 4.9 Trucks crossing the Ambassador Bridge at the Windsor–Detroit border. *Source:* Heather Nicol.

that economy in turn affected understandings of security. By the late twentieth century, the NAFTA had fostered a new sense of connection between Canada and the United States, predicated on and sustained by a new market model. That market model was expanding to include other mutually positioned interests and policies. (The contours of this permeable border were to appear in other separately negotiated NAFTA-era documents; see Hale, 2011; Konrad and Nicol, 2008.) As a result of the NAFTA, trade between Canada and the US increased so that economic dependence strengthened between the two nations. NAFTA-style cooperation was increasingly viewed as a template for some kind of "NAFTA plus" that would embed post–Cold War security arrangements to deal with newly identified security risks. Initially these were sidebar agreements, and it was in this context that a series of new agreements were negotiated, including the 1995 Shared Border Accord and the 1999 Canada–US Partnership (CUSP). These accords, which encompassed issues such as terrorism, smuggling, and cross-border crime, amounted to discourses of the meaning of border.

SHARED BORDER ACCORD

It is common knowledge that by 2001 trade between Canada and the United States more than doubled under the FTA and the NAFTA. This led to growing problems with infrastructure and border bottlenecks. For the Americans, the increase in trade under the NAFTA was coupled with unprecedented levels of immigration. Problems related to access and costs imperilled the infrastructure of cross-border trade: "as the Canada–U.S. Free Trade Agreement and NAFTA diminished the tariff and duty burden, new costs, on both sides of the border, began to appear—costs such as logistic and delivery charges" (Canadian Chamber of Commerce, ca. 2008).

More rather than less scrutiny at the international border was the result. But to place all of the responsibility for this change on the NAFTA is a bit simplistic. For example, Sands (2002) contends that the cooperation on which post-NAFTA and post-9/11 agreements could build was actually created by the Customs Modernization Act (CMA) of 1992. Following from this, on 25 February 1995 Prime Minister Chrétien and President Clinton announced their support of the Shared Border Accord, which had four key points: the promotion of international trade; the facilitation of movements of people; the provision of enhanced protection against drug smuggling and illegal migration; and the reduction of costs for governments *and* users. The accord's stated mandate was to "develop a vision for the border that develops and preserves its open character, while protecting our communities" (Canada, 2000). The Canadian Citizenship and Immigration Resource Centre, in an online posting in 2009, argued that the Shared Border Agreement was a benchmark document in that it seemed "as if the declaration would involve a merging, to a certain extent, of Canada and America's border security policies ... through steps as simple as insuring compatibility of immigration databases, to extensive integration through joint immigration processing facilities, where immigration processing of both countries are undertaken by a joint U.S. and Canadian staff" (http://www.immigration .ca/permres-gii-securingborders.asp). In other words, a new era of security cooperation seemed to have begun, and it was indeed more complex than that initiated by the Kingston Dispensation.

THE CANADA–US PARTNERSHIP FORUM

The Shared Border Accord of 1995 was followed in 1999 by the Canada–US Partnership Forum (CUSP). CUSP counterbalanced the economic "border vision" with concerns about terrorism, smuggling (of people and drugs), and cross-border crime. It turned its sights on better managing mobility and trade and on better detecting cross-border crime and terrorism. Shortly before 9/11, CUSP was augmented by the US INS-CIC Border Vision and Cross-Border Crime Forum. The result was a border "vision" that called for streamlined and harmonized border policies and management. The goals here were expanded cooperation well beyond the border and collaboration regarding threats emanating from beyond Canada and the United States. Border policies and practices were streamlined and harmonized, and cooperation was expanded to increase efficiencies in areas such as customs and immigration, law enforcement, and collaboration on common threats from outside Canada and the United States.

So the CMA, Shared Border Accord, and CUSP set the terms for the over-hauling of border security practices after 9/11, meaning that the groundwork for a new border relationship had been laid before 9/11, when talks with the United States began over expediting border security and efficiency. All of these efforts, including the Shared Border Accord, in particular, were launched with much fanfare. They promised that the two goals that had initially seemed diamet-rically opposed—a secure *and* free-flowing border—were achievable, and this set the stage for a new way of thinking about bilateralism (Konrad and Nicol, 2008). The Shared Border discourse was instrumental in developing the Can-ada–US Partnership (CUSP) of 1999, which turned its sights on better managing mobility and trade and on better detecting cross-border crime and terrorism. Shortly before 9/11, CUSP was augmented by the US INS-CIC Border Vision and Cross-Border Crime Forum. All of these agreements comprised "an agenda for the 21st century, outlining a vision which streamlined and harmonized bor-der policies and management" (Konrad and Nicol, 2008: 171).

Thus, the tidy assumption that borders were "open" under the NAFTA and "closed" after 9/11 is much too simple. Precisely because it was clear that borders under the NAFTA were less and less effective at moving people and cargoes at the required speed across the northern border, Canada and the United States again began exploring a more workable "bilateral border" in the late-1990s. The NAFTA's "one border" vision was not sustainable. This border vision "did not attempt to decouple security issues from territorial controls: according to the initial agreement, cooperation was to be facilitated by border processes, policies and procedures which facilitated the flow of goods and people" (Nicol, 2006: 58). This decoupling, in the sense of developing a robust set of security protocols, only occurred in the late 1990s and early twenty-first century, as new security arrangements sought to better control "people."

American policy-makers argue that CUSP was a necessary "mechanism for the two governments, border communities, and stakeholders to discuss issues of border management." The guiding principles that evolved from the discussions included these: streamlining, harmonizing, and collaborating on border policies and management; expanding cooperation to increase efficiencies in customs, immigration, law enforcement, and environmental protections at and beyond the border; and collaborating on common threats from outside the United States and Canada (Seghetti, 2004: 4). The result was an emerging border regime that relied on pallet X-ray systems, potassium-40 prototype systems for bulk mari-juana detection, vapour detection systems for cocaine, and a number of other technological initiatives. At the same time, efforts were made to set in place joint initiatives such as NEXUS, PORTPASS, and CANPASS; these were passenger processing systems that relied on technologies such as licence-plate readers and identity cards (Nicol, 2006). In the name of facilitating the movement of people, individuals were more closely scrutinized than ever.

In addition to these developments was the beginning of the trend to move inspection sites away from the site of the border itself, by developing new ways of managing cargoes and by creating pre-clearance systems. The resulting border regime was increasingly dehumanized and increasingly managed by risk-assessment protocols. And, where borders already existed, there was a tendency to see them "reinforced"—that is to say, increasingly rationalizing services and programs. A series of high-volume crossings becoming targeted as "portals," and with major highways labelled as "corridors" connecting the continent (Konrad and Nicol, 2008). This mapping of North American economic integration would lay the foundations for border management after 9/11.

The resulting border management technology was considered "neutral" because it relied more and more on technologies such as the Nexus card or selected biometrics so as to depersonalize the crossing experience. But when viewed through the lens of a critical geopolitics and critical geo-economic analysis, this neutrality is questionable. Instead, Sparke (2006) suggests that under the NAFTA but prior to 9/11, the border embedded neoliberal interests within North American border-crossing technologies. He contends that using the NAFTA, US neoliberalism reworked the border to make it more market-mediated and to embed citizenship privileges within a framework that privileged economically rational actors. The border technologies that mediated cross-border trade thus privileged neoliberal rationalities; indeed, they established the border as a neoliberal institution. This new border rationality was transformative. It promoted an economic relationship that played to North American market integration and that was managed by technologies of neoliberalism, much like those that assessed financial risk for large investment and insurance corporations. It was also conducive to universalizing US standards in security and foreign policy.

"AMERICA" WRIT LARGE

How so? In a broad sense, the NAFTA represented part of a globalized economic strategy that itself was a response to changes in the US economy brought about by the end of the Cold War. For the United States, this treaty reflected a desire for increased global influence. While supported by a globalized geopolitical discourse that espoused neoliberal values, especially during the Ronald Reagan administration, it was firmly rooted in a deep and foundational US desire for security and national autonomy. The United States had invested heavily in the NAFTA, which in geopolitical terms they saw as opening Latin America and

the Caribbean to American products and capital. Mattli (1999) suggests that
the enlargement of the European Community worried Americans; the NAFTA,
besides promoting neoliberal ideology, would "indicate to the rest of the world
that we, the United States, can make progress in opening up borders and con-
fronting trade barriers either bilaterally or multilaterally" (185).

The NAFTA, by internationalizing and integrating North American markets, reduced the need for "foreign" policy with respect to North American
economic decision making, although it could not be claimed that the treaty was
an effective integrating governance body in general (see Clarkson, 2008). But the
NAFTA would prove useful in fast-tracking security arrangements that affected
the transport of goods within the North American marketplace, although in
other areas it was not so effective (Nicol, 2008; Clarkson, 2008). Indeed, while
there is a propensity to think that the events of 9/11 were a "deal-breaker," securitizing the Canada–US border had been on the agenda even earlier. A discourse
calling for greater integration between Canada and the United States had been
emanating from Washington in the days and months before. Even before 9/11,
Canadians had been feeling pressure to reorganize their border. In the aftermath
of that event, with the media replaying the events of that day, there was popular
pressure as well. Meanwhile, there was political pressure to negotiate a flurry
of new cross-border security agreements. And there was diplomatic pressure as
well. Then US Ambassador to Canada, Paul Celluci, argued the American case
with comments intended primarily for a business audience. Those comments
were reported by McDuff (2012): "Talks of even closer economic ties with the
States than under the current free trade agreements already include a suggestion
by Paul Cellucci, the [former] American Ambassador [to Canada], of redesign-
ing border controls. He wants to speed trade traffic, curb illegal immigration
and nab criminals" (http://www.issuesnetwork.com/articles/mcduff20010813
.html).

What has happened since then has built on a new US hegemony emanating from financial market calculations of security risk (see de Goede, 2008;
Beck, 2000; Sparke, 2005). The resulting borders have done more than symbolically reinforce existing boundaries. They have also enforced neoliberal border
technologies that in turn reinforce US hegemony in North America by implementing economic- and security-oriented border management processes that
are increasingly diffuse.

REFLEXIVE NATIONALISM AND THE FREE TRADE AGREEMENTS

Aggressive neoliberal free trade rhetoric demanded a freer flow of goods as well
as the reconcentration of capital-regulatory functions within the United States.
In the late twentieth century, Canadians feared, much as they did in the 1930s,

the loss of economic markets should the border restrict trade. The neoliberal context in which the NAFTA was served up was tied to a conscious decision on the part of Canadians to explore North American trade possibilities. The problem was that it came with many strings attached, and these had implications far beyond the immediate issue of imports and exports.

The narrative of globalization had, by the eve of 9/11, created the impression that not to open borders would be to be left behind in the global rush to new markets. Given the rise or regional trading blocs, such as the EU, MERCOSUR, and ASEAN, it was difficult to see how the Canadian economy—and by extension the Canadian nation—could succeed without the NAFTA. Fears about job losses coincided with the NAFTA's implementation, as did worries about the NAFTA's impact on the Mexican border and economy. Cavanagh and colleagues (2002) suggest that the NAFTA's role as a neoliberal trade agreement was precisely what distinguished it from broader socio-political and economic projects such as the EU: "the negotiators argued that free trade alone would lift all boats. We argued that strong controls were needed to ensure that trade and investment supported social goals, rather than the narrow interests of large corporations" (59–60). In general, where there was resistance, American anti-NAFTA sentiments were directed towards the Mexican border, not towards Canada. In Canada, as in Mexico, the NAFTA would create a common space for what was predominantly American-style capitalism. Thus, neoliberal ideology was extremely significant in furthering US hegemony and Canadians' economic dependence.

In the 1980s, the FTA universalized neoliberalism with its attendant rhetoric about the private sector, deregulation, and free markets in North America. By the 1990s, policy-makers no longer viewed this rhetoric as controversial; indeed, they incorporated it into a discourse that rendered free trade and neoliberalism a "normative" (i.e., sound) economic policy. Canadian parliamentarians and policy-makers associated with the majority government fully endorsed the NAFTA, even though they had opposed the FTA not too many years before. But if Canadians felt that they stood on the threshold of enhanced integration and bilateralism, mediated by an open border operating in the interests of economic rationality, this did not mean they embraced Americanization. Clarkson (2008) reminds us that there was and still is a pro-liberal corporate agenda supported mainly by the business community in Canada. Increased trade is viewed positively by Canadian manufacturers and by Canadian companies with interests in US markets. Despite corporate and high-level support from all nations, the message of "integration" initially received a mixed response among ordinary citizens. For example, the Conservative government under Prime Minister Brian Mulroney, which that initiated the FTA in the 1980s, was defeated afterwards, partly because it was viewed as "forcing" free trade on Canadians and partly because Canadians viewed the friendship between Canada's Prime Minister Mulroney and US President Reagan as "cronyism."

In the late twentieth century, few Canadians saw themselves as having interests in common with the business elites that were pushing for continental integration. Instead, they evaluated the NAFTA through a critical nationalist discourse. Consistent with historical fears, many Canadians viewed the NAFTA as a threat to Canadian cultural and natural resources. Between 1981 and 2002, the percentage of Canadians advocating a "North American identity" was between 3 and 6 percent (41). This is consistent with studies that explored Canadian and American responses to the NAFTA during the same period. Rankin (2004) found that while better educated and more mobile citizens were more likely to support trade liberalization, their criteria for doing so, in both Canada and the United States, were ultimately related to culture and political symbolism rather than individual economic interests. Regarding the NAFTA, for example, Rankin noted that "in the symbolic politics of the NAFTA, national identity is a critical reference point for Americans and Canadians with limited information about the specifics of trade liberalization" (337).

Rankin found that identity, culture, and sovereignty were critical factors in North Americans' responses to supranational integration: "supranational arrangements have not yet developed enough in the public mind as viable alternatives to the national construction for supranational affective attitudes to determine public opinion on policies of trade liberalization" (348). Rankin's work ascribed considerable importance to how cultural assemblages referencing sovereignty, patriotism, and nationalism determine attitudes towards supranational projects. A borderless North America was more often correlated with a loss of identity, nationality, and cultural distinctiveness, and sometimes, for Canadians, with fear of Americans' ultimate designs. Political cartoons of the era reflected this (see Figure 4.10). Regarding the NAFTA, Canadians supported engagement with the United States even while advocating for "distance." They assumed that neoliberal economic relations were legitimate but wanted to protect Canadian cultural products, identity, and sovereignty.

This concern ran through political debates of the time. As one Quebec representative observed in 1995, "even while the [NAFTA] was being hammered out, the Canadian government was backing away from one of its fundamental responsibilities intended to support cultural development. Knowing that Americans produce 97 per cent of the films we see, we cannot help but be concerned by the lack of vision of the Canadian government of the day" (*Debates* no. 118, Parliament of Canada, 1 November 1994).

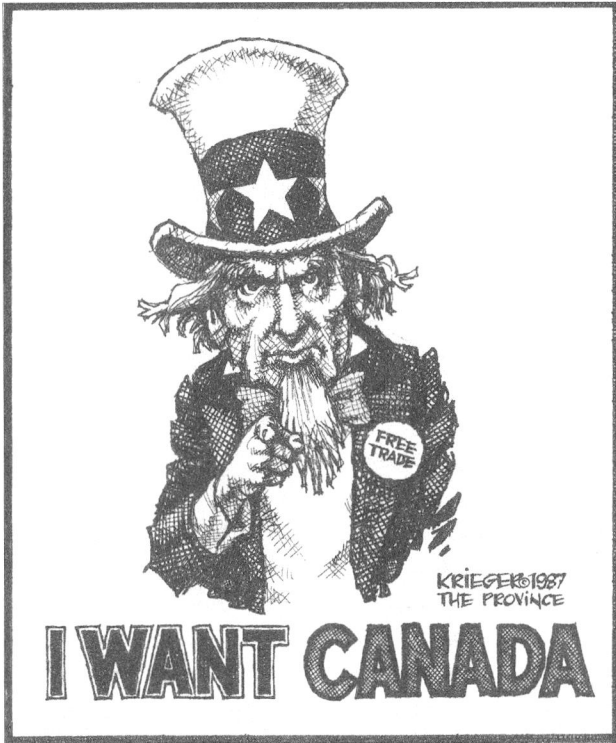

Figure 4.10 "I Want Canada" cartoon. *Source*: Robert Kreiger. Used with permission.

CONCLUSIONS

For much of the twentieth century, the Canada–US border reflected collective assessments rooted in the relationship between national territorial control and expansion. The work of borders, on both sides, was to create and solidify societies that were coterminous with national territory. Both countries were building national economies that reinforced this territoriality. In the mid- to late twentieth century, a series of agreements and arrangements overhauled the border's function. Many in North America believed that increased cooperation between Canada and the United States would deliver security, prosperity, and economic development as well as bring hope to the world, by showing how peaceful relations between neighbouring nations were possible. But the promises made by strengthened security, military interoperability, and seamless free trade came to be broken by US universalism, coupled with Canada's dogged devotion to its own territorial independence. These stimulated the construction of reflexive border metaphors that challenged as much as they facilitated cooperative ventures (see Nicol, 2012: 161).

This process began well before the Cold War, when the debate over Arctic borders demonstrated the importance of sovereignty and territorial integrity to Canadian national discourses. Contrast this with the Cold War discourse on which US geopolitics was based, where Canada was seen almost exclusively as an American buffer zone. All of this generated a meta-geography that could only end with Canada's seamless incorporation into the US national security space. Each of these representations built upon, rather than replaced, the foundational security/trade cooperation developed in the 1940s and 1950s (Nicol, 2012), adding yet another layer of complexity and contradiction.

So while 11 September 2001 is constantly being cited as the date when "everything changed" with respect to border management in North America, it might be more accurate to say that the shift to common border policies and US-style securitization began much earlier, through the NAFTA and various common defence and security agreements. It was the NAFTA, though, that provided the strongest glue, for it internationalized and integrated North American markets, thereby eliminating the need for foreign policy with respect to North American economic decision making. That agreement institutionalized arrangements that heightened Canada's economic dependence on the United States, and this in turn drove Canadian security cooperation post-9/11, as we shall see in the following chapters.

The current North American border regime did not begin in 2001, although the architecture of border security has been very much defined by the US security politics since then. This hegemonic control over bordering processes would not have been possible if the Canada–US border had been imagined and managed differently throughout the nineteenth and twentieth centuries. In many ways, this new securitization is the capstone to a series of securitization dilemmas that have challenged both Americans and Canadians since the early nineteenth century and that have shaped the Canada–US relationship. The United States pushes for ever closer integration; Canada by turns facilitates and resists this. The two Canadian responses are not necessarily counterpoised and indeed are often mutually constitutive. Some have called this paradox "ambivalence" (Thompson and Randall, 1994) or even anti-Americanism; it is useful, however, to view it as an active and ongoing duality—as both a concession to US hegemony and a reaction to it.

Chapter 5

CONTROL IN THE TWENTY-FIRST CENTURY
EMBODYING AND SITUATING THE BORDER

In his book on borders in the global context, Popescu (2012) argues that we should consider international boundaries in terms of the Big Picture. Perhaps we need to take a step back and examine North American borders in this light. He suggests that worldwide, there have been three major interstate border-making episodes in the twentieth century alone. The first of these was after the First World War, mainly in Europe; the second was after the Second World War and extended into the 1960s. This latter episode encompassed the decolonization era and the Cold War (43). The third round of interstate border-making was in the 1990s, after the Cold War, and resulted in "the dramatic increase in the number of state borders" (94), a process that has carried on into the twenty-first century. There is, of course, no guarantee that these new borders will not be challenged and reworked in the future, for there is no template for getting borders "right" for all times and all places.

The way in which the Canada–US border evolved in the twentieth century conforms rather well to Popescu's model. In North America, as elsewhere, the most recent round of global border-making has involved much "debundling" of sovereignty, territory, and identity to accommodate globalization. Here, as elsewhere in the world, international borders are being unpacked so as to move their management to new locations, and many of those locations are not on the territorial boundary itself. Muller (2010) describes this as a new era in which border security is being transformed by technologies that are causing borders to proliferate to the point that borders "cross people" rather than the other way around (Balibar, 2002). New laws and governmental institutions (and even non-governmental ones) are taking over the management of the border through what we might call back office functions such as the building of databases and detention centres. Indeed, Walters (2006) goes so far as to argue that the major purpose of border governance is no longer to fix borders in place, thereby compartmentalizing spaces as means of surveillance and control. These days are long gone.

A multitude of researchers tell us that border management agencies must now be seen to operate within states as well as at their margins (see, among others, Walters, 2006; Popescu, 2012; Muller, 2010; Deleuze, 1990; Balibar, 2002). Indeed, the reach of these same agencies is sometimes extraterritorial. They work in ways that are independent of international borders. They also create large and powerful government institutions that operate outside the line, not just along them (see Nicol, 2011). An example is the US Secure Flight Program.

The Secure Flight Program, overseen by the US Transportation Security Administration (TSA; a branch of the Department of Homeland Security [DHS]) was implemented with controversy after 9/11. It was described by the TSA as " a behind-the-scenes program that enhances the security of domestic and international commercial air travel through the use of improved watch list matching. By collecting additional passenger data, it improves the travel experience for all airline passengers, including those who have been misidentified in the past. When passengers travel, they are required to provide ... Secure Flight Passenger Data (SFPD) to the airline" (TSA, http://www.tsa.gov).

What the TSA does *not* tell us here is that this US institution operates extra-territorially. This means, for example, that Canadians are required to release their information to the TSA, even for flights within Canada. These security protocols are sensitive to socio-economic class, in that neoliberal categorizations of "risk" in terms of creditworthiness, income, employment, and citizenship status are embedded in security documentation if not directly collected by TSA protocols: airlines often link Reward Card data to TSA data for example. All of this means that Canadians must meet security standards that are designed primarily for travel in the United States to met US-determined standards. Recently, though, the TSA has partnered with US Customs and Border Protection (CBP) to offer expedited pre-checks to Canadians as well as Americans at certain airports and on certain flights. Still, creditworthiness and Reward Cards are no help to people with names that sound a security bell with US officials. According to Canadian Liberal MP Joseph Volpe, it was precisely for this reason that the new (in 2011) regulations were more than an inconvenience—they were restricting his ability to fly within Canada. In opposing the implementation of Bill C-42, An Act to Amend the Aeronautics Act, he voiced his frustration:

> I want to point out that this document finds its origins and is an extension of and materially similar to in the atrocity of the American do not fly list, resonant in, maintained and operated by Washington ... I am on that stupid list and cannot get off it. So was the minister of defence, Bill Graham. The Canadian minister of defence was on an American do not fly list and was unable to board a

domestic aircraft in his own country. That is how insane this do not fly list is …
I could not get my name off that list for love nor money. First, people could
not find out where it was and then they could not find out who to talk to. Then
after six weeks of trying, we finally got a phone number, a 1-800 number in
the United States, which told us to send our birth certificates, our passports,
our marriage licences, our driver's licences and in six weeks to three months, a
message would be sent back us, telling us whether we could get off that list …
I am not going to send all my documents away to some black hole in some
basement bunker in the Pentagon. That is not what a Canadian member of
Parliament does when he wants to board an airplane in his own country to fly
from home to work and back.

The Bill to which Volpe was speaking reorganized Canadian law to provide
the necessary authorization for Canadian compliance with the TSA program.
Bill C-42 allows airlines to pass on passenger information to "a foreign state" for
flights over that country. The legislation was necessary so that Canadian airlines
could comply with the new TSA secure flight program, which required airlines
to submit personal information about passengers seventy-two hours before a
flight's departure. Since the bill was passed, passengers leaving Canada on a
flight that crosses US airspace have had their name, birthdate, and gender subject to screening by US officials. If you have the same name as someone on a no
fly list—and many people do, including Volpe—you may be questioned, delayed,
or even barred from the flight. If your name does not appear, you receive your
boarding pass.

At the time this book was being written, some of the difficulties with the law
were merely "growing pains." That said, there is a stronger lesson to be learned.
Fortmann and Haglund (2002) write that the TSA program speaks to the way in
which Canada–US security cooperation is consistently envisioned. Hale (2011)
suggests that "although concepts of shared border management between the
United States and Canada survived 9/11 for a time, particularly through the
processes of the Smart Border Declaration of December 2001, they gradually
succumbed to pressures for increased bureaucratic centralisation of border
management and widespread societal insecurities expressed in demands for
increased sovereign American control over national borders" (34). The potential
co-option of individuals' data has contributed greatly to the deterritorialization
of US border control, and not only at airports.

The Secure Flight program is less draconian than other security measures
that had been envisioned but not implemented. In 2009, newspaper articles
heralded a new era in which all visitors to Canada were to be scrutinized by
fingerprints and other biometric means. Push-back from Canadian authorities
has exempted Canadians from routine fingerprinting (see Muller, 2010), and

so far, biometric scans are required only for visa applicants from twenty-nine countries, who will also have their identity checked against US immigration databases. This is the result of the Immigration Information Sharing Treaty, negotiated by Canada and the United States as part of the Beyond the Border Agreement and signed the same year. The concerns, however, predate the new agreements.

Similarly, in interviews with Canadian border personnel in 2007, this researcher found that the visa exemption issue between Canada and the US had long been an irritant, a consequence of DHS's rather stereotypical assessment that Canada has a "lax immigration process." The Americans worry that Canada's immigration and visa requirements have left them vulnerable to those whose nationalities are not problematic for Canadian officials but might be for US officials. In 2011, when announcing the Immigration Information Sharing Treaty, Citizenship and Immigration Minister Jason Kenney claimed that it would facilitate "building on our countries' mutual efforts to protect our common borders and surrounding perimeter through improved screening." It would "prevent terrorists, violent criminals and others who pose a risk from entering Canada and the United States" (Koring, 2012). Defending its new policies, the Canadian government announced:

> Starting in 2013, the Government of Canada plans to introduce the use of biometrics, through the collection of a photograph and fingerprints, for nationals from twenty-nine countries and one territory who apply for a temporary resident visa, work permit, or study permit. Through automated and systematic biometric information sharing, both Canadian and U.S. authorities will be able to identify previously failed refugee claimants, deportees, previously refused overseas refugee resettlement applicants, and visitor visa applicants trying to enter our countries under fraudulent identities.
>
> Under the Treaty, information will not be shared on Canadian or U.S. citizens or permanent residents. Any information shared on travellers and asylum seekers will be handled responsibly and, as with other information sharing agreements, exchanged in accordance with relevant Canadian laws including the Privacy Act to ensure individuals' privacy rights are considered and protected. (http://www.cic.gc.ca/english/department/media/backgrounders/2012/2012-12-13.asp)

In earlier chapters, we reviewed how the Canada–US border has often been "remade" to suit perceptions of the time. The early twenty-first century is no exception. American policy-makers are preoccupied mainly with the Mexican border, but in its insistence on "one border" approaches, the DHS has painted the "northern border" with a similar brush. We will soon look more closely at how this "dangerous Canada" imaginary has been constructed to fit the new border metaphor, although we can see now that the metaphor is recycled, not new. But first we need to consider more carefully how borders are being remade with respect to perceptions about the need for enhanced security arrangements in the post-9/11 era.

RETHINKING BORDERS POST-9/11

The United States has long envisioned itself as a project that has escaped the confines of nation-state, as an exemplar for the western hemisphere if not the world. Meanwhile, Mexicans and Canadians have tried to carve out space for their own nations in North America. This puts a different spin on the history of borders in North America and on how North American and European integration projects are understood.

In many ways, North American borders appear to move in synchronicity with Europe's. They deploy modern technologies to effect security regimes rooted in data sets that access travellers' personal information; they are open to the flow of goods and capital in the globalized world; and they appear to be sustained by modern neoliberal regimes that promote democracy. With the new border technology, the process of evaluating who can enter and leave is often moved far from the border itself to an airport, a visa-processing centre, a detention cell, a credit bureau, or even purely mundane spaces. Over the past decade or so, it has been common to view borders in both North America and Europe as simultaneously "deterritorializing" and "reterritorializing" borders (Newman, 2005; Popescu, 2012). Borders, that is, are playing an increasing role in security but are also increasingly diffuse; they can now be found in quotidian spaces such as schools and stores, in public and private spaces, and in political and commercial venues (Newman, 2006).

More than two centuries of proximity have not turned Canadians into Americans in the same way that Europeans have come together under the banner of the EU (Brunet-Jailly, 2006; see also Chapter 7). True, the current motif of the NAFTA and NORAD cooperation has led many—in the security world, at least—to conclude that there is one "North American border model" that can be positioned against the European model (see Papademetriou and Collett, 2011). Remember that in Canada in 2013, the monumental underperformance of the much-hyped American retail giant Target reminded both Canadians and Americans that, in the words of one top company executive, "even though they speak the same language and look like Americans, Canadians have a different culture." Such thinking flies in the face of the notion that boundaries, being artificial constructs, are irrelevant in an era of globalization. But it is also true that within the North American security regime there have been multiple visions, although that of US homeland security has been monolithic. Drache (2004) has reported that even after years of having security discourses pushed at them, Canadians do not fear terrorism as much as Americans. He notes that when Canadians were asked to rank their most important concerns in 2007, health was at the top of the list, followed by the environment. Of course, this did not discourage the CBC from offering sensationalist coverage of the Toronto 18 "terrorists," arrested in 2006, nor did it discourage the Prime Minister's Office from promoting its own version of that event (see Muller, 2010).

Still, terrorism has consistently been a lower priority for Canadians. Even in 2015, as a new security bill was being negotiated in the Canadian Parliament as a result of the shootings at the War Memorial in the fall of 2014, the CBC reported that

> in March 2014, only four per cent of Canadians listed public safety and ter-rorism as one of their top three issues. That hardly budged over the next few months, registering at six per cent in August.
>
> But as Canada's Armed Forces became committed to the war in Iraq against the Islamic State in Iraq and Syria (ISIS) in the fall of 2014, the issue became one of the top three for 11 per cent of Canadians. That increased significantly to 18 per cent in the wake of the October 22 Ottawa shooting, settling at 16 per cent in mid-December. Similar data is not yet available following the Paris attacks.
>
> However, public safety and terrorism remains just one issue among many. At 16 per cent, public safety and terrorism were listed as a top-three issue as often as the environment was. And it still trailed at some distance health care (54 per cent) and job creation (35 per cent), the importance of which was unchanged by the events of October. (http://www.cbc.ca/news/politics/economy-not-terrorism-remains-canadians-top-vote-driver-1.2919792)

Newman (2006) reminds us that "the opening of borders does not, auto-matically, result in the hybridization of ethnic and national identity" (147). So it should not be surprising that in the aftermath of the NAFTA and 9/11, and even while debating new security and anti-terrorism legislation (as was the case when this book went to press) there is general support for a continuing close relationship with the United States, most Canadians remained committed to a very different national project. All of this suggests that the idea of security bor-ders and even security perimeters is not inherently a Canadian option—it has emanated largely from the DHS—and that Canadians feel no particularly com-pelling need to fortify their borders. That need has had to be "sold" more than once, as we will see shortly. Security cooperation, then, has been driven from the top down by the Canadian *and* US governments and is being implemented at the same time that the NAFTA's open border imperative remains in place.

REMAKING BORDERS

In post-9/11 North America, a dialectical relationship has been assumed between economic and security discourses, as if they were naturally and mutually exclusive. But much like the security/liberty paradox, which Muller (2010) decries as overly simplistic, the categorization of the border as either secure or free-flowing reinforces a self-defeating thinking about how national borders function. Why is it that people and goods do not enjoy equal mobility? Sparke (2005) suggests that neoliberal politics have been extended as "an invisible but powerful regime of governance" (113–14). Under that regime, goods, not people, are at the core of the "new economic constitution for North America." And that regime is increasingly trying to capture mobility through what Sparke (2006) suggests are the "corporate logos" of transnational companies (2).

For Sparke, neoliberal economic integration is the driving force behind new security technologies that read biometric data. Those technologies have created a nexus between corporate and security imperatives. He continues: "Various insignia of national identity that are today inscribed on specific national passport covers [have been] replaced by the corporate logos of transnational corporations," while "the class-organized, transnational world of credit card transactions, along with all their liberating and constraining market-mediated contradictions ... come to eclipse the more equalized world of belonging regulated ... by the serial sameness of national passports" (252). Sparke contends that this is a future "where the ambiguities of state control and state protection associated with passports would appear to be transcended by the ambiguities of corporate control and free market flexibility afforded by credit cards" (252).

Sparke's work draws upon concepts developed by Balibar (2002), who views borders as "differentiat[ing] between individuals in terms of social class" (82); meanwhile, states maintain their borders "in the service of an international class differentiation." These differentials play into the notion of a "polysemic" border, where borders are experienced differently by different people. Moreover, as we have seen, not all borders are encountered outside the state or at the firewall, where "control society" supposedly begins (Walters, 2006).

All of this creates, in the early twenty-first century, a circular and self-referencing situation: neoliberalism has become the monolithic narrative defining border structure and security discourses that promote specific border management technologies that further neoliberal goals. Part of the process is to create different citizenship entitlements: in other words, these border technologies rely on "emerging neoliberal norms of citizenship" that "appear to depend on new forms of class-based inclusion and exclusion" (Sparke, 2006: 253). These socially sorting technologies "have actually been intensified, at least in terms of border practices, since the crisis in confidence in US 'homeland' security" (253).

In other words, differential mobility of goods and people is a problem area for national security unless securitization is imagined as a project where, just like widgets and car parts, shipped with complex manifests describing origins and assembly points, "nationality" and other complex social descriptors can be "unpacked." When we bundle all people into a single category, whatever their citizenship and national origins, then we must scrutinize all movement. When we differentiate on the basis of biometric characteristics, that single package becomes a data set of untidy, socially constructed personal information such as gender, race, and ethnicity, all ranked according to desirability. The problem here is that there is a certain tyranny in the process: at the border, for example, one cannot be two nationalities at once, nor can one be transgendered. Nationality, age, gender, fingerprints, credit history, and a variety of similar pieces of personal and biometric information, once unpacked, define a spectrum of bits and pieces of code, which when scanned and compared, and perhaps recombined by a securitization lens, determine eligibility to pass, to be refused, or to be detained.

Border management, as it was institutionalized under the NAFTA in the late twentieth century, required new technologies to assess biometric data in order for the cross-border/border-crossing relationship to function fully. This was not because border management could not function properly by traditional means (i.e., by adding more capacity for "old school" border control, such as agents to stamp passports); rather, it was because to implement neoliberal governance, control would have to be implemented by different means, using tools such as retina scanners, fingerprints, voice detection, stress measures, and other biometric management tools. Only this would satisfy the demands of security delivered via risk management practices. Meanwhile, a broader but also different filtering system was demanded of border security. It needed to develop protocols to "commodify" the movement of people much as they would the movement of goods, using digital data and the equivalent of personal bar codes. This institutionalized risk management, which, as Muller (2010) reminds us, reflected "a preoccupation with precautionary risk and pre-emptive risk assessment," a preoccupation that has become "the motivating force behind contemporary border management" (14).

Recognizing this sea change in border management and governance, many scholars have begun to explore the relationship between neoliberal embodiment and biometric border management. For Muller (2010), a significant role of biometric border management today has been "to deal with in some satisfactory manner ... the reinvigoration and adapting of the function of the border ... The biometric state, with its panoply of technologies and approach to 'governing through risk,' is charged with securing the political community, commerce, the population and indeed liberalism itself" (24). There has been tremendous state investment in biometrics and related border management technologies. This means, writes Magnet (2011), that biometric technologies not only have been tasked with securing borders but are now also part of the corporate interests the border secures. Commenting on the more than $24 billion spent on national security between 2004 and 2011, and referencing the larger amount spent on security initiatives in the United States, Magnet observes that the anticipated expense in that country for

> adding biometrics to passports would be between $4.5 billion and $8.8 billion per year, again depending on the biometric technology used: passports with biometric fingerprinting, iris scanning, or facial recognition technology are more costly than those that contain biometric fingerprints only. In either case, the system is estimated to require $1.6 billion to $2.4 billion per year in maintenance … The biometric industry describes 9/11 as a tremendous business opportunity. For example, the biometrics group of the Canadian Advanced Technology Alliance was formed within six months of the terrorist attacks. The company's website asserts that "the events of September 11th have completely turned around the perception of the biometrics industry." (120)

The work of Magnet (2011), Sparke (2006), Muller (2010), Balibar (2002), and others can be contrasted with less critical understandings of economic and security arrangements post 9/11 generated by various Canadian and American policy-makers and security industry representatives, whose work is less invested in critical understandings of the biometric regimes they advocate and more focused on resolving the practical problems of day-to-day border crossing. It is often the product of think tanks created for lobby groups, political interests, and even policy-makers, who see a harder border as an imperative, perhaps as one demanded by their constituencies. Such discourses often counterpoise economic interests with personal mobility, arguing that privacy must be given up if liberty is to be secured.

All of this forges connections between the terrorism crisis, the deployment of biometric technologies, and neoliberal border management. That is to say, borders are concerned with facilitating neoliberal governance and broader economic goals through the use of technologies capable of assuaging concerns about terrorism. Deep contradictions are inherent in what have clearly become "totalizing" cosmologies of intervention. For example, US policy-makers raise alarms about illegal immigration and NAFTA job losses even while border management technologies and their ancillary "discourses of crisis" facilitate even broader implementation of NAFTA-like borders. There is a genealogy of sorts between the security agreements produced through neoliberal border management and the NAFTA itself. As Sparke (2006) and Balibar (2002) have argued, the neoliberal polysemic border has created a context in which neoliberal arrangements can dictate the terms of personal mobility.

But as Brunet-Jailly (2006: 6), Clarkson (2006), Nicol (2006), and others point out, the NAFTA was never meant to be a foundational agreement for these security arrangements. As a comprehensive tool for post-9/11 policy-makers to implement continental security measures, it is of limited use (Nicol, 2006). The NAFTA, in other words, has limited capacity to foster transnationalism, partly because there is neither the imaginative capacity nor the political will to transcend the importance of borders in either country. Rather, it is a cooperation agreement that has opened the door to further negotiations but is unlikely to be the basis for broader security arrangements (Clarkson, 2008). Why is this? According to Drache (2004), it is mainly because it is difficult to see the NAFTA as a "Big Picture" geopolitical event. The United States initially had less interest than Canada in a trade deal, so the passage of the FTA (the predecessor to the NAFTA) was no sure thing (Drache, 2004). It was not until the NAFTA was being negotiated that the Americans showed some enthusiasm, in the belief that there was much to be gained from securing Mexican markets (Drache, 2004). Drache contends that since 9/11, Americans have tended to see the NAFTA as an important piece of the security problem, and negative representations of that agreement as a "border breaker" have been cultivated through the American media as well as linked to illegal immigration discourses. Critiquing the NAFTA has become a new "brick in the wall" of a discourse that is increasingly opposed to free trade under conditions of continental partnership. All of this has positioned the US interest in taking hegemonic command of a single North American security arrangement as either inherently in opposition to economic integration or opposed to economic imperatives or increasingly weighed against illegal activity and terrorism. At the very least, it has politicized the NAFTA in a way that casts it in a negative light, as a source of security problems (Drache, 2004). In this way, those post-9/11 security discourses emanating mainly from Washington have repositioned Canadian and Mexican interests in economic integration as "chips" in a broader security game. Their integration into a continental economy is now viewed as making the United States more vulnerable, and Canada and Mexico may have to make the most security concessions in order to keep the NAFTA running smoothly.

If securitization agreements have rendered the NAFTA less potent, they have also led to a rigid standardization of North American security. Initiatives such as what is now called the Canada–US Beyond the Border Accord are meant to foster economic and security partnerships but are increasingly sensitive to tensions resulting from American security expectations. Economic interests are less compelling from an American perspective, since the US trade relationship with Canada is less critical for the US than Canada's trade relationship with the US is for Canada. This is why the relationship between security and economy is so important. Both have implications for how border making is understood and positioned in bilateral institutions. Neither is a "neutral" or technical issue. At the same time, "security trumps trade" has become an oft-repeated truism when it comes to understanding the importance of each piece of the relationships. So when it comes to border management technologies, we must always ask, "In whose interests and at whose expense are we implementing security?" It behooves us to critique how border security narratives are structured and represented and their impact on the territorialization (or deterritorialization) of power, by exploring the foundational documents that have institutionalized border management and practice. Over the next few pages, we explore those foundational documents from a critical and theoretical perspective in anticipation of Chapter 6, where we will discuss how risk is constructed and the "border work" it does. Few of us would argue that there are no direct links between US homeland security, emergency preparedness, and the variety of new instruments and agreements through which the US government is today constructing and managing North American borders. Those links are being forged incrementally. The process began in the late 1990s with the Shared Border Accord (see Chapter 4), followed by the Smart Border Declaration (discussed in this chapter), the Security and Prosperity Partnership (SPP), and, most recently, the Beyond the Border initiative.

DISCOURSES OF COOPERATION: BUILDING A SHARED BORDER NARRATIVE

The first significant cross-border agreement after 9/11 was the Smart Border Declaration of December 2001, followed by the Smart Border Action Plan of January 2002. Brunet-Jailly (2006) argues that Canada and the United States signed it because it conformed to their security history (8). By this he did not mean that it was uncontroversial, but rather that it was not subject to the decisions of international institutions. The Smart Border had four specific goals, which we can compare with those of the Shared Border Accord that preceded it. As we saw in Chapter 4, the Shared Border called for the two countries to (1) streamline, harmonize, and collaborate on border policies and management, (2) expand cooperation to increase efficiencies in customs, immigration, law enforcement, and environmental protections at (or beyond) the border, and (3) collaborate on common threats from outside the United States and Canada. The Smart Border also had four main cooperation goals: (1) the secure flow of people (separating low- from high-risk travellers), (2) the secure flow of goods (cross-border movement of low-risk, preapproved commercial goods and truck drivers), (3) investment in secure infrastructure (highways, bridges, technologies), and (4) coordination and information sharing in the enforcement of these objectives. The Smart Border was a defining moment in that it embedded the concept of biometric borders in ways once only imagined (Magnet, 2011).

In listing biometrics as its first objective, the Smart Border Action Plan ensured that these technologies would be central to remaking the border. Since then, the Smart Border Declaration has been the subject of five joint status reports. Over that time, the role of biometric technologies has expanded, and promoting their use has remained at the top of the bilateral agenda. Augmenting NEXUS-Air and other programs for expediting border crossings for business-people and other regular travellers, the declaration gave rise to various biometric initiatives designed to provide additional screening of persons designated as security risks. Moreover, since 9/11, Canada has required permanent residents to obtain identity cards equipped with a chip that can store biometric information. Biometric technologies can now be deployed to subject newcomers to Canada to a secondary identity test; in effect, the border has been outsourced onto individual bodies. In addition, the Statement of Mutual Understanding on Information Sharing provides for the two countries to share biometric information on immigrants and refugees. That agreement, too, grew out of the Smart Border Declaration (Magnet, 2011: 115).

The Smart Border and Shared Border documents are quite similar, in that both promote techno-economic interventions. Furthermore, the Smart Border agreement has retained many of the key points found in the Canada–US Partnership Forum (CUSP) (Konrad and Nicol, 2004; Nicol, 2005). Being a post-9/11 document, however, the Smart Border is more deliberately focused on terrorism (Farson, 2006). Indeed, "it was the ongoing border accord dialogue of the 1990s that made it possible for Canada and the U.S. to come to such a broad-scale consensus agreement on new border arrangements so quickly after 9/11" (Farson, 2006: 33). The Smart Border Declaration included a thirty-point Action Plan that was meant to expand specific technological interventions that would guide the future cross-border relationship (Canada–US Smart Border Declaration, 2001). The agreement included key provisions for addressing "security risks" while "efficiently expediting" the "legitimate flow of people and goods" across the border, although how risk and ill intent were to be determined was not specified.

Coté-Boucher (2008) suggests "the Declaration, accompanied by its action plan, could be more specifically labelled as a programme of government of movement" (144). This is because, much like the earlier Shared Border Accord, it was intended to secure flows of people and goods, boosting investment in "secure" infrastructure, "coordination," and "information sharing" in order to achieve these objectives. At the core of this agreement was a new commitment to common biometric standards and technologies: identity documents would be standardized, making it easier for US officials to scrutinize IDs, and biological information would be embedded in those IDs in machine-readable form. Passports would now be machine-readable and would be compulsory at the transnational travel. Biometric technology was simultaneously applied to the NEXUS program, the "trusted traveller" program that preapproved travellers deemed to be low risk.

Concomitantly, more document-reading machines were installed at border locations. Also targeted was the visa and visa waiver system, which now coupled border security to immigration policies. Canada and the US have very different immigration policies, and this concerns US policy-makers, who view this lack of coordination as potential terrorism threat. One result has been a Safe Third Country agreement, to the extent that it no longer allows immigrants to enter Canada through the United States and subsequently claim refugee status. Refugee claims can now be made only in the country of initial entry. Unresolved is the matter of visa waivers—something that the Americans find especially irksome. In 2009, concurrently with trilateral security negotiations with Mexico (the SPP), Canada implemented a visa requirement for Mexicans visiting Canada. It also established the Passenger Information Sharing System to facilitate the sharing of information about airline travellers and to calculate a "risk score." The latter agreement was also intended to develop Joint Passenger Analysis Units to screen passengers in advance, using a standard Canadian/American framework.

The Smart Border Declaration promoted all of these developments as "best practices." At the time the agreement was signed, the Canadian government declared: "Since signing the Smart Border Declaration, Canada and the United States have proven that tremendous progress can be made through close cooperation and a commitment to an effective philosophy of risk management" (Canada–US Smart Border Action Plan Update, 2008).

But these developments are wide open to criticism. For example, the best practices discourse has naturalized and neutralized the securitization process. Instead of problematizing risk or questioning the structure and nature of border activities, that discourse has reified and overdetermined borders (Balibar, 2002); then, in a tautological cycle of reasoning, it has recast those same borders as spaces in need of securitizing. Documents like the Smart Border Declaration promote a matter-of-fact, no-nonsense understanding of how borders operate with respect to efficiencies and policy goals, but they do so without heed to how they actually *create* insecurity. These matter-of-fact readings are then embedded in normative and uncritical understandings of political cooperation.

The Smart Border and the changes to border management it initiated were only the beginning of much more comprehensive border management rooted in a thorough reorganization of intra- and interstate relations. In 2001, after 9/11, the Canadian government passed a hastily drafted anti-terrorist act that allowed for investigative hearings and pre-emptive arrests (Roach, 2003: 8). This was followed by a 2001 security bill that "made it seem as though terrorism was the only threat to the security of Canadians" (10). Indeed, even when compliant, the many adjustments made by Canada to address US security concerns through the Smart Border Declaration did not seem to be enough: "The border agreements did not ease friction between the two governments. Canada protested that Canadian citizens born in the Middle East and Muslim countries were being singled out for photographic, fingerprinting, and registration in the United States" (11).

Moreover, the Smart Border Declaration, designed to keep trade flowing, seemed not to be so smart after all. Ross and Hira (2006) contend that a smart border means a border where stricter security will not impede the flow of goods, services, or people. They suggest that if there were greater investment in technology and border infrastructure, the trade-off between flow of goods and flow of people would not be an issue. Their solution would involve tightening the inspection of goods and people *before* they arrive in North America while facilitating the movement of both through pre-clearances.

But the US Patriot Act, passed in the fall of 2001, intensified border management instead of expediting it. For example, a Safe Third Country agreement was required to keep borders flowing. The agreement may have responded to US concerns about Canada's supposedly liberal refugee policy, but it did nothing to ameliorate other cross-border tensions, such as the ones generated by arguments that swirled around US softwood lumber tariffs and farm subsidies (11).

In keeping with the growing securitization mandate initiated south of the border—especially the demand for greater harmonization of Canadian and US immigration policies—the Smart Border Declaration was soon superseded as a comprehensive border agreement by the Security and Prosperity Partnership Agreement (SPP).

BEYOND SMART: THE SECURITY AND PROSPERITY PARTNERSHIP

The Smart Border Declaration was not the only or even most significant agreement or restructuring arrangement to follow 9/11. Further changes to government structures were made in the ensuing months and years, and new agreements between Canada and the United States were developed. For example, Canada established a new government department, the Department of Public Safety and Emergency Preparedness Canada (PSEPC, now Public Safety Canada), which took over the Office of Critical Infrastructure Protection and Emergency Preparedness from the Department of National Defence (DND). In some ways the equivalent of the US DHS, the PSEPC was to oversee all of Canada's domestic and border security agencies, including the RCMP and CSIS. It also took control of the Correctional Service of Canada and the National Parole Board; crime, terrorism, and border control were thereby crammed into a single mega-institutional oversight package. In addition, the Canada Border Services Agency (CBSA) was established in December 2003 within the PSEPC. The CBSA has folded together the Customs Branch of the Canada Revenue Agency (CRA) and Citizenship and Immigration Canada (CIC).

By 2007, Canadian government had implemented a host of changes in border management. Muller (2010) writes that Canadian policy-makers have "mimicked" their US counterparts and that differences in orientation have been relatively superficial. Others suggest that Canada has had little alternative in this, given the importance of the trade relationship between the two countries, as the NAFTA's health had proved to be too sensitive to the 9/11 attacks. Trade levels dropped significantly as a consequence of thickening post-9/11 borders. By 2005, it was clear that trade and security arrangements should be linked and improved upon to develop a more comprehensive North American border security regime. The NAFTA was revisited with the goal of heightening cross-border coordination. Some dubbed these negotiations "NAFTA Plus." The Security and Prosperity Partnership of North America (SPP), signed in 2005, was designed to bolster continental security without hindering flows of people and goods. It asked Canadians and Mexicans to "partner" with the United States to secure US borders (for the SPP's relevance, see Beylerian and Lévesque, 2004, 11). The SPP eventually failed. The rhetoric, political texts, agreements, and accords relating to its short life and ultimate demise have been explained most often through normative texts that take an institutional approach.

For the US government, the SPP talks had been an opportunity to resolve what it saw as pressing cross-border security concerns that had not been addressed by more conventional border accords. The continental partnership promised by the SPP had further shifted Canadian (and Mexican) national security towards the American model. But Gattinger and Hale (2010) have described the SPP's failure as a result of its lack of ability to create buy-in beyond the elite political and business classes. According to those advancing an institutional understanding, the SPP debacle amounted to a failure of governance— that is, of institutional coordination and support—rather than a failure to reach a consensus regarding the need to coordinate institutions.

Gattinger and Hale, and others, privilege the role of policy and formal politics. By contrast, critical geopolitical approaches examine how the SPP's assumptions about policy remedies exemplified the problems faced by border policy-makers arising from the fact that—as Kuus (n.d.) has described it—"state identity and interest do not precede foreign policy, but are forged through foreign policy practices." In other words, the SPP was a high-level forum on trilateral North American governance that assumed a common space could be established; but it failed to develop a blueprint for such a space by creating either a viable transnational identity or viable transnational foreign policy practices.

Why foreign policy? Because security institutions serve as much as vehicles for constructing foreign policy discourses as they do for implementing predetermined security interests. Indeed, they instrumentalize those discourses. The SPP's failure suggests that such policy differences are more important than we give them credit for. For example, many viewed the SPP as containing a number of political imperatives waiting to be implemented in order to enhance American national interests by reorienting security discourses within neighbouring states. True, the SPP was touted as a politically expedient document whose end goal was "to improve the safety and enhance the prosperity of the citizens of Canada, the United States and Mexico." This partnership promoted cooperation in areas as diverse as national security, transportation, the environment, and public health; that said, it was overwhelmingly oriented towards corporate and US security concerns. And while we have here stressed institutional perspectives, from realist perspective its security provisions reflected the "principal locus and mechanisms of the balance of power" (Beylerian and Lévesque, 2004: 13), and that balance, of course, favoured the United States.

The SPP failed, not necessarily because the partner states would not cooperate to develop a security discourse, or because appropriate institutions could not be implemented, but because the mechanisms for cooperation were understood to be elitist and poorly coordinated at best (Gattinger and Hale 2010); at worst, they were understood as instruments for furthering US geopolitical domination in the western hemisphere (Clarkson, 2008). Building on arrangements that Sparke (2005, 2006) suggests comprise a "neoliberal nexus," the agreement was meant to create harmonized security policies, including policies on immigration and refugees. But, at the end of the day, the SPP had little traction, and its impact was much less dramatic than that of earlier security accords. Perhaps this was because, as Sokolsky and Lagassé (2006) predicted, it did not develop a partnership among equals, but merely attempted to insert Canada and Mexico into a Washington-led initiative. Indeed, the US Department of Commerce had promised Americans that the SPP would "co-ordinate our security efforts to better protect US citizens from terrorist threats and transnational crime and promote the safe and efficient movement of legitimate people and goods" (SPP, 2009).

CONTINENTAL DREAMS

Although it advanced no blueprint for success, the SPP had been touted as a first step towards a continental security perimeter within which Canada, Mexico, and the United States would have harmonized their security policies (including immigration and refugee policies). Gilbert (2007) points out that

> in the SPP document alone, which numbers only a few pages, there are nearly a dozen allusions to the "people," and to their being "protected," "responded to," "invested in" and the promotion of their "full potential." The SPP thus signals a new interest in biopolitics, that is, a concern for the lives and bodies of the population, at the regional level. But it is not that a new kind of regional governance is being envisioned; in fact, the three countries insist that the SPP does not impinge upon their sovereignty. (78)

But not all would agree. The Canadian Citizenship and Immigration Resource Centre (2009) was more critical than others who responded to the SPP's perimeter discourses. It recognized that even with such a perimeter, there was no guarantee that the United States would soften its border security policies towards Canada. Indeed, it suggested that the Americans' "layered" approach to security required strong border controls to remain in place regardless of border cooperation. Canada would in effect be giving up or losing sovereignty over its own security and immigration policies with no guaranteed benefit at the end of the day.

Without question, the SPP focused overwhelmingly on US security concerns, building on the existing cooperation set out in trilateral agreements like CUSP, and on deeper ties that had influenced North American cooperation in the past, such as the NAFTA and the Smart Border Declaration. It also relied on north–south transportation corridors (Konrad and Nicol, 2008) and on the efficient articulation of corridors on either side of the border. For Clarkson (2008), the SPP was ultimately a highly artificial initiative that, much like other North American integration initiatives, failed to effectively imagine a common North American space that did not yet exist.

So the SPP failed. But post-9/11, a host of other US-led initiatives relating to security, immigration, transportation and shipping manifests, rules of origin, and "trusted company" pre-clearance programs have succeeded in reorganizing cross-border trade protocols. More recently, in fact, Canada and the United States have brokered a new security perimeter accord, the Beyond the Border initiative. At the time of writing, many of its details and potential impacts remain undisclosed, but there is little doubt that it will closely reflect the intent of the SPP and post-9/11 security agreements. According to the Canadian government, this accord pursues a security perimeter, which will be managed by now familiar techniques. As with its predecessors, "harmonization of security and immigration initiatives," "standard documentation," and "best practices" are this agreement's preferred terms for border management. In a joint statement with President Obama, Prime Minister Harper declared:

> We expect to use a risk management approach where compatible, interoperable, and—where possible—joint measures and technology should proportionately and effectively address the threats we share. Effective risk management should enable us to accelerate legitimate flows of people and goods into Canada and the United States and across our common border, while enhancing the physical security and economic competitiveness of our countries. (Canada, 2011)

Much like previous "accords" in the post-NAFTA, post-9/11 era, the Beyond the Border initiative hints at a partnership that could create US hegemony by other means. Moreover, while over the past decade, border partnership arrangements have generally not been marred by dissent, even so there have been moments when objections have brought to light hegemonic processes, usually to no avail. One now famous example involved the Western Hemisphere Travel Initiative (WHTI). The WHTI is essentially about enforcing documentation at air, land, and sea crossings in order to target or intercept terrorists, smugglers, and others engaged in illegal cross-border activities. When it was passed into law in 2004, North American travellers were warned that their documentation would have to comply with this US law, which claims to have established standards for the "western hemisphere." This has ended the long tradition of crossing the Canada–US border without a passport, and with it, perhaps, any hopes for real partnership.

TECHNOLOGY AND EMPIRE

Beginning with the pre-9/11 Shared Border Accord and CUSP, and up to the Beyond the Border initiative, a series of agreements have been set in place that have essentially redesigned the Canada–US border. Most of these agreements have responded to post-9/11 security discourses in ways that privilege pre-9/11 neoliberal orthodoxies even while reframing them as security issues. Canada has faced more and more pressure to synchronize its border policies with those of the United States. Border cooperation is no longer based on general agreements (like CUSP); it now specifically addresses cross-border drug trafficking, criminality, and terrorism, in response to American pressure for a hardened border. By applying border security as a control lever, the United States has transformed its hegemonic control of North American markets into a broader securitization discourse that has universalized US standards and management protocols through agreements such as the Smart Border Declaration, the SPP (now defunct), and now the Beyond the Border initiative. Countries like Canada are yielding to American pressure in order to retain close relations and maintain economic partnerships.

Another important trend is that the various agreements, accords, and border policies that now mark the Canada–US border are in a fairly constant state of flux, the only real constant being the influence of US security discourses. At this point, we need to pause to understand how border technology today is instrumental in managing security and perceptions of security in ways that promote hegemony. In other words, we need to focus not just on the technical programs that promote these new and now normative security arrangements, but also on how these programs advance specific geopolitical agendas.

In this section we adopt a historical and critical approach, one that assumes that current events and security measures are changing more rapidly than this volume can assess in a timely way. Still, it is worth reflecting upon events as they unfolded, while remembering that much will change even before this volume goes to press. For this reason, adopting a long-term, big-picture perspective is quite useful. This includes consideration of borders as security technologies that embed biometrics and securitization discourses. It is to the discussion of these issues that we now turn.

Popescu (2012) argues that "security" is now derived from the application of technological assessment to individuals as well as vehicles and cargoes. Security today relies on machines that read data embedded in passports, manifests, and ID cards and that detect radioactive materials, contraband, and human cargoes. It also relies on electronic data-sharing systems that identify suspect individuals. These strategies require new ways of thinking about border management and enforcement as well as new technologies and structures. They also require new institutional arrangements for implementation, enforcement, and management. This is because, since 9/11, border management and enforcement policies have become the equivalent of foreign policies (Nicol, 2011) as individuals, goods and services, money, and information are filtered, monitored, and tracked both across and within sovereign territories and as the dynamics of maintaining flows has become at best politicized under conditions of post-9/11 globalization, "the War on Terror," and illegal immigration.

For academics who critically analyze contemporary Canada–US border arrangements, scholars like Foucault (2007) provide important analytical lenses. To understand why, let us return to some earlier discussion in this text (see Introduction). Foucault asked how we understand what we know. According to Sohoni, "he describes how 'discourses'—or ways of thinking and talking about topics—shape what constitutes 'knowledge' at particular historical times. Discourses, however, are not closed systems of meaning, but draw upon meanings and values constructed by other discourses. Foucault (2007) also stresses that what is considered 'knowledge' reflects the power of individuals or groups to determine cultural meanings" (Sohoni, 2006: 828).

Following from Foucault, Deleuze (1990) and others who deconstruct border security practices focus on the diffuse agency of security enacted in new border technologies through the use of biopolitical filters and the inscription of individuals into larger data sets. In this context, it is worth repeating what we discussed earlier in this volume (see Introduction). We noted that Deleuze reprises Foucault, who saw the eighteenth- and nineteenth-century disciplinary societies as "initiat[ing] the organization of vast spaces of enclosure." He then asserts that today, "we are in a generalized crisis in relation to all the environments of enclosure," so that instead of living in a society controlled by identifiable disciplines and spaces, "in the societies of control one is never finished with anything—the corporation, the educational system, the armed services being meta-stable states coexisting in one and the same modulation" (5). This approach signals a break with past readings of border management and mobility (Muller, 2010). Walters (2006) argues that today's border management technologies have introduced a new mode of political agency and governance, a "control society." He is describing here a form of hegemonic control embedded in US border security, which is diffuse and networked and which does not require territorial control, because of the nature of the technologies themselves.

SECURITY, RISK, MOBILITY, AND BORDERS

Border security discourses rely on broad assessments of threats that are infinite, premediated, and sometimes incomprehensible (see Dillon, 2008; de Goede, 2008; Isin, 2004). To be effective, security discourses must premediate risk—that is, calculate and recalculate threats that have even a minuscule possibility of occurring. De Goede (2008) argues that "premediated risk" requires security managers, the media and cultural industries, and decision makers to "map out as many possible worlds, or possible paths, as the future could be imagined to take" (159). The result has been the rise of a security industry and community, and even security "gurus." But as Isin (2004) shows, that industry/community has been created by "neuroliberal" rather than neoliberal bordering and security practices. Here he is referencing the paranoia generated by premediation. That paranoia in turn generates a desire for 100 percent "protection." Another issue implicit in the new security regime is, of course, the idea that domestic security concerns among North American nations must become internalized, fused, and connected through common security policies so as to externalize existential threats. For example, the response in North America to 9/11 was to focus on externalizing military and terrorist threats. The goal in this was total protection.

This suggests that since 9/11, there has been a change in how "risk" is assessed in security discourses. Risk had once been determined statistically. As if on an insurance underwriter's life expectancy chart, risk assessments were based on an individual's membership in a larger category or group, that is, on societal demographics. Things are quite different today, in the sense that under previous risk management regimes, a sheep was a sheep, with four legs and a woolly coat, and was seen as a rather benign creature; today, by contrast, a sheep is a potential wolf in sheep's clothing: something on the surface looks like one thing but when examined closely reveals a darker side. The new border management strategies and technologies set out to discover the wolves in sheep's clothing; they examine individuals one by one to make sure they are who they say they are. Is this really a sheep? Does it act like a sheep? What is its travel history? How does it interact with other sheep? All of this is determined by resort to electronic and digital networks that have recorded these individuals' past activities (habits, travel history) and hold their biometric signatures. The latter tend to universalize the security practices of well-developed states like the United States in the sense that these powerful and technologically savvy states set the tone for "best practices," and we now see the increasingly global impact of US security agendas. This has globalized the security agendas of those states as well as the accompanying rules.

A new spatiality is thus associated with control society. That is why we need to be cautious when positioning US hegemony as a "territorial empire" or a "network of influence," and this is a point raised at the beginning of this book, for precisely this reason. The notion that the United States is a hegemonic empire rather than an imperial one is rooted in recent developments in border technologies, not just in grand geopolitical narratives. Many researchers (Walters, 2006; Nicol, 2011; Popescu, 2012) have pointed out that new border technologies tend to deterritorialize border control, for they can be implemented at sites like airports as well as at secure zones away from actual borders (including at detention centres). Also, they are structured in such a way as to promote harmonization and build on the fact that security power is now embedded in spatially diffuse social networks and practices and is strongly linked to communications and information technologies.

Coté-Boucher (2008) refers to "the demise of the Westphalian political imaginary which represented the border as a geopolitical locus of war and peace for European nations" (146). She contends that because of this landmark change, borders now are "physically extending beyond and inside [their] geopolitical location through a set of legal, administrative and technological procedures such as refugee containment, counter-terrorism measures and information-sharing" so that "the border thus articulates fluid control measures based on the use of information technologies to more restrictive procedures such as confinement" (142). As we have seen, for example, at the Canada–US border, the Smart Border Declaration saw this process begin as one that saw "the extension of the border into a multiplicity of sites for the surveillance of movement" (143). Amoore, Marmura, and Salter (2008) contend that neoliberal border management has resulted in a sort of social sifting, as a result of which transnational mobility is now linked to social status, which in turn is based on broader socio-economic assessments of class, income, ethnicity, and (more generally) marginality. These assessments infiltrate both sides of the border and are difficult to challenge.

Does all of this suggest that we have seen the end of sovereign borders? Definitely not, but we have seen a transformation (see Popescu, 2012; Nicol, 2008). Political geographer David Newman (2005) suggested some years ago that borders need to be understood as a continuum and that they can reterritorialize and deterritorialize simultaneously. Similarly, Coté-Boucher (2008: 147) raises an interesting issue: although Westphalian imaginary of border as a container for conflict now appears to be defunct, there still exist hegemonic borders, which perpetuate colonial practices on people and places in new and diffuse ways, and those borders are still being constructed. The exceptional exercise of state sovereignty and state control has been reinforced, not replaced by a security paradigm that has normalized security powers so that they operate as everyday, ordinary techniques of government.

In other words, in modern border management, there is an ever-present contradiction between state presence and state invisibility. The same point is raised by Balibar (2002) with respect to state violence and unlawful confinements, and Balibar in turn is echoed in Amoore, Marmura and Salter (2008), who observe an inherent conflict in traditional border imaginaries: borders represent "both an appeal to the limits in politics and of political community, and a technology of limits—a means of defining what is possible in the governing of life itself" (96). In this sense, borders are not found just at the edges of states. They can also be understood as multiple and as found throughout societies and places. Moreover, as Balibar (2002), Rumford (2008), and others suggest, borders remain overdetermined by the state in precisely those traditional spaces that once defined the edges of nation-states. This often obscures the more nuanced or polysemic ways that new borders develop through socio-economic sifting and neo-colonial discourses. Still, although sovereignty is no longer seen a matter of managing and protecting discrete territorial limits, Agamben (2005) suggests that in protecting such interests, states facilitate state power through evoking a state of exception, exercising full sovereign control, by deciding where laws are to be suspended and how (for example, human rights violations in detention centres). In this sense, diffuse borders do not weaken the state's power of the state; rather, they extend it inwards, onwards, and outwards.

It is true, then, that in North America, post-9/11 borders have become increasingly diffuse. This functions through exclusions and also through inclusions; for example by "cooperation" through intelligence sharing. For Coté-Boucher (2008), it happens by building an intelligence paradigm that "rests upon the national and international sharing of information by security agencies along circuits of information exchange" (149). So although networked, modern and seemingly seamless, security protocols in North America exist to build or force compliance with near neighbours, on terms set by the US (Nicol, 2011): "U.S security policies are implemented through agreements and border controls meant to incorporate neighbours rather than exclude them, but to incorporate them under the terms of US domestic security agendas instead of through foreign policies, diplomacy or broader treaties and institutional agreements" (263). New border technologies are able to exclude individuals, and they can also encompass, contain, and control individuals beyond state borders, at the individual *and* societal levels.

But what is actually diffuse or extraterritorial about such technologies? Are not the new technologies, as well as the traditional guards and the fences, the checkpoints and the bridges, found in or bounded by finite spaces? There are two ways to approach this question. As Walters (2006) explains: "Today, it seems, borders are becoming more and more important not as military or economic practices but as spaces and instruments for the policing of a variety of actors, objects and processes whose common denominator is their 'mobility' … or more specifically, the forms of social and political insecurity that have come to be discursively attached to these mobilities" (188).

Border posts are being militarized and fortified by new technologies, but to be effective, those locations rely on diffuse data sets and networked cooperation. They draw from all sorts of information to assess individuals, and as they do so, they generate new files to record and track those individuals. They use electronic and biometric data, and they can pull up information immediately as a border crossing takes place. They rely on machine-readable documents developed to specific information standards, and those documents have been pre-cleared or screened. In the wake of 9/11, a new border security industry has developed that is trying to screen *everyone* as if every individual was a real and present threat to national security (see Konrad and Nicol, 2008). This industry does not hesitate to create and share data sets; indeed, it regards all of that information as a security bonanza. As in the wolf-in-sheep's-clothing analogy made earlier, "biometrics do not signify merely a shift to more sophisticated technology, they represent a larger shift toward the concept of identification through individual characteristics rather than on the basis of nationality. This is driven by the realization that home-grown terrorism exists in numerous 'safe' countries, countries that cannot have wide-ranging visa restrictions placed upon all of their citizens" (Papademetriou and Collet, 2001: 6).

The theme of mobility informs all current border management and border technology development. Although it is increasingly clear that globalization will not bring an end to borders; it will, however, reconfigure borders to merge security imperatives with mobility ones (Nicol and Townsend-Gault, 2005). For example, after 9/11, in the context of North American borders, we were told that "security trumps trade." But that is nonsensical: trade and security are co-constitutive, and the former is being securitized as a means to promote the latter. Border management is now about managing mobility—about capturing data related to flows of peoples and goods in order to maintain if not strengthen the "exceptional" sovereignty claims of states (Salter, 2008). Border management, in that sense, represents the pinnacle of achievement in modern globalization efforts—borders *look* wide open when in fact they are closed. As we have already seen, building on his reading of Deleuze, Walters (2006) contends that implementing this sort of totalizing border surveillance and control has involved not just machines and technologies but a new *kind* of control that has affected the bordering process itself (191). Like Deleuze, he argues that a control society is one in which power is embedded in spatially diffuse social networks and practices and strongly linked to communications and information technologies rather than to bounded institutional enclosures. It is that society, he argues, that defines North American border practice.

It might be worth returning here to the idea of polysemic border raised earlier in this volume. Among many others, Balibar (2002) and Muller (2010) suggest that borders have proliferated and are everywhere. They are not contained by sites of control; rather, they operate through individuals and social relations, through data sets and practices, through the act of living itself. These techniques, implemented by highly sophisticated technologies and databases, may be an "alternative" to racial or ethnic profiling, but the data they scrutinize are codified by race and ethnicity, as well as economic status and other indicators. Moreover, in their erasure of the individual, and in their focus on the "dividual," they render the individual actor impotent and meaningless. Detached from identity and territory, the "dividual" prised apart in the data code can be manipulated to "fit" appropriate risk scenarios—in effect, to justify them. In this way the data themselves create the specific categories of risk—and security threats are all about risk categories. Those same data have also created the community of scholars, policy-makers, specialists, and other actors who develop responses to risks—responses that are self-referencing and almost entirely premediated.

Yet as noted earlier, actual borders have not vanished, and they continue to be viewed as sites of potential security threats. It is here that the normative assessment of risk occurs, be it at the airport, the land crossing, the port, or even the embassy. External borders, whether North America's or the EU's, are more numerous and daunting than ever. The Berlin Wall has fallen, but many other walls are being constructed.

So the real irony is that despite the current multiplication of bordering sites, border networks, and border technologies, we still build the spaces where borders are institutionalized and where these institutions are framed and represented. Such spaces are still considered normative in popular texts, and indeed, they provide the context in which border practices are understood by the public at large. For example, the US Customs and Border Protection website (http:// www.cbp.gov) displays photographs of US helicopters surveying Canadian soil for "terrorists," riding over rough terrain in search of illegal immigrants and drug smugglers, and searching and seizing cargoes. (Figure 5.1, one of many of the agency's online images, was pulled from its website in the fall of 2012.) All of these photos are action-oriented, suggesting a vigilant paramilitary force with dogs and weapons combating illegal activities at the border, which is cast as a site of ongoing threats and criminality. The border is thus vulnerable and dangerous and in need of biometric securing. This highly visual rendering of "border"

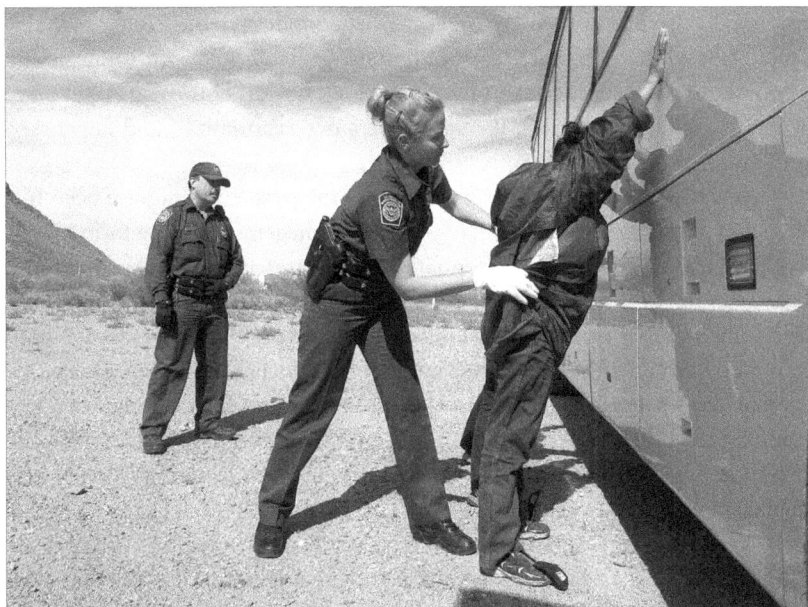

Figure 5.1 Image from the Department of Homeland Security's website that stresses the "active" and aggressive nature of border management—to the point of appearing quite "paramilitary." *Source*: DHS.

reinforces the need for resources to secure it tightly; that same rendering creates a imperative for biometric risk management, for *governing through risk,* as Muller (2010) and others describe it in a Foucauldian sense. (At the time this book was written, no similar representations were found on the Canadian Border Services Agency website, though we should expect these to appear shortly.)

Still, it is the US–Mexico border, not the Canada–US one, that has provided the new securitization paradigm. In its insistence on "one border," the DHS has painted the latter with much the same brush as the former. Later on, we will look more closely at how the United States has constructed a "dangerous Canada" imaginary. But before that, in Chapter 6, we will consider more carefully how security discourses are constructed as "speech acts," reinforced in popular and governmental texts that reference borderlines.

CONCLUSIONS

To understand the post-9/11 bordering process in North America, both in general terms and in the specific case of Canada–US boundaries, we need to begin with the premise that describing "the remarkable relationship" and all it entails is a simulacrum under construction rather than a critical analysis. As such, it fits into the second part of Popescu's (2012) heuristic three-stage model. But lest we think of the process as neat and orderly, as unidirectional, or as proving the empirical existence of predictive "macro stage models," let us recall, as Walsh (2010) tells us, that this practice of bordering is generally met with "strategic and symbolic acts of 'debordering'" (114). Moreover, not all "bordering" takes place at international boundaries. It can also be a deterritorialized and networked process.

The cooperation discourses so typical of the post-9/11 era have been furthered by border technologies that promote US hegemony in the form of networked empire, in ways both biopolitical and extraterritorial. They have also been promoted in ways that have securitized the everyday challenges posed by policy harmonization, cultural differences, and political diversity. We need to remember that although the meaning of borders has been appropriated by present-day securitization discourses focused on controlling immigration and stopping the illegal movement of people and goods, borders have historically functioned as more than sites for managing mobility. Only recently have border management agencies been appropriated as securitization actors.

One outcome of the new "cross-border management regime" is that it has resulted in a North American security regime that is somewhat different from that of the EU in terms of the technologies, corresponding attitudes towards integration, and the nature of border agreements (such as the Schengen Agreement). The latter employs a different border logic than has currently been developed in North America. Indeed, Papademetriou and Collet (2011), for their part, suggest that the real differences between the EU and North America are not just technical but political. They can be evaluated in terms of four areas: the collection and sharing of travellers' data; the use of new technologies to verify individual identities; the use of new technologies to monitor physical borders; and the building of partnerships to achieve border management goals. Moreover, they consider the drawbacks of the two principal securitization models—the American and the European—to conclude that even if the EU has serious concerns about the US approach to gathering and sharing data about individuals, a single global system is required to universalize security architectures and goals. In Chapter 7 we will return to the issue of universalized securitization and border management.

In the meantime, perceived threats to the US homeland have elevated geopolitical discourses that privilege border control and security there. The United States is a highly territorialized space with its own understanding of security. More precisely, since 9/11 the North American economic space (i.e., NAFTA) has been reconceptualized as a security puzzle, with the United States as the driving force behind building new and much-needed security arrangements. Yet when we look closely at the record of Canada–US security cooperation, we see that the post-9/11 border regime was being developed even *before* 2001. The bilateral responses to 9/11 and the ensuing agreements and protocols have been very much rooted in an neoliberal understandings of governance as well as risk. We are in the situation now, as the familiar old camp song goes, of "Same song, second verse / A little bit louder and a little bit worse."

Chapter 6

CONSTRUCTING RISK, SECURING BORDER

Who would wish for thousands to die in an act of terror? Who would gain satisfaction from watching airplanes crash into buildings? Hopefully, none of us. Today's securitization discourses seem to be the outcome of the horror and revulsion that day brought us. Our responses to it were and still are universalizing or totalizing. In the famous words of George W. Bush: "who is not with us is against us."

Yet securitization processes are not so straightforward. Indeed, "security" has been approached from a variety of perspectives (Balzacq, 2011; CASE, 2006; Williams, 2011; Bell, 2011; Muller, 2010; Bigo, 2002, 2006; Buzan, Waever, and de Wilde, 1997). Each of these "schools" focuses on why specific issues become securitized and how they are incorporated into broader structures of government, discourse, and action. Having said that, there are differences in how discursive and performative acts, institutions and agencies, and contexts are seen to interact. An important theoretical foundation here is the understanding of security as what Buzan, Waever, and de Wilde (1997) call a "speech act." According to that understanding, security is not a concrete, territorial "deliverable" (in the sense of securing a state-centred "disciplinary society"; see Foucault, 2007: 481) but rather an "enabling discourse." The political power embedded in security discourses lies in the degree to which the state or some other agency can make security appear to be real, tangible, and "concrete"—much like a public good or commodity, or much like the "prosperity and partnership" promised by the Security and Prosperity Partnership, discussed in Chapter 5. Buzan, Waever, and de Wilde see security as a performative act; others, though, have questioned how well this explains the securitization process. For Balzacq (2011), understanding security as such ignores the contextual basis in which securitization is received as well as the situated actions of mediating agents. He critiques this locutionary understanding of security mainly because "securitization can be discursive and non-discursive; intentional and non-intentional; performative but not 'an act in itself'" (2).

Other approaches to security studies include a critical approach that seeks "to make explicit the largely statist and military-oriented assumptions of traditional security studies as a means of opening the field to greater theoretical scrutiny and debate, as well as allowing it to address a broader range of issues" (CASE, 2006: 6). This approach has been associated post–Cold War analyses of international relations and is particularly useful for understanding changes in how security is understood more broadly (i.e., security can encompass the environment, energy, food supplies, and so on, besides "human security"). There are also those who take a more political approach to understanding security and securitization. But rather than reifying the traditional statist approach, for Bigo (CASE, 2006) it is important to understand the institutional context in which securitization takes place, "focusing on security professionals, the governmental rationality of security, and the political structuring effects of security technology and knowledge" (449).

For Williams (2011), a fundamental issue when discussing securitization is that there are important differences in how the various approaches to security define "extremity" (214). This approach suggests that the "realism" of post-9/11 security agendas in North America, as constructed by the Bush administration, succeeded precisely because it was articulated in a way that materialized extremity through symbolic action (the Twin Towers) and response (war and border security). This, I would argue, is how normative approaches have been structured in North America since then: threats are perceived, then they are defined through policy responses, and then those responses are evaluated in terms of their efficacy in addressing the perceived threats. But as Bigo (2006b) demonstrates, security is more than a *de facto* outcome. It is heavily negotiated and mediated by security professionals and policy-makers. Indeed, as Williams (2011) reminds us, security may refer to more quotidian than exceptional circumstances "in a local or particular context equating security with extremity may be misleading, leading to a failure to see how security logics can have effects even if they do not conform to the criteria of existential threat and emergency measure" (214).

American and Canadian government responses to post-9/11 border management, described in the pages to follow, can be understood in this way— that is, they reflect a particular discourse about security developed by a group of security professionals and decision makers. By promoting a particular understanding of security and relating it to an extremity such as 9/11, that discourse has generated new institutionalized understandings about security and security management. In the words of Bigo (2006b),

immediately after 11 September 2001 ... [a] "common sense" rhetoric emerged using the semantics of international disorder, failed states and the need for a more global security. It was simply more comfortable for many to use the old matrix of a bipolar clash by just "adapting" it to a new polarity: the West against the Others or the community of real states against all the other actors. The Cold War matrix and its reasoning were shaken but not disrupted, even if academic voices demonstrated its contradictions. Two groups organised inside the security professions and competed to define the most important threats. The first group, the Classics, mainly consist of criminal police, traditional intelligence services and armed services. They insisted on the role of borders and state actors, but wanted more money and technologies invested at the border or at the local level. The second group, the Moderns, mainly consist of special squads, private security companies, and think-tanks. They advocated a de-territorialised vision of security without frontiers, which were seen as obstacles in the struggle against the new enemy. They insisted on the rise of an interconnected global insecurity at all levels, where local events would in fact be the results of this global development." (387–88)

These theoretical discussions help us understand how, as a response to narratives of extremity as well as local insecurities, securitization became embedded in a series of narratives and approaches to "border." No longer simply the boundary between two neighbouring countries, the Canada–US border took on a new security significance precisely because of how discursive elements of security were artfully operationalized. In this case, though, we need to distinguish between the border security narratives operationalized for Americans and those operationalized for Canadians. This is because border security was operationalized in quite different ways between the two nations, each national discourse revealing important relations among the bordering, securitization, and representational practices that were deployed.

RECONSTRUCTING "DANGEROUS CANADA": RECYCLING THE METAPHORS OF THE SKETCHY BORDER

The ways in which risk definitions and security scenarios develop and play out internationally reflect, to large extent, the ways in which those processes have been explained and have become internalized within national governments. In the United States, intergovernmental relations that are highly ideological, polarized, and competitive. They have created and are continuing to create a problematic process along the Canada–US Canada border. This has been buttressed by a broadly defined security discourse based on hegemonic and increasingly fundamentalist ideologies. The result has been a carefully constructed narrative— or rather discourse—that generates a kind of knowledge about the "northern border." That discourse reinforces US security centrality, which, of course, seeks to eliminate competitive models. That, in turn, entails finding fault with how others determine their own security parameters, branding them threatening.

Since 9/11, but especially since 2006 or 2007, that is effectively what has happened along the Canada–US border. As Haglund (2007) has noted, "U.S. policy elites have begun to regard their northern border, the much-ballyhooed 'longest undefended border' in the world, with growing trepidation from the point of view of physical not societal security, i.e., the kind of security woes that were once thought to be exclusively related to the border with Mexico" (87). This is evident not only in the popular press and social media, where comments by less than credulous Fox News talk show commentators speak about Canada as a terrorist haven, but also in statements being made before Congressional security hearings. Take, for example, the comments of Representative Mark Souder at the 2006 "Fencing the Border" committee hearings: "And while we are spending millions of dollars over the next years to build that southern fence, what are we going to do about the northern border? Or about ports like Miami, where people come in every day and nothing is stopping them? We cannot hope that just building a fence is going to solve this immigration problem" (United States, 2006: 5).

As this book has underscored, Canada has been targeted as a security problem by the United States over the past decade or so, especially with regard to its immigration policies. Soon after 9/11, the Canadian border was rather deliberately constructed as a conduit for terrorists. It is nothing of the kind, but this misrepresentation has been tremendously resilient and has led to a discourse that positions the Canadian border as more "dangerous" than the southwestern border. This discourse has been built on the "dangerous border" metaphor that has always permeated Canada–US relations. It took root in the late eighteenth and early nineteenth centuries in the aftermath of the American Revolution, the War of 1812, and the Indian Wars; it resurfaced during the American Civil War and later during the Cold War. It reappeared in earnest with the "Millennium Bomber" incident of December 1999, when Ahmed Ressam was arrested as he attempted to enter the United States, notwithstanding that Canadian authorities had tipped the Americans that he was on his way. Since then, reports have persisted that Canadian citizens were involved in the World Trade Center attacks of 1993 and 2001; again, this flies in the face of the facts. In December 2002, multiple reports that Pakistani terrorists had illegally entered New York State prompted a large-scale manhunt that was heavily reported in the American press. Those reports were false—the story had allegedly been concocted by Michael John Hamdani, a Pakistani Canadian arrested for document forgery and human smuggling. Nonetheless, the story as first disseminated played to notions that the Canadian border was dangerous—that it was wide open and offered no protection, or that Canadian society harboured dangerous elements, criminals (read: immigrants) who threatened US security. Consider the following description of the border published online in 2003 by Capstone Policy

Analysis, from the Pepperdine School of Public Policy: "The Canadian border covers over three thousand miles of land, almost all of which is uncultivated countryside that is completely inaccessible by road or rail. Despite the immense geography covered by the US–Canadian border there are only a few roadway checkpoints that make the two countries accessible by car." This report then worries that terrorists could easily walk across the Rocky Mountains to infiltrate the United States: "Committed individuals willing to brave the wilderness and make the trek from Alberta over the Canadian Rockies into Montana can be picked up in Kalispell without having to worry about presenting documentation to any immigration official."

That is how the border is being represented in films and other popular media. In the film *Frozen River,* for example, the wild and dangerous Canadian frontier harbours criminals and human smugglers. Images such as this confirm Hataley's (2007) understanding that "central to American concerns about Canadian security has been the Canadian immigration and refugee system. Following 9/11, Attorney General John Ashcroft was clear on the need for increased security in light of potential terrorist threats when he commented that the U.S. was working on plans 'to help provide greater security for our northern border, which has become a transit point for several individuals involved in terrorism'" (2–3). Haglund (2007) explains that this discourse of a weak immigration system had several flaws:

> At the source of U.S. security concerns regarding the Canada-U.S. border is the perspective that terrorists can easily slip into Canada, as did Ressam and … many others, as a result of the country's immigration policies, especially as they pertain to the processing of refugee claims. According to statistics compiled by the United Nations High Commission for Refugees (and published in its 2003 Global Refugee Trends), Canada had an acceptance rate for refugee claims of 49.1 percent … The country's intake was disproportionately high because its acceptance rate was so out of line with the western acceptance average of 15.1 percent, an average itself exceeded by only two other OECD states: the U.S., at 21.8 percent, and Italy, at 16.3 percent. (90)

Yet the idea that Canadian immigration policy represents a threat to Americans retains its saliency (Rudolph, 2008), largely because Americans view those policies as lax and conflate immigration with terrorism. Furthermore, Canada is consistently perceived as a "drug haven." At a Congressional hearing of the Committee on Homeland Security, it was recorded that

> Jose Padilla, convicted of plotting terrorist acts in the United States was an American citizen who re-entered the United States from Pakistan at Chicago's O'Hare airport. The so-called millennium bomb suspect was apprehended in

the United States–Canada border. And Canada has been a major source of marijuana and a key transit country for the illegal immigration of other illicit drugs, precursor chemicals for meth and other contraband. It is clear, then, that an expanded fence on the southern border addresses only part of the problem. (7)

Discussions before the "Cargo and Container Security" House Appropriations Committee (2 April 2009) indicate how certain the Americans are that they are threatened by criminals and terrorists from Canada. Responding to the mistaken assumption that 9/11 terrorists came from Canada, Representative Sam Farr asked: "I'm interested on the Canadian side, because I remember some of the other hearings, that as of the—of the sort of risk factor that the Canadian border was a higher risk factor than the Mexican border, because of the known terrorists that had entered the United States, had come across the Canadian border; and that in fact, the ingredients of weapons systems were detected from trans-shipment across the Canadian border. Has that statistic changed now?"

Oblivious to the diplomatic and functional security relationship between Canada and the United States, Farr then asked the witness, Jayson Ahern, Acting Commissioner for US Customs and Border Protection, "Are we building a fence across the northern border?" When Ahern answered no, Farr, unaware of the economic ramifications of such a fence, replied, "Although Congress, I think, asked for it."

The clearest indications of the discursive power of rhetorical constructions of insecurity are found in various Congressional hearings and reports on border security published in 2010. One of these reports (US GAO, 2010b) asserted that the Canada–US border was "more dangerous" than the Mexican border:

> The United States and Canada share the longest common nonmilitarized border between two countries, spanning nearly 4,000 miles of land and maritime border from Washington state to Maine. The terrain, which ranges from densely forested lands on the west and east coasts to open plains in the middle of the country, is composed of both urban and sparsely populated lands with limited federal, state, and local law enforcement presence along the border. Historically, the United States has focused attention and resources primarily on the U.S. border with Mexico, which continues to experience significantly higher levels of drug trafficking and illegal immigration than the U.S.-Canadian border. However, DHS reports that the terrorist threat on the northern border is higher, given the large expanse of area with limited law enforcement coverage. (1)

Another 2010 report, this one on border cooperation (Haddal, 2010), contextualized these fears in ways that responded to political concerns and DHS operations. While noting evidence that apprehensions along the northern border were relatively few and were declining, it concluded that absence of evidence was not evidence of absence:

> The 9/11 Report pointed out that this lack of balance in manpower between the patrolling of the borders was due to Congress and the INS' focus on unauthorized immigration as opposed to potential terrorist threats. According to the commission, securing the northern border was not a priority despite evidence that terrorists had entered the United States from Canada, awareness that terrorist activity existed in Canada perhaps due to its more lenient immigration laws, and the previously mentioned OIG report, which criticized the Border Patrol for not having a coherent northern border strategy ... A possible issue for Congress concerns whether the increased numbers of Border Patrol agents and resources deployed along the northern border adequately address the 9/11 Commission's criticisms and are enough to effectively detect, apprehend, and deter potential terrorists from entering the United States across this border. (24)

The Congressional report suggests that American security actors have identified a tremendous variety of threats on the Canada–US border. The intent of all these reports is not to justify the invasion of Canada, nor is it to absorb Canada—neither step is necessary, given the diffuse nature of border control, and given how hegemonic institutions have privileged US foreign and domestic interests. Rather, the intent is to justify more intense security integration by evoking a "dangerously weak" trope. On 11 March 2011, Brian Masse, a Canadian MP, pointed out during a parliamentary debate that

> it has often been said that some of the 9/11 terrorists came from Canada. We have heard those statements from Hillary Clinton. We have heard them from Janet Napolitano. Even if they were to retract them after much attention because they are not fact based, it still would not matter. The impression has been left that we are weak and that we do not stand up for ourselves.

Do perceptions that the post-9/11 border is dangerous have a basis in reality? Not really. Haglund (2007) suggests that these kinds of statements reflect a knowledge deficit regarding the Canada–US security relationship. But the intended audience for the dangerous border discourse is not Canadian security experts. Largely, it is the Congressional appropriation committees that fund the DHS.

Since 2001, the dangerous Canadian border narrative has been repeated until Americans increasingly accept it as a reality. To illustrate this, the previously mentioned 2010 GAO report identified specific border crossings, which it then mapped by "potential threat" level. That mapping presented the

Canada–US border as a series of security hot spots (see Figure 6.1). Terrorism and known "terrorist cells," criminality, and smuggling were identified as high risks in almost every sector (8). Overall, the report positioned the threat posed by Canada as existential and as rooted in the physical presence of the border itself, in much the same way as had been done in the nineteenth century:

> A transportation infrastructure exists across much of the northern border that facilitates ease of access to, and egress from, the border area. CBP also reports that the maritime border on the Great Lakes and rivers is vulnerable to use of small vessels as a conduit for potential exploitation by terrorists, alien smuggling, trafficking of illicit drugs and other contraband and criminal activity. Also, the northern border's waterways can freeze during the winter and can easily be crossed on foot or by vehicle or snowmobile. The northern air border is also vulnerable to low-flying aircraft that, for example, smuggle drugs by entering U.S. airspace from Canada. Additionally, CBP reports that further northern border threats result from the fact that the northern border is exploited by well-organized smuggling operations, which can potentially support the movement of terrorists and their weapons. (8–9)

This is how the Canadian border has been rhetorically constructed as dangerous, to the point that it has become a cliché, and a humorous one at that. But that cliché "does work"—it orients and legitimizes US security discourses for the purpose of promoting US hegemony. The reports, hearings, and media accounts merely reiterated and reorganized the dangerous Canada motif by painting the northern border as a site of illegality that must be "secured":

> There is also a great deal of trade and travel across this border, and while legal trade is predominant, DHS reports networks of illicit criminal activity and smuggling of drugs, currency, people, and weapons between the two countries. The DHS reported spending nearly $3 billion in its efforts to interdict and investigate illegal northern border activity in fiscal year 2010, annually making approximately 6,000 arrests and interdicting approximately 40,000 pounds of illegal drugs at and between the northern border ports of entry. (US GAO, 2010: 1)

In focusing on the tiny fraction of cross-border traffic that was illegal and ignoring the vast majority of the traffic that was not, the GAO report succeeded in branding the Canadian border as a US security threat in very concrete terms in order to generate specific action. This report, made all the more powerful by the cartographic form in which it was presented, became the foundation for a popularized geopolitical assessment of Canada–US relations. The GAO report was followed by a flurry of media accounts that reported security "failures"

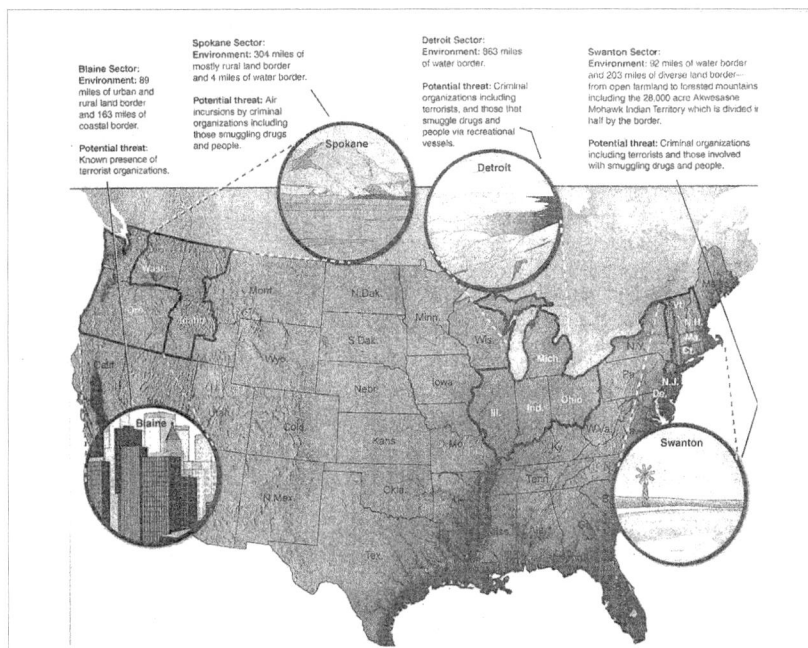

Figure 6.1 The Canada–US border as depicted in a recent post-9/11 border mapping. "Problem spots" are indicated. *Source*: US GAO, 2010 Report to Congressional Requesters.

and again positioned the Canada–US border as "more dangerous" than the Mexican one. Northern states were alarmed and demanded more accountability. On 2 February 2011, the *Washington Independent* reported that "Sen. Carl Levin (D-MI) is calling for increased security at the northern border after a Government Accountability Office report found that less than one percent of the U.S.–Canada border has an acceptable level of security" (http://washington independent.com). Newspapers across the northern states reported with alarm on this sudden state of insecurity, even though there had been no specific event to justify it.

In the end, the 2010 GAO document proved to be more of a blueprint for interagency action and funding appropriations than for security infrastructure development and planning. It was one of a series of reports that rehashed Congressional hearings and debates over the northern border, that reinforced the security discourse, and that turned alarmist viewpoints into functional language, complete with maps. It concretized a potential threat by mapping it, and those maps lent precision and authenticity to what had been a vague and general assessment. But in doing so, it also generated hysteria among the media, which exaggerated and recast the security threat. Thus, a year after the 2010 GAO report was released, one media outlet reported breathlessly that "in contrast to the extensive and routine sharing of intelligence and other cooperative efforts that exist between the federal agencies with responsibility for protecting the homeland from threats coming across the Southern border, a new Government Accountability Office (GAO) report concluded that just the opposite is happening on America's Northern border with Canada" (Kimery, 2011, online). This report went on to recharge the 2010 GAO report with quotations from persons of interest. For example:

> "What we have is a criminal—even a terrorist—element in Canada that poses a serious threat," [an] official familiar with GAO's report on Northern border security told Homeland Security today. Continuing, he said that terrorists, just like south of the border, can utilize established organized criminal enterprises in Canada operating on the border to easily get into the United States—"and as the [GAO] report highlighted, there are plenty of unsecured areas on the US/Canadian border where these illegal enterprises can transport people into the US."

Of course, threat generalization is not unique to the Canada–US border. Bigo (2002) discusses these tropes of securitization and how they are meant to generate unease, here and elsewhere. Though ubiquitous, they are not benign. Nor are they, Bigo reminds us, an expression of traditional responses to a rise of insecurity, crime, terrorism, and the negative effects of globalization." Instead, these unsettling security discourses are cultivated as "the result of the creation of a continuum of threats and general unease in which many different actors exchange their fears and beliefs in the process of making a risky and dangerous society" (63). The process rolls out as "professionals in charge of the management of risk and fear especially transfer the legitimacy they gain from struggles against terrorists, criminals, spies, and counterfeiters toward other targets, most notably transnational political activists, people crossing borders, or people born in the country but with foreign parents" (63).

A key point made by critics of conventional understandings of security discourses as matter-of-fact statements about real-world events is that there is an important yet often undisclosed and active relationship between the imperative of border management to exclude others and broader geopolitical assessments of the "world out there." For example, Sohoni (2006) has documented how the social media have linked immigration to terrorism and in this way constructed immigration as an existential threat. She concludes that there is substantial evidence of a resurgence in "nativism" in post-9/11 America, linked to identity narratives and cultivated through partisan political and popular discourses. In other words, border perception and management is geopolitically contextual *and* is mobilized and justified through narratives of a supposed common national identity and a common "other." And all of this is constructed in relation to neighbours and friends as well as to terrorists and foreign peoples. It is part of the prism through which the United States has positioned itself as the central North American securitization agency, and this perspective is promoted aggressively in popular, political, and academic texts.

Such accounts suggest not only that the brand of North American security that informed border management was US in origin, but that American exceptionalism remained alive and well and busy recycling popular myths regarding America's natural right to Canadian political territory. Take Sapolsky's (2005) rather provocative article, in which he tells Americans that "confrontation surely lies ahead unless Canada recognizes both its growing dependency on its neighbor to the south and the renewed intensity of America's security concerns. It is time to give Canada some attention and a bit of a warning. Canada is easy to squeeze" (36).

It is not hard to understand how, in the face of aggressive rhetoric of this sort, a dangerous border metaphor was constructed after the events of 2001. More puzzling is how we position the popular geopolitics of the dangerous Canadian border in relation to the cooperative lens through which US decision makers have attempted to universalize their security paradigm (Rudolph, 2008; Papademetriou and Collet, 2011). One way to understand this uncomfortable mix of cooperation and aggression is in terms of the degree to which the domestic security imperative in the US has been constructed in ways that are taken to represent normative ideal practice. We call these "best border practices," and they consist of a mix of technologies, protocols, agreements, and policies that are supposed to represent an ideal form, whether ideal means effective, efficient, or most cost-effective. After all, border control is not there to detach the United States from neighbouring countries, but to bring neighbouring countries into the fold—to create common ground and then to control the commonality.

The problem is that these idealized objectives are *not* objective; rather, they are grounded in deep-rooted cultural and identity narratives. "One of the interesting consequences of 9/11 has therefore been how it has seemingly turned the border inside out—placing Canada on the frontline of security for the United States, rather than reflecting the Canadian border as a security system designed to mediate a relatively benign relationship between Canada and the United States" (Konrad and Nicol, 2008: 165). This is why Clarkson (2008) calls Canada the American security "glacis" and recognizes the important relationship as one of inequality rather than partnership. Indeed, in making a similar point (albeit from a vested US perspective) Brookings Institution Senior Fellow and neoconservative Michael O'Hanlon (2006) remarked to the House Committee on Homeland Security that

to the extent Canada and Mexico make it hard for terrorists to use their countries as staging bases or way stations, the United States benefits from an added
line of defense of its own country … If Canada and Mexico improve their own
monitoring of persons traveling into and out of the country, only modest additional improvements may be needed in border security along the U.S.-Canada
frontier, and other lines of protection in the broader homeland security arena
may become more effective.

IMAGES OF SECURITY: THEORIES OF DIFFERENCE

Despite its obvious exaggerations, the discourse about the dangerous border has
gained considerable traction in the United States. Haglund (2007) suggests that,
given that the 9/11 terrorists had entered the United States legally, the construction of the dangerous Canadian border is a reflexive one, "the logic being that if
the U.S., as the target of the terrorists and therefore taking security more seriously than most other states, can be so ineffective at keeping out those who mean
it harm, then how much less attentive to security must Canadian authorities
be?" (91). Indeed, the discourse is tautological and iterative: the United States
has positioned itself as the gatekeeper of its own national border and national
society; it then justifies that role by suggesting that it is primarily due to Canada's
weakness and inherently "dangerous" society that borders must be maintained.
But such arguments are not important because they are logical. Rather, they are
efforts to link immigration to terrorism and thereby retool the anti-terrorist
discourse as a political agenda. Those arguments "do work," in other words. They
also do work, as both Haglund (2007) and Harvey (2006) remind us, in the sense
that they increase anxiety among Canadians: What would happen if a terrorist
attack on the United States was launched from Canadian soil? For much of the
post-9/11 era (or at least until the events of 2015, when, in the face of ISIS and
the Parliamentary shootings, Canada began to shape its own new anti-terrorist
legislation in the form of Bill C-51), this may well have been the single greatest
fear among Canadians, and it has been constructed largely by the US "War
on Terror" securitization discourse. Still, these same fears have also fuelled a
rather reflexive popular imagery—a "nefarious" US is increasingly portrayed in
popular Canadian dramatizations of its border relationship with its neighbour to
the south. Indeed, in commenting on perceptions of Canada–US relations that
found their way into discussions leaked in Wikileaks, Clark (2010) reported:
"When American TV and movie producers want action the formula involves
Middle Eastern terrorists, a ticking nuclear device, and a (somewhat ironically,
Canadian) guy named Sutherland." "Canadian producers don't need to look so
far—they can find all the action they need right on the U.S. border."

The same discussion goes on to report on the substance of leaked cables relating to Canadians:

> Now a handful of the cables show U.S. officials … explaining to colleagues in Washington the U.S.'s "overwhelming" importance to Canada and complaining about the increasingly negative stereotypes of the U.S. government on Canadian TV … The CBC program *The Border,* the embassy contends, regularly pits Canadians against nefarious U.S. authorities as they fight a "new war" at the border. While the war is supposed to be against criminals and terrorists trying to cross the border, many of the immigration team's battles end up being with the U.S. government officials, often in tandem with the CIA-colluding Canadian Security and Intelligence Service.

All of these venues promote specific versions of the Canada–US relationship through their representations of security discourses. They create images and perceptions that evolve into truisms and that in turn constitute how border relations are understood. Most North Americans are familiar with humorous television and film renditions of inept Canadian Mounties stopping Americans at the border (specific episodes of Conan O'Brien, or *That '70s Show*). These have a certain traction in the United States. Similarly, Canadian films and TV programs depict Americans as aggressive and their border security as "over the top" but ultimately incompetent (CBC's *The Border, The Trojan Horse,* and *Intelligence,* for example). Each of these stereotypes promotes popular perceptions that resonate with national populations. More theoretically speaking, they contain popularized geopolitical codes (see Flint, 2006) that encourage geopolitical assumptions. Those geopolitical perceptions orient foreign policies and world views; they also reflect assessments concerning the relations of nation-states to one another and to the world as a whole (Ingram and Dodds, 2009; Nicol, 2011). They inform "the dominant discourses of security and insecurity" (Flint, 2006: xi), yet they are also coded by more general perceptions about the meaning and significance of geographical space itself (see the discussion in the Introduction to this volume). So it is important to understand that geopolitical constructions of borders are largely fantasy and that they contribute to the construction of what Benedict Anderson (1983) has called "imagined communities." Cox (2002) reminds us that television, radio, newspapers, and films contribute to the creation and positioning of these imagined communities; they foster an "us" and a "them." These images are powerful, for "unity is being forged not only among a people but against other peoples. The nation belongs to 'us' and not to 'others'" (184).

Such imagery references what Bigo (2002) has called, elsewhere, a "continuum of threats and general unease" (63) that has positioned immigration as a "threat" rather than an opportunity. Immigration, that is, has been coupled with existential threats such as terrorism and cross-border criminality, and it is mediated or managed through "the prism of security." Bigo tries to avoid presenting the struggle as an ideological one between conservative and liberal positions, or even as an "intertextual competition" between agencies. Instead, he examines why the discourses of securitization continue to be so powerful even when alternative discourses are well known, and why the production of alternative discourses has so little impact on the political arena and indeed on daily life. Bigo's work emphasizes the way politicization of security, as well as the mobilization of security technologies, enables some actors—especially political actors, the media, security professionals—to create a "truth" by building discursive links among crime, unemployment, and migration.

A case in point is how US fears of radical Islam have focused attention on Canada because of its high levels of Islamic immigration. Magnet (2011) documented the 2006 arrest of the Toronto 18 and the almost farcical attempt to build a terrorism case that followed from it:

> Making clear that the perils of Canadian immigration are connected to the racialization of those crossing the border, a commentator in the *Los Angeles Times* argued, "Security controls are famously lax in Canada because politically correct Canadians do not differentiate between 76 year old Madame Dupont coming to visit her grandchildren and bearded young men from Islamic countries" … Voicing the same problematic views about newcomers to Canada, Douglas MacKinnon … former press secretary to Bob Dole, argued that "the Canadian government not only willingly allows Islamic terrorists into their country, but does nothing to stop them from entering our nation." Analyzing the durability of the myth of the 9/11 hijackers makes clear that the imagined whiteness of the Canadian state is changing. However, the instant that Canadian bodies are no longer racialized as white, we see that the bodies of people of color are falsely collapsed into the category of "terrorist." The transformation and increased surveillance of Canadians in the U.S. national imaginary was accelerated as a result of media and government coverage of the arrests of the Toronto 18. (101)

In other words, the security discourse creates its own truths. For Bigo (2002), the problem is that

> the concepts of sovereignty, security, and borders always structure our thought as if there existed a "body"—an "envelope, or container"—differentiating one polity from another. The state justifies itself as the only political order possible as soon as it is accepted that sovereignty, law and order, and a single body are the prerequisite for peace and homogeneity. (67)

Indeed, as Foucault (2007) observes, this type of thinking advances a territorial claim concerning governance in that "The relationship of a state to the population is established essentially in the form of what could be called the 'pact of security.' Previously the state could say: 'I will give you a territory' or 'I will guarantee that you will be able to live in peace within your borders.' This was the territorial pact, and guaranteeing borders was the major function of the state" (481).

SITUATING BORDERS: CANADA'S SECURITY DISCOURSES

It is clear that despite the increasingly diffuse and varied nature of security enclosures, the site of the border itself has not vanished but has multiplied (Loyd, Mitchelson, and Burridge, 2012). The fact that airports and exceptional spaces of state power (see Salter, 2008) can create borders at a multitude of new sites well away from the international border—or, more accurately, that "borders are everywhere" (Balibar, 2002)—does not delegitimize the study of national borders and how they change over time (Jones, 2012). It just makes it more complicated. Indeed, the study of borders as actual places remains central to understanding how the idea of national borders has been adapted to serve new discourses of management and the proliferation of sites of management. It must also be understood that such technologies have been incorporated into new imaginations of borders and into border metaphors themselves. These are mutually embedded and can be understood in ways that reference both the macro- and the micro-context of border making, its materialization, and its deeply co-constitutive nature (see Newman, 2005).

Borders have become a metaphor for vulnerability because they are the sites of potential security "threats." It is here where the assessment of risk occurs—in the airport or at the land crossing, in the port or even the embassy. Each of these is a border of some type. In this sense, external borders, whether in the EU or North America, are more numerous and daunting today, "thicker" in many ways, than ever. The Berlin Wall has fallen in Europe, but outer walls have been constructed by protocols, agreements, and technologies, all of which are enacted in specific places and at specific points. The same is true in North America. The tariff wall has fallen, but the security wall is now under construction everywhere goods and people are mobile. This new wall-building process began in earnest September 12, 2011.

Konrad and Nicol (2008) suggest that Canadians initially saw the heightened security measures post-9/11 as an affront, but indignation soon turned to practical measures to expedite security, enhance flows of people and goods, and re-establish a positive cross-border relationship. These were important components of border negotiations in the early days after 9/11. One of the first laws enacted in Canada in the post-9/11 era was the Anti-Terrorism Act, passed by Parliament in October 2001, which Bell (2011) argues set the stage for Canada's security architecture. It also led to the security certificate program and the Immigration and Refugee Protection Act. In 2004, Canada issued its first national security policy (Securing an Open Society); by 2006, Canada's emergency preparedness program had been reorganized to create a multi-layered and broadly linked department of security providers and managers. In part, this reflected the success of the right-wing political discourse in Canada, which muted resistance to US policy demands. But not all of these developments can be understood in this way. Similar ideas about security came to be embedded in Canadian political processes. That is, policy-makers and government officials responded to Canadian security matters in terms of US imperatives, but they made them on their own. There is no clearer example of this than the introduction of anti-terrorist legislation in February 2015, through Bill C-51, under debate in Ottawa as this book went to press.

The question is Why? From one perspective (Fortmann and Haglund, 2002; Haglund, 2007), it was the result of the previously described security relationship between Canada and the United States dating back to the Kingston Dispensation (Chapter 4), so the real question was whether that relationship could survive new iterations of post-9/11 securitization. Or would these break the camel's back? Canada since 9/11 has increasingly raised security concerns in the United States (ibid). American security officials have expressed fears that the Canada–US border has become attractive to potential terrorists, who gather in Canada to plan attacks in the US, as well as to drug smugglers and illegal immigrants.

Canadian officials—and Canadians generally, for that matter—are well aware that American policy-makers have constructed Canada as a security threat. This has led to tremendous accommodation but also to resistance to US-style security measures. This chapter ends by exploring these themes, beginning with the issue of accommodation.

COMMITTEES AND CARDS: REAFFIRMING PARTNERSHIP AND RESISTING HEGEMONY

After 9/11, Canada's Standing Senate Committee on National Security and Defence, which had convened in July 2001 to discuss national security and defence, turned its attention to terrorism. After meeting with US officials and lawmakers, that committee reported that "it is clear that both Canada and the United States need to do more to secure their borders and to prevent the movement of contraband, illegal aliens and terrorists" (Canada, Standing Senate Committee on National Security and Defence, February 2002). The committee also observed that "while Canada's ability to prevent its territory from becoming a haven for those wishing to enter the United States illegally, or to smuggle contraband into the United States, has been called into question, the United States faces problems that are just as serious" (Canada, Standing Senate Committee).

The committee was anxious that the Canadian side of the Canada–US border be seen not as a problem but as part of the solution. Thus, its discussions reflected the broader goal of crafting a Canadian response to 9/11 that would help alleviate US concerns while developing approaches that the Canadian public would support. This involved a review of security and intelligence rather than a proposal for military support for the invasion of Iraq or support for expansion of the War on Terror to other "Axis of Evil" countries (Canada, Standing Senate Committee). Subsequently, Canada restructured its approach to national security. For example, it passed the Anti-Terrorism Act (Bill C-36) in 2001, and it created an Integrated Threat Assessment Centre (ITAC) in 2004. Also in 2004, it articulated a new framework for national security: *Securing an Open Society: Canada's National Security Policy*. This restructuring also involved reorganizing security enforcement. Muller (2010) argues that the Canadian Border Services Agency (CBSA) was in fact created in this way, to follow the lead of the US reorganization of homeland security.

Since then, developments in Canada–US security cooperation have led to the standardization of technologies, processes, and agreements (see Konrad and Nicol, 2008). The cooperative agreements and protocols influencing Canada–US cross-border mobility were documented in Chapter 5. National security is now seen to be heavily invested in managing the crossing of international borders. A case in point is the Beyond the Border agreement, signed by Stephen Harper and Barack Obama, which has drawn Canada and the United States into a perimeter security arrangement. The agreement states: "We share responsibility for the safety, security, and resilience of Canada and of the United States in an increasingly integrated and globalized world. We intend to address security threats at the earliest point possible in a manner that respects privacy, civil liberties, and human rights" (Canada, Canada's Economic Action Plan, 2011, http://actionplan.gc.ca/en/page/bap-paf/beyond-border-shared-vision-perimeter-security-and-economic-competitiveness).

What are we to make of this apparent consensus? Does it reflect a new continental security space whose contours align with North American market integration (see Clarkson, 2008)? Does it reflect a truly bilateral consensus or the imposition of US security hegemony (Nicol, 2011)? Does it reflect a homegrown Canadian version of security (Bell, 2011) or an American one (Muller, 2010)? How is the Canada–US border represented in this new metaphor of equanimity and cooperation?

The terms of reference agreed upon since the talks between Harper and
Obama in February 2011 are a clear indication that the security perimeter is not
intended to create a transnational space of governance and world view so much
as to develop a security regime that is sensitive to economic imperatives. These
imperatives include access to US markets for Canada and strengthened US
security through the continental application of US-approved standards related
to terrorism, criminality, immigration, food and drugs, and environment. The
terms of reference suggest that

> Canada and the United States have their own well developed and transpar-
> ent regulatory regimes. For example, both governments follow good regula-
> tory practices, such as regulatory impact assessment and open engagement
> of citizens and stakeholders in the rule-making process. Notwithstanding
> the strengths of current approaches, both countries do operate independ-
> ently, and they recognize the opportunity to work together in order to bolster
> transparency and better align analysis in support of regulations, including for
> example, measures that would provide early notice of regulations with poten-
> tial effects on trade. Their mutual desire to better align and cooperate in these
> areas reflects the commitment of both countries to evidence-based, predict-
> able, cost-effective regulatory approaches that are carefully targeted to enable
> businesses to continue to innovate and grow without compromising the high
> standards of public health, safety, and environmental protection that their cit-
> izens expect. (Canada, Economic Action Plan)

A telling statement is that the project will "align analysis in support of
regulations, including for example, measures that would provide early notice
of regulations with potential effects on trade." Clearly, security measures have
tremendous implications for trade, so the regulations in support of trade may be
very broad indeed. The measures and policies Canada adopts to placate American security concerns will impact the degree to which cooperation on trade can
be assured. The Canada–US Perimeter Security and Economic Competitiveness
Regulatory Cooperation Council speaks pointedly to this through business sector concerns:

> Canada and the United States share cultural, social, and environmental val-
> ues that have led both countries to develop robust and efficient regulatory
> protections for their citizens. However, Canadian and US regulators do not
> always maximize—or the laws under which they operate do not allow them
> to maximize—opportunities to align regulatory approaches that achieve
> common objectives. Alignment is imperative, given the integrated nature of
> our supply chains and robust trade relationship. In some cases, the resulting
> differences do not increase regulatory benefits, and instead impose needless
> additional burdens and costs for businesses and consumers. These costs can

be particularly acute for small- and medium-sized enterprises—the corner-stone of economic activity between our nations—which may not have the resources to customize products to meet unnecessarily divergent regulatory requirements. Identifying, preventing, and addressing unnecessary regulatory divergences requires regulatory cooperation between Canada and the United States. (Canada, Economic Action Plan)

This raises a question: Is "security perimeter" to be understood in a material way (i.e., the obliteration of national border spaces in continental North America) or in a metaphorical way (i.e., the harmonization of security management, infrastructure management, and intelligence gathering)? In other words, does a security perimeter have a physical space or does it entail a new relationship that includes virtual walls? Is it a cosmopolitan space, in the sense that Europeans see their EU project, or an extension of US universalism and networked empire, as Harvey (2003) and others suggest?

POST-9/11 SECURITY

The language of the Beyond the Border agreement is instructive here. The need for the plan is rooted in the common threat of criminality and terrorism; thus, one of its key goals is to develop "common understanding of the threat environment; aligning and coordinating our security systems for goods, cargo and baggage; and supporting the effective identification of people who pose a threat, which will enhance safety and facilitate the movement of legitimate travellers (Canada, Perimeter Security and Economic Cooperativeness, 2011: 4). This presupposes a common threat environment, and, at least until the recently identified ISIS threat now influencing national security discourses, most security experts would argue there is not. For Canadians, the threat of terrorism on their soil has not been as frightening a prospect as the threat that terrorists might use Canadian territory as a staging ground for an attack on the United States (Fortmann and Haglund, 2002; Harvey, 2006; Haglund, 2007; Hataley, 2007). This is buttressed by US fears—which, as we have seen, have been magnified through social media and the press—that "Canada is not only home to terrorist 'sleeper cells' waiting for a chance to cross the border and attack the United States, but also that crossing from Canada has become a favoured route for illegal immigrants, drug smugglers, and potential terrorists" (Hataley, 2007: 4). Whether or not the new terrorist threat, that of homegrown domestic attacks, will significantly change this over the long term, and how, is beyond the scope of our discussion as the answer remains to be seen.

So the big question remains: whether this threat environment now makes American-style security "Canadian," or whether the US, as the major provoker, and target, of Islamic terrorist threats, will continue to define the threat environment and response. If the latter, can the United States expect the security of Americans—which is arguably a domestic policy—to be the number-one priority of all countries, or even neighbouring countries, especially those that approach security and border management from a slightly different perspective? The evidence so far is mixed. In 2005, 64 percent of Canadians supported closer security cooperation with the United States; that figure, though, had fallen to around 50 percent by 2011. According to Fortmann and Haglund (2002), this

> preliminary evidence seemed to be that America was taking the challenge more seriously than Canada, as one would have expected it to, given that the US and not Canada was the target of the terrorist attacks. For a time it even seemed as if Ottawa was more committed to protecting Canadian sovereignty than to ensuring Canadian and American security, and there was much early official rhetoric, after 11 September, focused on Canadian "values," whatever these were supposed to be. (21–22)

Now, in 2015, unlike in earlier years, nearly three-quarters of Canadians support greater securitization. But this new attention to security measures comes in reference to the Canadian government's impending anti-terrorist bill. This attention to security seems to have domestic roots and is not overtly the same as the issue of compliance with US hegemonic pressure for securitization, as we discuss below. This does not alter the fact that since 9/11 and more specifically since the Iraq War, countries like Canada and Mexico have been yielding more and more to US concerns in order to foster close relations and maintain economic partnerships. While some American security narratives have suggested otherwise (see Sapolsky, 2005), the evidence is simply overwhelming: Canada is tied through its military security agreements to continental defence; security cooperation already exists and has done so for over half a century. Setting aside their resistance to the Iraq War, Canadians have not challenged their country's continental defence relationship with the United States. So it is not that security themes are being compromised by Canada's military arrangements, which are at the crux of the reflexive relationship with the United States regarding recent border adjustments. It is that the United States has extended its security reach into non-traditional areas, such as immigration and refugee policies. This is clear in how Canada's political elites have offered the United States formal support when it comes to issues even when the US stance diverges sharply from the global consensus. Examples include the Kyoto Accord and climate change more generally. It is also clear in the way security experts now insist that Canada has no choice but to comply with US "best practices" in border security. Hataley (2007), for example, writes:

By far the biggest challenge however, will be overcoming traditional conceptions of what the border between Canada and the United States represents. The image of the border has a real effect in terms of material and manpower resources that are applied, or not applied, to create border infrastructure. Canada needs to take a lead in re-conceptualizing the border. The "longest undefended border in the world" is no longer a suitable description for the Canada–United States border. Canada Border Services Agency, the federal government department responsible for border security at ports of entry, must, as the president of the Customs and Excise Union has argued, have a security and public safety mandate rather than a revenue-generating one. Internally, Canada must act to assure the United States that Canada is not the weak security link, especially where it concerns new arrivals to Canada. (5)

Clearly, the Beyond the Border Agreement remains the border plan for the future. So the open question now is how Canada's new domestic security agenda, focused upon internal threats of terrorism, will become fused with this ongoing "Americanization" of a North American security agenda.

SUSPENDERS AND A BELT

Like the United States, Canada has a compelling security discourse that links immigration to border management, even though immigration from abroad does not generally proceed across the Canada–US land border. Thus, Canadian support for a security perimeter or a Beyond the Border agreement furthers problematizes immigration from non-American sources. In this sense, post-9/11 Canadian security discourses have become highly reflexive: even as they facilitate diffuse and continental forms of securitization, they have created the impetus for reinforcing the state. They attempt to ensure that Canada is considered a "partner" in North American security rather than the object of security concerns. In this way, securitization, surveillance, and even joint security agreements promote a continuing focus on state borders and discrete states. Canada practises surveillance and constructs securitization discourses and policies in cooperative ways that enhance rather than erode the state's exceptional power. This is evident in the most recent rounds of securitization efforts represented by Bill C-51, put forward in February-March 2015 and designed to enhance Canadian surveillance of its own population. In this way, the rhetoric of security provides the impetus for greater state control (Bell, 2006). State control is still concerned with defining hard territory but governs through biopolitical means: "the subjection of people to security and surveillance techniques, while occurring 'at a distance' and compelling modes of self-governance on the one hand, paradoxically also signals the presence of sovereign authority in modern affairs of state, especially when examined in relation to the post-9/11 management of borders and refugees" (151).

This is why US hegemony is no longer about boots on the ground, poised to take territorial control, nor is it about corporate America, whose collective chequebook threatens the existence of the Canadian state. When Canadian support for a security perimeter problematizes immigration from non-American sources it feeds into a strategy of biopower that facilitates US interests by repatriating them—in other words, by making them "Canadian."

In this way, the formal discourses of the Canadian government are able to recast enhanced "security" along the border as both a Canadian project and cooperative one: "We share responsibility for the safety, security, and resilience of Canada and of the United States in an increasingly integrated and globalized world" (Canada, Economic Action Plan). By implication, according to this document's wording, to neglect security would be to court economic failure. As we have seen, this coupling of security and economy has created a totalizing discourse that is difficult to resist. It is rooted in asymmetrical power relations and powerful methodological nationalisms promoted both within the US Congress and in the United States at large, but also within the Canadian state.

At the same time, though, it would be wrong to see even hegemonic security discourses as monolithic. There are, indeed, other points of view. One of these is that no nation, even the United States, can afford to stand alone. The irony of the current security climate is that it can only operate through cooperation and that this cooperation is based on a military cooperation agreement signed before the Cold War. Thus, if the Beyond the Border agreement (still under construction) signals that Canada and the United States need to cooperate to succeed, this brings us back to Fortmann and Haglund's (2002) assessment of the post-9/11 security climate:

> [T]here would seem to be, over the longer haul, a definite logical link between the porosity of the border and the sustainability of the Kingston Dispensation. For if the border stays relatively hardened—if it remains "Mexicanized"—for too long a period, this will have to be taken as prima facie evidence that the normative basis of Canada–US security cooperation has eroded, with all that this must signal to governments on either side of the line. We doubt that such a signal would be something any Canadian government would wish to receive, nor would it be something any American government would desire having to send. Thus we conclude that, not without some strains, the Kingston Dispensation will hold. (22)

By this, Fortmann and Haglund mean that from the perspective of a realist or state-centred discourse, security cooperation between Canada and the United States is imperative. The glue is not a diffuse border control regime initiated in the post-9/11 era, but a traditional military agreement rooted in the previous century that embeds US hegemony in its structural conditions. So while neoliberal border technologies entrench and expand the state's reach beyond the border, cooperation agreements like Beyond the Border create the rhetorical glue for conjoining the interests of states in ways that promote hegemonic interests. The metaphor of the border represented by the Beyond the Border perimeter is thus highly reflexive. While north of the border it promises ease of access and seamless border crossings—indeed, a borderless North American model—south of the border it means more border agents and surveillance, more virtual if not real walls, and meeting increasing demands to control the flow of people and goods. As Sokolsky and Lagassé (2006) so aptly put it, it means suspenders and a belt. For our purposes, this metaphor may be the most appropriate representation of all.

DIFFERENT VISIONS OF SECURITY

Americans support greater border security along the Canadian border, and as we have seen, this security perimeter discourse has been accompanied by a persistent discussion in Congress about building border fences with Canada. Canadian are well aware of this. About a year before the most recent perimeter accord was signed, the *Globe and Mail* reported that "the issue of a possible fence emerged as both countries prepared to release their Beyond the Border joint initiative that aims, in part, to improve border security through co-operation" (29 September 2011). The US government was at this point clamouring for a co-operative security perimeter agreement in the shape of the Beyond the Border agreement, at the same time that it was arguing for the greater use of fences, surveillance technologies, and even drones and surveillance balloons, along the "northern border." Even as talk of a new "security perimeter" in Canada's Parliament progressed, competing talks were taking place in the US Congress regarding the erection of a "wall" along the Canada–US border. The spectre mirrored Bigo's (2006b) postulation concerning the presence of two powerful and contradictory security discourses in post-9/11 America, embodied in the "Classics" and the "Moderns."

So while we have seen a degree of support on both sides there has also been, of course, a strong reaction to the various harmonization projects that encourage compliance with new border management practices and infrastructures. Maher Arar provided one such case. Although it can be argued that Canadian officials were complicit in what happened to him, the response to the detention and torture of a Canadian citizen in Syria did deep and abiding damage to any consensus regarding the acceptability of "exceptional" security in the War on Terror or continuing efforts against emerging new terrorist groups like ISIS. Indeed, it has also triggered a larger debate that counterposes individual liberty and security. Since then, several times a year, a story emerges in the Canadian media concerning security abuses at the border or beyond. These refresh the problem of individual rights versus generic security measures, and leave us questioning in whose interests such measures really are. It is not just a question of whether the ends justify the means.

In Canada, instances such as the Arar case have been seen as evidence both of American hegemony and of the need to resist that hegemony, especially where people and rights are compromised. That case occasioned a tremendous amount of ink spilled over the Canada–US security relationship, and opinions were vociferously offered. The broader issue seemed to be that returning Canada to the fold of esteemed ally through mutual security arrangements, like those involved in the Arar case, weakened it; Canada as a US partner means Canada as a US subaltern helpmate; Canadian sovereignty is threatened by US security imperatives. This sort of understanding generates a strong counter-current to the increasing pressure for Canada to Americanize its security arrangements, one that is difficult for US policy analysts to understand because most American policy-makers deeply believe they are meant to be the nation of "standard-makers." This in turn has created deep ambivalence among Canadians and promoted considerable resistance. Windsor MP Brian Masse argued in Parliament in 2011, when speaking in the House to Bill C-42, that Canadians must "push back" in order to maintain integrity and control over their borders. He suggested, moreover, that "we feed into their system … They try to spin these programs as being successes" (Masse, 1 March 2011, https://openparliament.ca/debates/2011/3/1/brian-masse-1/only/).

So it is not surprising that the harmonization of border security has become a flashpoint for resistance as well as a conduit for compliance. Even so, because it represents the potentially weaker discourse, some have dubbed opposition to the plan as "shrill doom saying." Is it? Or does it underscore the complexity of security visions themselves?

Muller (2010) suggests that in terms of security discourses, "the problem" of "securing identity comes to be constructed so that biometrics is the obvious clear and only answer" (41). We have seen that in the American case, the imperative to use such measures more often is usually pitched in terms of the insecurity posed by "the other." But in the case of Canada, the imperative is not so clear and security cooperation remains contested by members of citizens and citizens groups. Parliamentary texts dating to 2011 (when the Beyond the Border agreement was introduced to Canadians) show a political system both preoccupied with criticism of governmental approaches to cooperative border security with the United States and at the same time negotiating and implementing the same security agreements. The contentious nature of Canadian federal politics has been such that in the past, many of these discourses gained little traction. The failure of Canadians to adopt a national ID card in 2003 (Muller, 2010), the failure of the SPP (discussed in Chapter 5), and a variety of others types of resistance to full-blown US-style security measures point to a different governmental rationale and a different view of the meaning of border itself. This is, of course, where what happens with the 2015 security legislation and its potential impact on border management, after Bill C-51, will be telling.

Canadians have since the negotiation of the NAFTA been relatively consistent in their desire for an open border between Canada and the United States. Those who travel are used to crossing the border easily, while political and business elites are sensitive to the problems that border restrictions pose for the economy and trade (Drache, 2004). So there is less insistence in Canada on border security, and less likelihood of seeing Canada as the object of any existential threat of the same proportions as 9/11. At the same time, Americans clearly see the border as a critical place for enforcing security measures. But the idea that the Canada–US border must be "protected" is not a newly minted security discourse as much as a recycled one whose grand narrative continues to pay little attention to protecting existing economic interconnections. As we saw in the previous section, the American perspective is based on an amalgam of border stories, anecdotes, and metaphors that—as Magnet (2011) reminds us—have both racialized Canada's population (via immigration issues) and attempted to contain and externalize it.

All of these perspectives have generated a variety of US and Canadian views ranging from full support of US security concerns to no support at all. Some believe that the border should facilitate trade but hold firm against implementing US-style security interests. Others argue that this can only be done if US concerns are met in a timely fashion and reframe US demands in ways that result in "corrections" to Canadian security practices. Still others—and these are mainly but not exclusively American—identify the border as a site of great US vulnerability and as a conduit for cross-border crime and terrorism. Thus, the Canada–US border is now seen both as a serious obstacle to trade and as a trade facilitator; security is critically important, but security measures are problematic. Let us examine some of these arguments.

THE VULNERABLE BORDER

The border is very often described as facilitating trade through a number of cross-border protocols, agreements, and practices that privilege US protocols and concerns over others (see, for example, Granatstein, 2010), and policymakers are encouraged to follow this pragmatic approach, which reframes US demands in ways which result in "corrective" action by Canadian security practices. In the United States, however, as Vance (2008) suggests, the border has increasingly become "a symbol not of the close social, political, and economic relationships of two friendly neighbouring nations but rather one characterizing the border as a 5,000-mile-long weak link in the (U.S.) national defence system" (239). Such differences in perspective play strongly on different understandings of border—such as a wall or a gate, and a site for containment or for facilitation of trade. They also reflect that one's position on the issue is strongly determined by the side of the border on which one stands.

For example, discussing how individual corporations are affected, Vance reports from her own work on Canada–US cross-border relations that "a distinct difference arose between Canadian and U.S.-based firms" (247). In 2006, US firms were less likely to show an interest in maintaining contacts with Canadian firms; at the same time, Canadian firms were forced to redouble their efforts to "connect," for a variety of reasons having to do with border impediments and exchange rates, perceptions of cost, and actual costs of border security (248). She suggests that "firms located in western New York were far more likely than those in southern Ontario to discount the importance of their cross-border suppliers and customers" (248). On the other hand, the same border saw Canadians on the other side who "did not express any plans to reduce their dependence on the U.S. market. Themes that commonly emerged through interviews with Canadian firms emphasized the efficiency of the border and the improvements that have been made in terms of cross-border movement since 2004 ... Canadian firms seem to be downplaying the impediments related to border-crossing activities and are continuing to prioritize their strong ties to the United States" (248–49).

For Vance, the result has been the development of a "dichotomous perspective of physical versus economic security," which has contributed to what is now commonly seen as a technological "fix" in which the "security and trade framework focuses on improving coordination and information sharing within and between sectors" (240). However, she suggests, lengthy delays and problems have persisted despite such efforts. As such, the normative way of understanding the Canada–US border and its security policy and management is as an economic and security problem requiring political intervention to create compromise and coordination. This perspective informs current border management at Canadian border posts and also, to a lesser extent, at American ones. But here, "dichotomous" is really the emphasis on border management itself, which has polarized interests in security and economy. The decision made after 9/11 to halt movement and close borders and points of entry contributed early on to a perception of security vulnerability at the border and led "to the widespread perception that U.S. borders, including the border shared with Canada, could not be allowed to maintain pre-9/11 levels of permeability—lest dangerous goods and undocumented or otherwise 'illegitimate' people be allowed to pass through and terrorize U.S. citizens" (239–40). A dichotomous framework has characterized the dominant discourse regarding functions and meanings of the border ever since. "The border as a security mechanism (hindering illegitimate and, consequently, legitimate movement) has been contrasted with definitions of the border as an efficient conduit for frequent and meaningful social and economic interactions and therefore unfettered risk. Both extreme positions have been argued in a climate of elevated tensions and fear" (240).

This dichotomous security discourse is supplemented by the types of racialization noted by Magnet (2011), Bell (2011), and Côté-Boucher (2008). It is also "being reconceptualized through the trope of terrorism. In imagining the border as a site of terrorists and in constructing the terrorist threat to the United States through the bodies of immigrants and refugees to Canada, Americans have racialized Canadians" (Magnet, 2011: 124). According to this construction, the Canada–US border is easily transgressed by non-Causcasian Canadians, more specifically those of South Asian and Arab descent. It is these groups that have been particularly targeted since 9/11. It is around this point that Bell (2011), Côté-Boucher (2008), and Magnet (2011) converge, offering a very different response from that of Rudolph (2008) and others. Why? Because, they argue, the Canada–US border is consistently being portrayed as a problem, or more specifically as a site of vulnerability because Canada's "lax immigration policies" need fixing. The result? According to Magnet (2011), it has been changes to Canada's immigration and refugee policies. These changes are accompanied by high-tech biometric screening processes, all of which are designed to detect what she calls "criminalized bodies."

> Thus vast expenditures on new technologies able to visualize newly identified Canadian threats become central to the border. Just as Ruiz shows that diseased Mexican immigrants came to stand in for the U.S.-Mexico border, terrorists—in the form of the 9/11 hijackers and the Toronto 18—are used to symbolize newly identified threats to the U.S. This helps explain the reasons for large bilateral expenditures on biometrics and their role as a ubiquitous border technology in accords signed after September 11, 2001. (124)

Some argue that inherently different racializations sustain northern and southern US border discourses; this idea, however, is increasingly being challenged by those who contend that the DHS's "one border policy" has "Mexicanized" the northern border. Which is to say that in the south, Magnet (2011) writes, "anxieties about the southwestern boundary are represented through the construction of the border as a line of infection … or as an unstoppable epidemic of immigrants overwhelming the boundary between North and South."

This has "discursively conceptualiz[ed] the U.S.–Mexico border through the trope of infectious disease has material ramifications" (124). Following this line of thought, many researchers argue that biometric security technologies are bringing a new racial dimension to the US northern border in ways that have contributed to its "Mexicanization." Côté-Boucher (2008), however, puts a finer point on the issue, reminding us that the Canada–US border is different regarding the degree to which undocumented migration occurs. This border is not militarized, "as is its United States–Mexico counterpart, nor has it been abolished, as is the case for a number of internal European borders. Yet, in the wake of the 'war on terror,' the Canada–United States border has come to assume increased importance as a locus of security in North America" (143). The term "Mexicanization," itself a racialized and pejorative term, is used in the sense that it has been in Canadian newspaper articles and policy talks, and it reflects a fear admitted to by Canadian scholars that a lack of differentiation between the Canadian and Mexican borders will be the end point of security cooperation. Will the US no longer see us as "kith and kin," the paradigm ushered in by nineteenth- and early-twentieth-century constructions of Anglo-Saxon racial stock (see Chapter 2)? As Andreas (2005) notes, the Canadian experience has been intense US political scrutiny, as well as "alarmed" media attention, much like what Mexicans have long had to contend with. Recent politicization of the border has "unsettled the traditional special US–Canada relationship and brought to an end what had been a mutually convenient low-maintenance approach to border control matters" (448–49). This, even though "the Canadian government has attempted to resist and reverse the Mexicanization process, making great efforts (with some success) to differentiate and distance Canada from Mexico" (450).

Of course there are exceptions, and no discourse is monolithic. As Vance suggested earlier, some Americans rely for their livelihood on cross-border trade, shipping, or an integrated continental market system and so are just as likely as Canadians to worry about cross-border economic access. Nonetheless, all of these positions have created a normative discourse regarding the dichotomous border and its pragmatic economic implications. These have gained real traction among policy-makers as well as among those whose job it is to develop security programs to monitor cross-border flows. Security and economy have been bundled together as border functions demanding policy intervention as a result. This is because they are seen as equal and opposite problems, not because the tensions thus constructed are understood as deep-rooted and normative to border management in North America.

EXPLAINING THE DIFFERENCE

I raise the question of difference here because it goes to the heart of what security means for Canada–US border representations. It seems there are several very different ways to understand security events in relation to "border." One is to assume that the structural imperatives of what Bigo (2006b) has called the "Moderns" vision of security offer a general view of security that has been robust enough to incorporate borders and to impose harmonious border management projects on Canada and the United States. From this perspective, the US model of security has become the Canadian one because it offers a compelling and comprehensive understanding of threats and responses. It has been implemented not through imposition but also through discourses of security that promote the "inevitability" of specific responses, including the voluntary acceptance of specific security measures. These responses rely heavily on biometrics (Muller, 2010), border agreements, and "partnership" cooperation. Cooperation agreements attempt to link Canadian and US security interests as if the border did not exist. Their influence on Canadian security policy, as evidenced, for example, in the Beyond the Border agreement, suggests that to achieve this larger goal, a never-ending security campaign, is normative. As Bigo (2006b) explains, they find their roots in post-9/11 America, when

> the neo-conservatives became the dominant voices in politics, marginalising the traditional "cynico-realists" around George W. Bush. The Moderns in the field of security maintained, for a while, a quasi-monopoly on thinking because of the homology of positions between the neo-conservatives and their own views. The attacks were seen by both as proof of their vision of a global network of terrorism. They linked the Twin Towers with the anthrax fear as a symbol of a new type of violence, called hyper-terrorism. Hyper-terrorism constituted active networks of terrorists across the world, including sleeper cells, recruited along an ideology of radical Islamism, prepared to kill themselves, and more or less connected at a central point: Al Qaeda. These groups, which were ready to kill on a large scale, animated merely by hate against the civilised world, could only be successfully combated through a permanent state of exception allowing less judicial control and permitting all the available information to be shared through exchange of personal data among a transnational group of security agencies recognised as useful data providers, regardless of any claim of national sovereignty. The war on terror is then, for them, a never-ending war, a long fight at the global level aimed at establishing a global order with a benign empire as the leader of an ever growing number of democratic regimes, good neighbours and areas under transitional process towards peace and state building until a global democracy secures the world. (388)

But polls suggest that Canadians have been more ambivalent about taking security cooperation to new lengths. As we have already seen, one such poll reported that between 2005 and 2011, "a total of 63 per cent of Americans and 50 per cent of Canadians support a closer cooperation on national security, down from 73 per cent of Americans and 64 per cent of Canadians from the beginning of the study in 2005" (pollingreport.ca, 8 September 2011). Another 2011 poll indicated that 68 percent of Canadians now believe that Canada "will compromise too much power over decisions about immigration, privacy and security to get a perimeter security agreement" (Dana Gabriel, 28 March 2011, http://beyourownleader.blogspot.ca). The jury is out on whether opinions have changed much since then. Certainly Canadians have in the past been split on the issue of the acceptability of government Internet monitoring especially if terrorist activities are being monitored (see http://www.ipsos-na.com/news-polls/pressrelease.aspx?id=6233, which links to an IPSOS poll dated August 13, 2013). Americans have somewhat higher rates of acceptance for a variety of National Security monitoring activities, including the monitoring of phone calls (see http://www.people-press.org/2013/06/10/majority-views-nsa-phone-tracking-as-acceptable-anti-terror-tactic/), and these rates are rising, not falling, over time. Still, these data agree that the unquestioning acceptance of security narratives of the sort Bigo calls "Moderns" remains less developed in Canada, even after the terrorist event of 2014 unfolded on Parliament Hill. Moreover, Canadian security professionals clearly support and are acting on a project of greater harmonization and integration, although there has been no real public disclosure or discussion of security issues related to the Beyond the Border initiative.

Why is this so? There are several possible explanations. One is that Canadian policy-makers have been co-opted. Bigo (2006b) writes that "as security is increasingly seen as global, the leaders of small states have to rely on information provided by those that are more powerful. They also have to put their faith in them and suspend concerns about their own capacity to decide." Thus, by definition "the competition over who is capable of deciding about exceptions at the global level needs to be oligopolistic or monopolistic. Small states cannot lead or even participate on an equal footing in the coalition against global terror" (390).

Benjamin Muller, a noted security scholar, has argued in response to ideas presented in this volume that "the notion that there is little resistance to this, or whether resistance is futile—fails to admit the extent to which the Canadian state has consciously chosen to devote little or no significant resources towards developing the intellectual capital required to mount an effective critique and pose a counter strategy to the U.S. approach to border security." According to Muller, the larger size, population, and economy of the United States, and its wealth of think tanks and intellectual capital for security research "devoted solely to thinking about the management of the Canada–U.S. border, which Canada not only can't match but which barely exists, places Canada in a situation where it is easily washed aside with Bushisms such as you are 'with us or against us'" (personal communication, 2013).

For Muller, political myopia and intellectual shortcomings have helped create this situation, and this is probably quite true, although many Canadian policy-makers would undoubtedly disagree.

Gilbert (2005) takes a slightly different tack in her analysis of the same events. Her concern is with the "logic of inevitability" that has come to frame "the options that have been placed on the table with respect to the future of the Canada–U.S. relationship" (204). For her, these are not inevitabilities so much as carefully framed discourses that reify particular perspectives. It is no accident, then, that many security options have been crafted by right-wing think tanks or those with vested economic interests. Much like Sparke (2006), she suggests that "the cooperation between the two countries that has ensued in areas such as security and immigration [has] effectively established the conditions to make deeper economic integration more feasible and more likely. There is yet another dimension to this discourse … The fatalistic logic has been mobilized to make more acceptable the neoliberal precepts that lie behind the various proposals" (204). For Gilbert, then, it is not that the United States has pressed Canada to change its domestic policies (although undoubtedly it has) or that there were very real threats of reprisal for non-compliance. It is simply that neither "the big idea" of the SPP nor the North American Monetary Union (NAMU) has materialized.

So how are we to reconcile the two Canadian positions—*for* perimeter and *against* US hegemony? Conventional wisdom would say that they have resulted from separate realities—elite versus non-elite, nationalist versus neoliberal, regional versus national, pro- versus anti-American. But the truth is that these are not separate realities; they are mutually embedded. Post-9/11 security has rationalized the harmonization of security policies, practices, and institutions, as well as law enforcement, and meanwhile cross-border security cooperation agreements have sought to strengthen the Canadian state in ways that privilege certain positions and peoples. This is complicated, Bell (2011) suggests, because other, larger contextual issues are at work. She argues, following from a Foucauldian understanding of governance, that there is a more general liberal problematic of security to consider. Following Campbell (1998), Bell (2011) asks how security claims are mobilized through reference to Canadian values. In other words, she treats Canadian security developments since 9/11 as truth claims made by a number of Canadian actors, including political institutions, the media, and politicians. So instead of simply positioning such developments in terms of coercion from American neighbours, she discusses post-9/11 security in Canada as part of the broader problem of liberal governance and the "problematic of security." For her, "Canada's new national security policy operates through language and practices that take elusive risks to the health and safety of the population as an opportunity for action, and is made possible through an expansion of surveillance ... The biopolitical governance strategies of Canada's national security policy treat the problems of political freedom, equality and democratic accountability posed by encroaching security measures as largely negligible in the face of indeterminable danger" (2006: 148).

So the trope of inevitability is just one local manifestation of a much more widespread discourse that differentiates between the people to be protected (generally certain types of Canadians and Americans) and the people who are a threat. It ties that threat to specific (Canadian) ethno-national and ethno-cultural frameworks, which are racially and spatially coded. In this way, much like those that surrounded the Anglo-Saxonism described in Chapter 2, new frameworks of accommodation and resistance to border security become socially constructed along racial lines. But again, we need to assess those racial or biopolitical frameworks in terms of the issue raised in the introduction to this chapter—that is, we need to see them as discourses that define securitization and that must be understood through their discursive *and* contextual/structural relationships. As Bell (2011) reminds us, this is how we will be able to select those securities that best reflect collective justice and Canadian values. In Chapter 7, we push this point further when we explore whether the Canada–US relationship can be seen through the lenses of cosmopolitanism and transnationalism.

CONCLUSIONS

While Gilbert explains how relative compliance for new measures is achieved, it is well to remember that the sorts of agreements they reference have provided the syntax for resistance to networked hegemony as well as to the universalization of American values and norms, in historically grounded ways. We are not, after all, talking about annexation but about neoliberal, universalized best practices. Is this convergence between Canadian and US security discourses the result of the fact that no effective alternative has been offered, or is it because no alternative is really tenable under the present day's tenacious securitization discourses and geopolitical practices? Muller, as we have seen, argues the latter, Gilbert the former. Along the Canada–US border, the ongoing resurgence of resistance to US hegemony has made security discourses an opportunity for fomenting nationalism. But as Gilbert (2005) reminds us, the language of inevitability should also be understood as another very Canadian response to the changing geopolitical relations introduced since 9/11.

Support for security cooperation in North America is embedded in an understanding of Canada as economically dependent on the United States and in a logic that equates cooperation with neoliberal connectivity and societal well-being. Resistance, for its part, entails more nationalistic discourses, as well as discourses that reference the marginality arising from biometric technologies and securitization practices that reduce people to pieces of code. Let us not forget that border security's impacts are not simply economic or political; security practices are not simply lines that can be forgotten once crossed (van Houtum, 2012). Rather, border security is an emotive and identity issue as much as it is one that speaks to exclusion and exceptionality, citizenship and identity. It is also what van Houtum rightly refers to as a "simulacrum": the representation of a virtual reality that is "a simulation, a manifestation of a copy, but with its own reality" (50). There is a well-developed approach to understanding border management as a pragmatic economic or policy-making problem, but this should not prevent us from looking more deeply and critically at the implications of this "simulacrum issue" from a theoretical as well as geopolitical perspective. In other words, we must ask where the Canada–US border works within a larger framework of border studies and geopolitical perspectives to reflect or embody ideologies, beliefs, values, and, ultimately, the instrumentalization of power.

So, support for or resistance to new technologies and policies is not just a reflection of national differences: Canada versus the United States. Nor is it simply a matter of history. Indeed, it is a much messier process, one that has created a problematic process among the Canada–US border. Loud protests have been raised in the United States by the business sector over border policies that impede trade. Agreements to date have seen "security trump trade" and have positioned border management not along nationalistic lines but as a dialectical opposition between two opposing understandings of national interests. Risk definitions and security scenarios develop and play out in an international context in ways that largely reflect how national governments have internalized such processes. In the United States, intergovernmental relations are highly ideological, polarized, and competitive (Nicol, 2011); they are also supported by a broadly defined security discourse based on hegemonic and increasingly fundamentalist ideologies. In Canada, a similar discourse has arisen, but it has been "Canadianized" through a series of debates and political manoeuvres. The United States views Canadian immigration and security policies (and indeed, Canadian foreign policy more generally) as problematic. This reflects the neoliberal imperative to create a kinetically mobile North American market by securing mobility itself (Sparke, 2006).

It also plays to well-entrenched ideas about borders as walls and not bridges and to Canadian and American racial intolerance (Magnet, 2011; Côté-Boucher, 2008). This is the other piece to the national security discourse promulgated by the United States. Increasingly, the Canada–US security relationship is being honed to ensure a "perfect fit." Hataley (2007) writes:

> In December 1999 the Mackenzie Institute warned publicly that Canadian trade with the United States could be damaged if Canada did not do something about the Canadian immigration and refugee system and if Canada did not take action against the known terrorist organizations operating within Canadian territory. In December of the same year the Canadian Security and Intelligence Service (CSIS) confirmed not only that Canada's immigration and refugee policies were attractive to terrorist organizations, but also that a number of terrorist organizations had already taken advantage of the rules to establish a presence in Canada. Following the 9/11 attacks, Stewart Bell of the *National Post* reiterated the claims made by CSIS and added that given Canada's proximity to the United States and the openness of the border, Canada had become "a logical staging point for attacks against Americans." (4)

This type of reasoning is now common because Canadians are now much more likely to engage in policy harmonization for the sake of protecting their trade relationship with the United States and their place in the continental economy than in order to forestall any perceived terrorist threat. Andreas suggests that the root of the contradiction—trade versus security since 9/11—also has something to do with the actual geopolitical foundation of the Canada–US relationship. Konrad and Nicol note that one of most interesting consequences of 9/11 was that it repositioned the meaning of the Canada–US borderlands by putting Canada on the front line of US security. For Stephen Clarkson (2008), however, it was the Cold War that provided the template for today's Canada–US security relationship. This has meant there is little new organizational and institutional capacity.

Moreover, this lack of experience in any modern post–Cold War Canada–US border security relationship has fostered in the United States a rather truncated understanding of security issues along the Canada–US border. It has contributed to what we have already identified as the "Mexicanization" of the Canadian border. Mexico had been the only other "border template" the Americans had for addressing common continental border security issues except for the DEW Line, constructed by the United States and Canada across the Canadian Arctic in the early postwar era.

What specific geopolitical imaginations support the new rounds of control-oriented border making and the reterritorialization of North America? Recent rebordering has required the construction of a geopolitical imagination within a post-9/11 world so as to accommodate economic globalization in a way that favours US international and domestic concerns. So while facilitating buy-in among Canadians, these new geopolitical imaginations must accommodate or even encourage support for US-style continental hegemony. And again, this relationship is symbolically understood through a series of metaphorical juxtapositions. Rather aptly, a *Globe and Mail* editorial cartoon from February 2011 satirized this assessment by superimposing a Group of Seven painting (an iconic Canadian image) over a cynical cartoon rendering of plans for Canadian border integration with the United States.

All of this suggests that there are several discourses within the Canada–US security debate. On the US side, those discourses are louder and more monolithic: US security first. On the Canadian side, things are more complex. Kilroy (2007) suggests that "for Canada, the 'threat' of a loss of sovereignty to the United States appears to be the greatest stumbling block to increased security cooperation" (9). Yet that may well be just what security now demands.

Chapter 7

CANADA, THE BORDER, AND US HEGEMONY
COSMOPOLITANISM? OR NOT?

Why end this book with an assessment of cosmopolitanism's relevance to North American borders, especially since much of the literature on diffuse borders and cosmopolitanism has been written from a European perspective? It is not just to understand whether the concept of cosmopolitanism is robust enough to capture the historical and contemporary development of borders and transnational spaces within North America. It may also help us expose the underlying hegemonic and not-so-liberal values embodied in the various national security/neoliberal globalization/Pax Americana discourses which impact upon our borders. Cosmopolitanism is often viewed as a result of globalization, and in that regard one of the functions of border discourse is to manage cosmopolitanism as a narrative, vision, and value. The questions raised in this chapter are: Has the United States developed a sort of exceptional cosmopolitan perspective in its border and related national security practices? How does its universalized security perspective fit within the theoretical complexity of cosmopolitanism? Does it contradict and defy cosmopolitan values?

So far we have focused on hegemony as the process that best captures and explains how borders and border metaphors have been mobilized in the Canada–US relationship and North American geopolitical discourse. This has created an ongoing process of integration and rupture, and the border remains an active site for creating both transnationalism and nationalism. What can cosmopolitanism, or even a critical cosmopolitan assessment (see Rumford, 2008), add to the mix?

As we touched on in the introductory chapter in this volume, the study of cosmopolitanism in contemporary scholarship tends to be primarily a European activity—a critical analysis of a discourse useful for understanding postwar Europe. It is a multiperspectival field of research that analyzes everything from urban cosmopolitanism to globalized risks. As such, it is generally positioned in contradistinction to American universalism (Beck, 2006) or as a sort of exceptional cosmopolitanism (Brennan, 1997). David Harvey (2009) tends to be skeptical of cosmopolitanism, viewing it as a deeply despatialized yet oddly racialized discourse, while Delanty (2009) argues that it is best understood from a critical perspective.

Unlike Europeans, North Americans are more likely to explain differences between North American and EU boundary and political logics in normative or traditional ways than by accessing cosmopolitan theory. For North American political scientists and sociologists alike, however, the main point of interest between the American and European systems relates not to evidence of cosmopolitanism but to the existence of supranational or overarching institutions that in the latter have created a different type of integration project (Brunet-Jailly, 2006). For Clarkson (2008: 470), this different governance structure is important, but there is more at stake—in terms of civil society's access to centres of power and the increased autonomy that North American integration offers for transnational business interests. For others, however, what counts is the differences between how empire is conceived, structured, and practised (Agnew, 2005; Beck, 2006; Beck and Grande, 2007, Brennan, 1997; Harvey, 2003). Overall, the consensus is that the United States may practise a global hegemony, but this does not make its outlook "cosmopolitan."

This chapter addresses a similar issue, but from a slightly different perspective. It asks, Does the new border, or, rather, the diffuse border, have the same "cosmopolitan currency" in North America as in the EU? Or does US universalism diminish the capacity for producing multiple cultural, ethnic, and egalitarian spaces (i.e., cosmopolitan ones) by promoting linked neoliberal goals of prosperity and security while excluding those who stand in contradiction to those goals because of their poverty, their political ideas, or their race, religion, or nationality? Are we seeing that borders are being reimagined in North America, not as hinges for building common viewpoints (despite the rhetoric of partnership that advocates universal peace, human rights, and free markets) but as means to generalize and universalize US standards, norms, desires, and expectations? Beck and Grande (2007), among others, argue that cosmopolitanism is the prescription for achieving a democratic and inclusive society. Do American post-9/11 securitization projects lead us down this path? For Beck, the answer is no.

To grasp why, we need first to understand how cosmopolitanism has been defined with respect to European border studies. There is a broad literature that will only be glossed in this chapter. The idea of cosmopolitanism originated in antiquity, and indeed "cosmopolitan" comes from the Greek words *cosmos* (universe) and *polis* (city). David Harvey (2009) traces the development of the idea of cosmopolitanism through the writings of Kant and Heidegger to the modern sensibilities of human geography, suggesting that cosmopolitanism is both problematic and geographically "banal."

There are many different ways to understand what cosmopolitan means. These vary from the idea of cosmopolitanism as a project of modernization (Nava, 2006), to the idea that cosmopolitanism refers to a "vision of global democracy and world citizenship" (Vertovec and Cohen, 2002: 1). It can refer, as it did in twentieth-century America, to a sort of elitist view of the well-travelled individual, or a communist perspective (Brennan, 1997), and it has also been used in anti-Semitic discourse ("rootless cosmopolitans"). It has been used to characterize "transnational frameworks for making links between social movements" and "post-identity politics of overlapping interests and heterogeneous or hybrid publics in order to challenge conventional notions of belonging, identity and citizenship" (Vertovec and Cohen, 2002: 1). Moreover, as Vertovec and Cohen suggest, some "use cosmopolitanism descriptively to address certain sociocultural processes or individual behaviours, values or dispositions manifesting a capacity to engage cultural multiplicity" (1). Beck and Grande (2007) contend that cosmopolitanism is both a pre- and post-national term, one that has been rediscovered by "debates on globalization," which see it "as a positive counterweight to the organizing power of the market and of the nation-state" (12). For them, cosmopolitanism has two specific meanings: one is a social science concept, the other relates to a "way of dealing with cultural difference" (12). Borrowing from Vertovec and Cohen (2002), they view cosmopolitanism as in dialectical opposition to the nation-state, in that its goal is to overcome "the dualities of the global and the local, the national and the international" (12). Cosmopolitanism, then, can be defined in a number of ways as (a) a sociocultural condition; (b) a philosophy or worldview; (c) a political project towards building transnational institutions; (d) a political project for recognizing multiple identities; (e) an attitudinal or dispositional orientation; and/or (f) a practice or competence (Vertovec and Cohen, 2002).

Cosmopolitanism is today commonly used in border studies as a discourse that speaks to how the borders of Europe have become polysemic and thin: "they are no longer at the border, an institutional site that can be materialized on the ground and inscribed on the map, where one sovereignty ends and another begins" (Balibar, 2002: 88). But at the same time, "borders are being both multiplied and reduced in their localization and their function: they are being thinned out and doubled, becoming border zones or countries whether one can reside and live. The quantitative relation between 'border' and 'territory' is being inverted" (92). The founding of the EU, with its increasing emphasis on outer rather than national boundaries, and on borders implemented through multiple sites of land, air, and sea entry, has led to a style of thinking about and inscribing borders that is less concerned with defining national spaces and more

concerned with creating a European identity that overrides individual nationalities. For Europe, this constitutes a "cosmopolitan project."

The particular way in which cosmopolitanism is used in this volume comes
from the work of Beck (2006), Beck and Grande (2007) and Brennan (1997). The
focus here is on comparing European and American transnationalisms as they
involve borders and bordering devices and evaluating their fit within broader
discussions of cosmopolitanism. We recognize Harvey's (2009) criticism that
cosmopolitanism as theorized by Beck has spatial and logical deficiencies, but
I am specifically concerned with Beck's (2006) and to a lesser extent Brennan's
(1997) proposition that North America is not cosmopolitan, especially as this
relates to the European Union. David Harvey's (2009) critique of cosmopolitanism, for example, situates American cosmopolitanism within a more generally
flawed theorization of what cosmopolitanism is, and that is a somewhat different
project. Indeed, for Harvey, cosmopolitanism at least of the sort he defines as
neoliberal, which is dominant today, presupposes the existence of a fictitious,
abstracted, isolated, and deracinated individual when no such creature actually
exists.

But if the validity of the concept of cosmopolitanism is acknowledged,
there is a clear disconnect between the North American project and what Beck
(2006), Delanty (2006, 2009), and others have called Europe's political and social
cosmopolitanism project. The EU has looked historically to expand its integration project, while in North America various categories of threatening peoples
continue to be discursively constructed and materially excluded through border
management policies and practices. The border is being remapped as a site
where "hot spots" of threatening human and non-human agency are fended off
and where territorial spaces reinforce national citizenships and territorialized
identities. More open immigration discourses are being replaced by more stringent ones. Given the discussion in earlier sections of this book, it hardly bears
repeating that discourses in support of limiting citizenship and immigration in
the United States are increasingly supported by a series of new laws and enact-
ments since 9/11. US border policies, increasingly mediated by assessments of
nationality and ethnicity, have achieved canonical status in the border and security literatures. Discourses supporting the reterritorialization of citizenship and
immigration are taking place within legislative and decision-making bodies. The
United States continues to enact much of its foreign policy through the lenses
of security and the so-called wars on drugs, terrorism, and crime (Nicol, 2011),
and simultaneously, border technologies are being reworked in order to identify
and contain terrorists, illegals, and "threats" in general. Those technologies, too,
have achieved canonical status in the literature. All of this has changed attitudes
towards non-citizens. Political attacks on US "birthright citizenship" for the
children of those whose immigration status is in doubt (i.e., for the children of

"illegals") followed the 2010 American Congressional elections. Immigration is increasingly being situated as a matter of the state's discretion rather than as a matter of rights, citizenship, and universal claims to hospitality. Repressive immigration laws have been linked to more stringent border management laws, including those relating to detention and incarceration (Loyd, Mitchelson, and Burridge, 2012), visa entry requirements, and documentation protocols.

Since 9/11, acts such as the Patriot Act and the Western Hemisphere Travel Initiative in the United States, and corresponding changes to visa and entry requirements and to refugee status determination in Canada, have problematized mobility. Discourses of "illegality," "patriotism," and "terrorism," which reached their zenith under the Bush administration, continue to frame legislative responses to border management and citizenship and have curtailed post-national engagement. There is a growing gap in terms of definitions of and attitudes towards citizenship and who has citizenship rights, a gap that hinges on more border management and mediation in North America and on more diffuse forms of citizenship and identity in the EU. For Beck, developments in the United States, which is seemingly so open to globalization, do not herald true cosmopolitanism but rather a series of "one-way universalisms" that promote US-style governance and values that are opposite of true cosmopolitan engagement. Indeed, Delanty (2006) argues that universalisms are counterproductive to the cosmopolitan imagination.

The point is that in North America today, border control is, as it long has been, a state-centred activity. It has been discursively created to promote greater oversight and intervention. Border surveillance has been "loaded on" at the edge of territorial control—along the external land and sea borders. In other words, the contemporary North American border takes its meaning from the very processes it now controls: immigration and economic activity. It is a national border first and foremost. This is far less true in the EU, where the Schengen Agreement and similar border accords have produced a less uniform wall that is far from coterminous with individual nation-states (Beck and Grande, 2007; Beck, 2006; Balibar, 2002). Moving between countries in Europe often requires little more than activating an indicator light signal on the motorways.

Still, Beck and Grande (2007) argue, it is not supranational institutions that create the potential for cosmopolitanism, but rather how projections of commonality are structured. In other words, Europe is also a frame of mind. In the EU, state boundaries are fluid and new identities are being cultivated to reflect a degree of cosmopolitan transnationalism; that has not been the case in North America. This is not to say there are no spaces of transnationalism in North America—clearly there are. The point, though, is that the continental security project unleashed by US imperatives has set out to standardize and universalize American values, practices, and politics. Contrast this with Europe's emerging cosmopolitan spaces—whether such cosmopolitanism is viable or not—which seemingly connect the local to the global in ways that bypass nation and state. Beck (2006; Beck, Sznaider, and Winter, 2003; Beck and Grande, 2007) sees in the EU a globalization from within rather than a breaking of the chains that bind the local to the national and that reimpose supranational and even universal standards.

DIFFUSE BORDERS AND BORDER FLUIDITY: EUROPE AND NORTH AMERICA COMPARED

Beck and Grande (2007) speak to the relationship between the United States and the world, and we can examine their thinking specifically as it relates to continental boundaries and security in North America. Does their "Pax Americana" explain the continentalization of a US hegemony project, or is the North American security perimeter truly the "cosmopolitan project" (equal partnership) that political texts have described? Do US bordering discourses instead render Canada–US relations in ways that are consistent with efforts to reinforce US "methodological nationalism" rather than continental partnership? Is the United States still a state *and* a society, as Beck and Grande (2007) claim, in contrast to the cosmopolitan empire that is Europe? Is there evidence in North America of borders becoming more generalized throughout society (Rumford, 2008)? Overall, in answer to these questions, most scholars suggest that North America is less cosmopolitan and that borders remain more rigid and state-centred.

There is another perspective, however, which we are less able to evaluate in the context of this volume. That is, the idea of cosmopolitanism as it has been argued by theorists is itself flawed. Embedded in this idea is that Europe is not as cosmopolitan as academics would have us believe (Rumford, 2008; Entriken, 2004), while North America is a little more cosmopolitan than we might think (Harvey, 2009; N. Smith, 2003; Brennan, 1997). Rumford (2008), for example, argues that a cosmopolitan Europe may in fact be unachievable—that cosmopolitanism is not intrinsic to the EU and that "it is wishful thinking to expect institutions of cosmopolitan democratic governance to spring up" (7). This is in response to Beck and Grande's (2007) idea that the EU should proceed in this direction. But while Beck and Grande advocate a kind of European cosmopolitian "universalism," they do not mean universalization in the sense of US "universalisms" that demand conformity to US ideals and practices (see Beck, 2006). Rather, for them, universalism "à la cosmopolitanism" represents a sort of outwardly oriented nationalism (Beck and Grande, 2007). The goal is a global discourse on democratic governance to which all are welcome and in which all are included.

Rumford (2008) is critical, however, of the "new cosmopolitanism" that has emerged as an academic discourse that seeks to develop institutions with global reach and global forms of solidarity (7). He is skeptical of this possibility, and his synthesis of cosmopolitan theory is enlightening. In most of the literature, cosmopolitanism is positioned as following from globalization, but according to Rumford, this is ill-conceived and prescriptive. For him, cosmopolitanism is "wishful thinking" in a Europe that is truly not cosmopolitan. Notwithstanding its claim to have made cosmopolitanism "the big idea," European cosmopolitanism is best understood critically, in relation to a critical analysis of globalization.

But globalization itself is a highly contested term (see Beck, Sznaider, and Winter, 2003). For some, it is even synonymous with "Americanization" (Agnew, 2005). Moreover, as Balibar's (2002) understanding of "fluid borders" suggests, fluidity is not simply an unintentional outcome of globalization. It is something to which the many EU border programs and funding projects attest. European transnationalism or "cosmopolitanism" has been not a spontaneous event but rather the outcome of decades of "border work" in this area (Scott, 2009), and has seen large amounts of funding and the deliberate cultivation of a cosmopolitan discourse.

Indeed, while arguing that the EU is attempting to create the foundations for a new regional community, Scott (2009) also draws our attention to how Europe is less homogeneous and cosmopolitan than we might expect, and how it works to create current levels of "cosmopolitanism":

> The EU is a composite polity endowed with several state-like functions but without many of the mandates and treaty-level competencies enjoyed by sovereign states. The EU has an executive, a legislative and a court system yet it, at the writing of this article, lacks a constitution and a common foreign policy. Similarly, in a manner reflecting its institutional mosaic, the EU is a geopolitical actor with different, often conflicting agendas. Some aspects of the EU's geopolitical agenda appear to correspond to traditional Realpolitik and state-based pursuits of self-interest. At another level, however, the EU strives to make an ideational and moral difference in the world, acting as a "force for good" and promoting a set of values that includes democracy, human rights, social cohesion, gender equality, a market economy, peace and stability, minority rights, and international solidarity. (233)

BORDERS AND COSMOS

These cosmopolitan debates lead us to speculate on how best to understand the most recent rounds of border management and the institutionalization of security as a governance discourse in North America. Are agreements to create a security perimeter best understood with reference to cosmopolitanism, the idea being that this form of transnationalism is attempting to universalize values of security, standards of security, and new institutions of equal and democratic continental governance? Or has the putative globalization of terrorist activity been met by a methodological cosmopolitanism, to borrow the language of Beck, which privileges US universalization, at least to the shores of the EU? Are North American borders really that much less diffuse than EU ones? And does the idea of networked empire apply equally to the United States and the EU?

True, some scholars suggest that European cosmopolitanism has been overstated (Rumford, 2008; Entriken, 2004) and has not been achieved; but also true, cosmopolitanism has produced, according to Beck, a distinctive type of European transnationalism, or more precisely a distinctive type of discourse that aspires towards cosmopolitanism. Much like the United States, Europe aspires to create a field of influence but for European values. The EU uses much the same type of border technology as the United States at its outer frontiers and indeed it has inculcated a post-9/11 security regime in much the same way as the United States. Unlike the US, however, the goal has been to facilitate rather than restrict continental travel.

So it is not the use of different detection and encryption technologies that differentiates the regions, nor is it the approach to border management itself. The EU's external frontiers have thickened rather than disappeared. Still, there is simply no way in which US ambitions for continental, hemispheric, and global influence can be understood in the same way as the EU's ambitions for Europe and the world beyond. They are just too ambitious, even for the EU. US security discourses have significantly different ambitions. They are designed to implement a space for US corporate interests in North America and the world *and* a space for US standards to ensure national security on a continental and global scale. The result may not be the absorption of Canada—the SPP's demise and several centuries of resistance, among other things (see Clarkson, 2008), suggest this is unlikely. However, the NAFTA and the "smooth border" have made absorption unnecessary.

In the final analysis, then, it is probably quite accurate to conclude that the EU and North American boundary projects have created spatial entities that have both commonalities and differences. On the one hand, notwithstanding Balibar (2002), Beck (2006), and Beck and Grande's (2007) positive comments on European integration, there are those like Rumford (2008) and Harvey (2009), among others, who harbour doubts that a cosmopolitan empire has been the result, or even that it is possible. Rumford suggests that while there are cosmopolitan dimensions to European borders (in that they are increasingly determined by actors other than nation-states), Europe is not "cosmopolitan," and that to claim cosmopolitanism as Europe's big idea is misleading. Borders are still central to Europe and the EU project. In North America, the difficulty is in seeing borders as EU-like with respect to the outcome of border "partnerships" and accords. Even while negotiating such accords, the United States builds fences and demands conformity to its national security standards. The real problem for Canadians (and Mexicans) under these circumstances is the growing democracy deficit as bilateral arrangements are increasingly replaced by the accommodation of unilateral interests. This is a sort of cosmopolitan colonialism, in the sense that Beck defines it, and there is no overarching EU-like governance structure to overcome it.

This is not to say that unilateral Manifest Destiny–type discourses and relations will always provide the underlying logic of US international relations or bilateral relations with Canada. In this regard, Neil Smith (2003), David Harvey (2003, 2009), and others have argued that there have been distinct "movements" in the evolution of US neoliberal globalization that have taken different shapes and forms than Manifest Destiny or even Wilsonian idealism and Cold War anti-communism. Rather, it is to say that few options are now available other than the hegemonic grounding of Canada–US relations and border management. There is a historical inertia to bordering that is now linked to a post-9/11 resurgence of national geopolitics. Given that US border management is now grounded in a DHS bureaucracy and Congressional politics (see Hale and Marcotte, 2010), as well as in a powerful popularized discourse that has created both risk and reflexivity along the border, it is difficult to see how the EU border model—a border that has created possibilities for new spatial configurations of identity and governance in Europe—can replace the thick layers of border control that are materially and metaphorically grounded in North America. The North American model has become a project of reifying nation, of drawing borders that in their "thickness" disguise their outward orientation—in that outward orientation is not welcoming to strangers but desirous of controlling them.

This is why, in an earlier work written with Konrad (Konrad and Nicol, 2008), we suggested that borders are increasingly borderlands, extending and pushing back even while organizing border management into thicker, more substantial, and more geographically precise crossing sites that both reify the line and make it broader and more diffuse. This does not suggest that North American borders are becoming increasingly polysemic and thin, but thicker and multiplying rapidly, unlike Europe's. According to Hale and Marcotte (2010), "border management policies apply not only at national borders or 'ports-of-entry' but well beyond them, requiring substantial co-operation not only with other North America governments but on other continents as well" (101).

Does this mean we can understand North American borders as equally "cosmopolitan"? Using the concept of cosmopolitanism developed by Beck (2006), Beck and Grande (2007), and Balibar (2002), for example, the short answer would seem to be no. The degree to which border management, functions, and now even perceptions have been shaped by US domestic security concerns argues against this likelihood. American cosmopolitanism seemed possible in the early twentieth century during the Wilson presidency, and it seemed so again in the late twentieth century as the Clinton administration spoke of global responsibility. Even the NAFTA border may have represented a prototype for North American neoliberal cosmopolitanism. Today, however, borders may be polysemic, diffuse, and in many ways similar to those of European regimes, but the meaning, purpose, and vested interests of security are all very different than they once were. Americans do not aspire to obliterate the differences between American and Canadian society through territorial control; rather, they wish to harmonize the continent economically and politically, including in terms of immigration policy, in order to extend America's "reach." As Hale and Marcotte (2010) argue, the idea is "to maximize the advantages to be derived from open trade, investment and travel with the United States while maintaining policy discretion in dealing with broader economic issues and trends" (105–6). For example, the SPP, one of the first post-9/11 forums to openly suggest expanded integration, or "NAFTA plus," was intended to link economic and security interests so as to define a trilateral community (Canada, US, Mexico). There was no talk of "the people" of the SPP, or of building a common SPP identity, as there would have been in an EU project. Similarly, who, at the end of the day, are the "people" of the new Beyond the Border agreement?

So there is, in North America, no socio-cultural project equivalent to the EU, regardless of North American economic and security arrangements. There is only a US security strategy that seeks global influence, but this is not the same thing. Security harmonization and North American economic integration still speak to a US-directed process of amalgamation.

EMPIRE OR NOT?

It is clear that the cosmopolitan vision that Beck and others have imagined for EU countries does not yet exist in North America. Even so, Americans have little trouble conceiving of their political project in global terms, although they balk at the appellation of such a system as "empire" and always have (Beck, 2006; Bender, 2006; Kramer, 2002). This has several important consequences. The first is that the hard and powerful tools of empire—military conquest and direct rule, the usurping of territory and the destruction of sovereignty—are increasingly unlikely to be deployed in any US attempt to achieve hegemony, especially for overtly American imperatives. The mixed results of early-twenty-first-century events, as they unfolded in Iraq, Afghanistan, the Ukraine, and elsewhere have increasingly given pause to the use of "hard" power, even in the face of the emergence of an ongoing ISIS crisis that began in 2014. Neoconservative and even moderate US policy-makers continue to extol the virtues of "Pax Americana" as a global model—that is, the promotion of American ideals of peace, democracy, human rights, and neoliberal markets—and it is clear that Americans continue not only to desire world influence but also to position their geopolitical understanding of world events in terms of US global leadership. Cosmopolitan? Not particularly. It means instead that states whose visions do not conform are seen in oppositional terms. Consider this extract from the National Security Strategy for the United States of America (2006), which serves as a case in point:

> It is the policy of the United States to seek and support democratic movements and institutions in every nation and culture, with the ultimate goal of ending tyranny in our world. In the world today, the fundamental character of regimes matters as much as the distribution of power among them. The goal of our statecraft is to help create a world of democratic, well-governed states that can meet the needs of their citizens and conduct themselves responsibly in the international system. This is the best way to provide enduring security for the American people. (1)

This document, and an associated series of twenty-first-century companion pieces (see Table 1 for a list of documents up to and including 2010), defines the US national strategy, and in so doing demonstrates the continuing relevance of Pax Americana to create a larger universal system that meets American values and needs. As such, "imperialistic" or "unilateral" might be better words than "empire" to describe how the US has set its strongly global economic and political agenda. This relates not just to issues of climate change, landmines, accessible abortion, and international criminal courts, but also, closer to home, to border security and management agendas that impact what is still considered to be the War on Terror and totalitarianism. In the context of the latter, the 2006 Security Strategy vowed that "America will lead in this fight, and we will continue to partner with allies and will recruit new friends to join the battle" (1).

By 2010, after the exit of the George W. Bush administration, this national security strategy message remained, although it was much more muted:

> Our national security strategy is, therefore, focused on renewing American leadership so that we can more effectively advance our interests in the 21st century. We will do so by building upon the sources of our strength at home, while shaping an international order that can meet the challenges of our time. This strategy recognizes the fundamental connection between our national security, our national competitiveness, resilience, and moral example. And it reaffirms America's commitment to pursue our interests through an international system in which all nations have certain rights and responsibilities. This will allow America to leverage our engagement abroad on behalf of a world in which individuals enjoy more freedom and opportunity, and nations have incentives to act responsibly, while facing consequences when they do not.

Table 1   US National Strategy Documents, 1998–2010

National Security Strategies

- The National Security Strategy of the United States
  The White House, March 2010

- The National Security Strategy of the United States
  The White House, March 2006

- The National Security Strategy of the United States
  The White House, 18 September 2002

- A National Security Strategy for a New Century
  The White House, December 1999

- A National Security Strategy for a New Century
  The White House, May 1997

- National Security Strategy of the United States
  The White House, August 1991

National Defense and Military Strategies

- The National Defense Strategy of The United States of America
  Arlington, VA: Office of the Secretary of Defense, June 2008

- The National Defense Strategy of The United States of America
  Arlington, VA: Office of the Secretary of Defense, March 2005

- The National Military Strategy of the United States of America: A Strategy
  for Today; A Vision for Tomorrow
  Joint Chiefs of Staff, 2004

- Shape, Respond, Prepare Now—A Military Strategy for a New Era
  Joint Chiefs of Staff, 1998

- A Strategy of Flexible and Selective Engagement—National Military Strategy

Source: Defence Alternatives, http://www.comw.org/qdr/offdocs.html#nss

More recent security texts, like the US Defense Strategy released in January 2012, mixes Manifest Destiny with a more global commons theme: "it promotes our strategic priorities, including sustaining a global presence while strengthening our focus on the Asia-Pacific region; deterring our adversaries and fulfilling our security commitments; investing in critical alliances and partnerships, including NATO; combating violent extremists and defending human dignity around the world; and preserving our ability to respond quickly to emerging threats" (http://thehague.usembassy.gov). Indeed, as Hurrell (2005) reminds us:

> It is in this context that hegemony as a tool for promoting both formal and informal empire has become normative in the U.S.—a normative relationship

now equated with globalization. The promotion of US interests in a globalized age has come ever more to involve deep intrusion into how different societies are to be organized domestically. This is a structural change. If states are to develop effective policies on economic development, environmental protection, human rights, the resolution of refugee crises, the fight against drugs, or the struggle against terrorism, then they need to engage with a wide range of international and transnational actors and to interact not just with central governments but with a much wider range of domestic political, economic, and social players. If you want to solve problems in a globalized world, you cannot simply persuade or bully governments into signing treaties and are therefore inevitably drawn to become involved with how other people organize their own societies. This trend has been reinforced by the transformation of the security agenda and ... is one of the most important factors that has reshaped the debate about legitimacy and, once more, complicated the exercise of hegemonic power. (163)

So while it is in the context of Pax Americana and its implications, rather than Manifest Destiny, that the facilitative role of borders now needs to be understood, this does not signal any sort of cosmopolitan agenda. As we discussed earlier, Manifest Destiny and American exceptionalism are constituent beliefs embedded in the discourse of Pax Americana, but they are not cosmopolitan as much as universal in scope. The latter reflects the US desire to universalize its model of democracy, human rights, and free markets (Beck, 2006), while the former have been more aligned with military and territorial ambitions—the annexation of Canadian or Mexican territories during the nineteenth and early twentieth centuries, for example. Ambition for territorial control, although very real less than a century ago, is today more muted. It is, after all, not territory but coercive power that matters today, and among the most important venues for coercive power are security protocols and agendas.

Such thinking implicates North American borders—and, for the purposes of this study, the border established along the 49th Parallel and Great Lakes system. We have seen throughout this volume that borders are powerful actors in facilitating the US hegemony project and have been for centuries. In the latest iteration, the way in which the Canada–US border has been discursively constructed in the United States has "given primacy to discourses enabling security over competing policy objectives" (Hale, 2011: 40). It also made these discourses hegemonic by linking them to unilateralist public policies and by making them integrative as well (40).

This means that continental security agreements will need to reinforce American primacy, and indeed this seems increasingly the case. True, the SPP had limited traction for a variety of reasons, not the least of which was that the United States continued to unilaterally impose its security imperatives as if the SPP negations were not under way: the WHTI in particular (Moens, 2011: 59;

Hale and Marcotte, 2010). Since then, however, security negotiations have not stalled but continued apace with little fanfare or discussion through the Beyond the Border initiative.

Overall, the universalism of American values as the only values of significance has operated quite differently from what cosmopolitan theories prescribe. This in turn suggests that even if borders are reorganized through partnerships—as in the case of Canada–US border agreements—equality and transnationalism are unlikely. Instead, such agreements encourage reflexive responses to partnership as much as they *promote* such partnerships, and this may be the real takeaway message of the SPP's demise (Moens, 2011). The situating of the border through popular representations, governmental, and even "scientific" discourses has played a critical and reflexive role in Canada–US relations throughout history, as well as supported the continental expansion of US domestic and foreign policies and their transformation in non-American territories. It has nourished national identity and indeed understandings of nationalism (that is to say, it has equated society with nation), even while transforming Canadian society to conform to US values and norms.

PAX AMERICANA WRIT LARGE: SITUATING CANADA

The United States has envisioned itself as a project that has escaped the confines of the nation-state to become an exemplar for the Western Hemisphere. Here, unlike in many parts of the EU, borders are not disappearing but are becoming the sites through which formal integration programs are promulgated and enacted. These sites are located at land, air, and water borders, and increasingly they are encountered in the walls and technologies that police the line. Policy-makers may implement decisions based on broader political discussions, not that one is isolated from the other, as we have seen, but that one relies on the other for legitimacy and implementation.

Moreover, this is not a North America "of the regions," as in Europe (see Scott, 2009; Molchanov; 2005), such that all levels of government attempt to develop transnational spaces and levels of governance at the local level; rather, it is a model that creates these institutions from the top down. This requires states' institutions and symbols to create the conditions for control. Common spaces are thereby externalized, not internalized, and security perimeters apply to the process of building walls to filter the outside world, as well as robust internal borders along boundary lines. Unlike in the EU, there are no targeted regional borderlands through which identities and differences are "eased" and smoothed over. In the North American case, this easing seems to require the reinforcement of nationalist sentiments rather than their diminishment.

What is important, therefore, is not whether the United States is a true empire or not, or even whether it is "in decline"; rather, what matters is that we examine how US hegemony exerts imperial power through borders in ways that mobilize US geopolitical discourses and that reference familiar American historical themes that naturalize and rationalize US power over continental North America. Chapter 1 led us to understand that geopolitics, borders, and hegemony are interlocking pieces of the same puzzle; in this chapter, we want to understand how that hegemony is instrumentalized along the Canada–US border. How does it function when it is practised not on a distant "Third World" of US creation, a rogue nation, a global periphery, or a terrorist state—places where racialized immigration practices or deeply exploitative production systems "distance" negative economic impacts and "legitimate" hegemony (see Salter, 2004)—but instead on those next door, who are seemingly not so different from Americans? In this book we challenge (as does Dalby) the idea that the measure of such hegemony, or even empire, is taken only in terms of violent or dramatic intervention on the global periphery (Dalby, 2008; Bender, 2006)—that hegemony refers solely to how the United States has created a global periphery and Third World (Slater, 2008). As Dalby (2008) observes, "if one looks at … the places where American power has been most directly exerted … it is in the peripheral regions, and especially those where valuable resources are to be found … American involvement in 'civil wars' … suggests a pattern of intervention that might be called imperial, but it is also important to note that American foreign policy is usually more frequently conducted by cooperative ventures, suggesting some kind of hegemony rather than dominance" (429–30).

This passage identifies the essence of how the United States has positioned the Canada–US relationship within a North American hierarchy and not a cosmopolitan or cosmopolitan partnership discourse. The United States is hegemonic in North America as well as globally. Canada is by no means a Third World country, but it has a small military and little global power. Moreover, while it is strategically important to its southern neighbour, Canada has otherwise been viewed as insignificant relative to the United States and US interests. But at the same time, among liberal democracies, Canada is one of the world's economic success stories and is not usually viewed as on the "global periphery." Nonetheless, US security concerns have increasingly positioned Canada as a nation whose interests are best served by serving those of its neighbour.

I contend that this demotion of a successful G8 country—rhetorically if not politically and economically—to little more than a US client-state can tell us much about current geopolitical discourses of border management and the prospects for more traditional agendas.

METAPHORS OF UNIVERSALISM

The geopolitics of the Canada–US relationship offer an interesting window onto how US hegemony works to cultivate a sense of "sameness," but not equality, through cooperation. And the border is instrumental to this relationship, for it mediates how hegemony is instrumentalized. The idea of Canada as America's periphery is not a late-twentieth-century development. It has been part of an ongoing historical project to bring about economic, military, and cultural dependency. This dependency agenda has rankled generations of Canadian nationalists and created an anti-American backlash.

In an even more general sense, the themes now attached to the Canada–US border—Canadian sovereignty, illegal immigration, the need for security, anti-terrorist technologies, and so on, always in the context of free trade—are not new either. Those themes have deep historical roots in Canadian border management strategies and within the reflexive Canada–US relationship. Free trade, illegal immigration, cross-border terrorism, and territorial protection have been important building blocks of the Canada–US relationship and of North American society since the early to mid-nineteenth century. They have been recycled in the geopolitical imaginings of generations of Canadians and Americans—popularized in political texts, newspapers, and editorial cartoons, in literature, film, and television, and in other discourses, towards quite different ends in either nation. The NAFTA and the US obsession with security since 9/11 have reworked and rekindled many of these themes and in doing so have reorganized and even reinvented familiar geopolitical processes, which are evoked and understood in new ways, and which are reified in border management practice and metaphors. For example, (American) Manifest Destiny and (Canadian) National Policy relied on similar symbolic renderings of the border as a wall, a fence, or a frontier, but with different understandings of the relationship and with very different roles for border management. The result has been a shifting over time of the metaphors applied to the Canada–US border: a wall, a fence, or a gate.

Border metaphors strongly highlight the reflexive nature of Canada–US affairs, for they situate that political relationship not only in terms of identity and nationalism but also in terms of continental and indeed global geopolitics. Yet as we noted earlier in this volume, the Canada–US border has been explored only superficially in the literature, which is more concerned with defining and rationalizing recent security agendas and recommending policies than in exploring the evolution, functions, and meanings of the border as a material site and as a site of perceptions. As a consequence, the border's significance has been lost. The tendency has been to explain current Canada–US border arrangements in terms of functions and across a limited time horizon; neglected by this work has been the history of security arrangements as tools facilitating Canada's reflexive relationship with the United States.

The ideal of "partnership," although touted in Canada–US accords, and implicated in the SPP imagery, has been far from realized in Canada–US relations even though institutions have been identified through which to foster it. The Shared Border Initiative, for example, which comprised the foundation for the security perimeter agreement, announced its goal as follows: "To preserve and extend the benefits our close relationship has helped bring to Canadians and Americans alike, we intend to pursue a perimeter approach to security, working together within, at, and away from the borders of our two countries to enhance our security and accelerate the legitimate flow of people, goods, and services between our two countries. We intend to do so in partnership, and in ways that support economic competitiveness, job creation, and prosperity" (United States, 2011). But security integration is a moving target, and its negotiation is a reflexive process—so much so that the previously discussed SPP initiative (see Chapter 6) was replaced in 2011 by federal-level discussions concerning a Canada–US security perimeter. The details of the Beyond the Border agreement, signed by Barack Obama and Stephen Harper in February 2011, have so far been kept well out of the public spotlight, marked only by public announcements from time to time, which again play on the "partners" metaphor.

So while the cultural connections between the two countries remain strong, as attested to by federal initiatives as well as by regional "nests" of political, social, and economic interactions, the push for continental integration has not been as strong as in the EU. Or rather, the push for cooperation and integrated markets has retained features that cannot overcome existing layers of national interest on either side. The result has been security cooperation rather than broader structures for continental governance. In Europe, increased security and immigration concerns led to common policies and approaches within a supranational framework; in North America, this has not occurred. The EU is more than a series of intergovernmental agreements; it is, in fact, a sweeping supranational project that has demanded new sovereignty arrangements. This has not been the case in North America, where border walls have thickened and grown higher since 9/11 and attention to border security has increased rather than diminished (Nicol, 2005). Yet it would be incorrect to call the arrangements that do exist in North American vestigial or even "old-fashioned" (see Nicol, 2005): they are neither—instead, they are moving towards a more deeply embedded networked empire of neoliberal globalization. But even at that, it would be wrong to refer to this type of globalization as "cosmopolitanism" in the sense that Europeans apply that term (i.e., in the context of democracy and equality).

THE POPULAR GEOPOLITICS OF US UNIVERSALISM

The focus of this volume has been on how states use borders to project the idea of "borderlessness," specifically with regard to the Canada–US border. Border technologies today perform a conjuring trick—they pretend to be integrated through dominant discourses that promise "security perimeters" and "expedited" traffic; they promote equal partnership and "best friendship" with the goal of lowering rather than raising territorial walls. A new border security industry has developed in the wake of 9/11, one that increasingly attempts to screen everything and everyone as if they were a real and present threat to national security (see Konrad and Nicol, 2008). This representation of borders requires the metaphor of walls, to be sure. But it also requires the understanding that those outside are not automatically equal—their equality can be assured only through participation in US-centred security discourses. Geopolitics must be imprinted on biopolitics. This is very much the point of a now-infamous media exchange involving right-wing US talking head Ann Coulter (sounding much more 1812 than twenty-first century) on Canada's position vis-à-vis the United States:

COULTER: They better hope the United States doesn't roll over one night and crush them. They are lucky we allow them to exist on the same continent. We could have taken them [Canada] over so easily.

ALAN COLMES: We could have taken them over? Is that what you want?

COULTER: Yes, but no. All I want is the western portion, the ski areas, the cowboys, and the right-wingers ... when you're allowed to exist on the same continent of [*sic*] the United States of America, protecting you with a nuclear shield around you, you're polite and you support us. (http://mediamatters.org/research/2004/12/01coulter-canada-is-lucky-we-allow-them-to-exist/132376)

In this light, security is not just about exclusion; it is equally about the terms of *inclusion* under conditions of hegemony. As such, the current security concepts in which we are interested are rooted not just in the "clash of civilizations" discourse but also in broader debates concerning how the United States has externalized its power to expropriate Canadian policy instead of exercising the imperialistic aspects of that power over Canadian territory in a traditional empire-building sense. The United States seeks to internalize Canada and to institutionalize US control over Canada without actually taking Canadian territory. Indeed, its present-day project would make "taking" this country unnecessary. That this is what US security partnerships with Canada are seemingly attempting to do. Those partnerships have become hegemonic in North

America and especially in Canada in ways that work "through" Canadian society and government in an imperialistic sense rather than "over" Canadian society in a classical colonial sense.

CONCLUSIONS

It is important to understand that American ideas about homeland and security are not post-9/11 constructions; rather, they relate to a previously existing ideologically charged notion about the protection of "America" and the centrality of US power interests within a global setting. This reflects a great deal of categorical ambiguity, as well as, arguably, territorial ambiguity. The articulated notion of American "centrality" actually goes back to the nineteenth century. It is in this longer historical context that "national security" and the physical management of bordering practices enter the equation and become tools of hegemony, principally of the United States as it attempts to cast a North American if not a hemispheric or even global shadow. Rather than move towards a European model, in the sense of embracing a more cosmopolitan perspective, this situation has contributed instead to a security agenda that, in the twenty-first century, has embedded ideas about how hegemony must be exercised, which is by managing borders by increasingly diffuse, technological means.

Why the need for diffuse technology? Are borders not still "fixed" in today's world? Are not the guards and the fences, the checkpoints and the bridges, finite spaces? The erection of walls and surveillance technologies at North American borders and the posting of armed guards on both sides of the Canada–US border have replaced what had long been a rather open port of entry; yet it is really more on the Canadian side that traditional security functions have been enhanced, with border guards now armed with guns and given greater powers. So while it is true that the border has been sharpened in ways that include quasi-military and policing functions, it is important to understand how bordering practices promote increasingly diffuse and extended boundaries that proclaim cooperation even as they thicken and promote unilateralism. Walls are not welcome because walls limit the territorial transgression power of states to control linear zones along the boundary. The new border technologies encompass, contain, and control beyond state borders, even when they are embedded within those borders.

If new technologies have made border posts look more militarized and fortified, but at the same time, those technologies require diffuse data sets and networked cooperation to be effective. They draw upon all sorts of information to assess who individuals are, and they create new files to track and record those individuals. They use electronic and biometric data, as well as information that can be pulled up immediately as a border crossing takes place. They rely on machine-readable documents that have been pre-cleared or screened and developed to specific information standards.

In North America, the eye of the storm that swept through security policy after 9/11 was linked to a broader process of achieving international hegemony. National security, with terrorism as *raison d'état,* has been an extension rather than a reinvention of that project. *Before* 9/11, national security matters were usually presented as important because they were exceptional. *Since* 9/11, securitization discourses are no longer "exceptional" because threats to security are everywhere. *Everything* must be secured. As a consequence, political agendas have appropriated security and indeed created totalizing security regimes under the guise of national security. Politicians can then take whatever actions are needed to serve the national interests they themselves have defined. Everything must now be securitized under this regime's control, including human life. This is clearly an impossible task, but it generates heated political rhetoric. It is in this context that the debate about "American Empire" can be revisited—at least in relation to its impact on Canada. As we have seen, the concept of empire has been debated with respect to how and where hegemony is executed, and increasingly, hegemony has come to mean US power to shape other societies and economies. More generally, the notion of empire is rejected in favour of a networked harmony.

The post-9/11 era seemed to suggest that "America was back," that it had reformulated a world power presence on the basis of the War on Terror. But the economic collapse in the first decade of the twenty-first century has worried those who watch the United States. Jack Granatstein (2011), long an advocate of Canada–US border engagement and cooperation, has suggested openly that we need a border wall along the Canada–US border to keep a chaotic and disintegrating American society out.

There have been more or less serious discussions about the decline of American empire, and there is a rather expansive literature on the subject that will not be broached here (see Dalby, 2008). I raise the point here because it foregrounds corresponding arguments that "Europe is back" (see Beck, 2006; Delanty, 2009). That latter argument is contextualized in discussions about how conceptualizations of borders in the EU have created a cosmopolitan society, something that has as yet proven impossible in North America because of the US position on borders, values, and "Pax Americana." This raises the possibility that Europe is "cosmopolitan" not because it has no borders but rather because "borders" are different in concept and management: they "have multiplied and border work has shifted to include both state and non-state actors, new borders and the dissolution of old borders, as well as the fact that the important borders in Europe—the Europe defining ones—are becoming determined less by

European nation states than by the EU, which has the power to shift, dismantle and construct new borders" (Rumford, 2008: 54). It is important to consider, in this light, whether the opposite is occurring in North America. Perhaps our challenge now is to produce a scholarship on Canadian transnational discourses post–World War II, and to evaluate more fully the contribution of this narrative to the Northern American story of cosmopolitanism.

Chapter 8

CONCLUSIONS

US rallying cries for Manifest Destiny and Canadian concerns about US expansionism have both relied on a similar symbolic rendering, or imaginative construct—of border as wall, fence, gate, and now bridge—to counter existential threats posed by immigration, drug trafficking, and terrorism. These images have in turn generated categories of historical and contemporary national threats. In Chapter 1, we probed nineteenth-century representations of borders as "walls"—a metaphor that served an important purpose, which was to recast the Canada–US relationship in reflexive and dialectical ways, with the border as more than a flimsy barrier to US continental expansion. In its alternative metaphorical roles—as wall, door, and line—the Canada–US border has evolved both as a response to and in cooperation with US imperatives. Its creation was not simply the result of judicial agreements, treaties, and the occasional border skirmish. The force of US Manifest Destiny, the desire to annex Canada, and (eventually) the imperatives of free trade and continental markets were intertwined.

By the late nineteenth century, the rise of naturalized geopolitics as a national discourse had reinvented the Canada–US relationship. This was foundational for the present day's immigration and profiling practices. As they fostered a naturalized geopolitical discourse, Canadians and Americans reassessed their relationship, which had been based on classic geopolitical struggles for territory and were framed by civilizational discourses that encouraged "othering." From now on, "othering" would be carried out along racial lines, with a complex set of metaphors defining the border as a site where the two nations were divided yet "sutured" together (see Berland, 2009). This is not to say that such understandings of the border were uncontested, or that they did not vary between regions. But such differences were stitched together and given coherence, rightly or wrongly, so that a series of metaphors representing the relationship symbolized by boundaries in terms of identity, history, and power gained traction.

In Canada, the border has sometimes been perceived as a wall defending Canadians from Americans and sometimes as a gate facilitating greater inter-action between the Canadian and US marketplaces. In the twentieth century, tariff walls metaphors thus were to be overcome through "smooth border" pro-cesses. By late in that century, with the rise of neoliberalism—and with the NAFTA as a continental discourse of integration—Canadian and US economic relations were intertwined to the point that the border was viewed as "open" and bridged by policies of free trade. This was a response to the need for greater mobility of goods and capital in the age of globalization. These developments prepared the ground for the securitization agreements of the post 9/11 era. New border technologies were implemented to control the border, and those tech-nologies challenged the transnational context of borders themselves. Post-9/11 border practices and management regimes have embedded US hegemony as well as more general practices of "control" in North America (Walters, 2006) in ways that the advocates of Manifest Destiny could only have dreamed of.

As we saw in Chapter 5, Coté-Boucher (2008) argues that borders now are "physically extending beyond and inside its geopolitical location through a set of legal, administrative and technological procedures such as refugee containment, counter-terrorism measures and information-sharing [where] the border thus articulates fluid control measures based on the use of information technologies to more restrictive procedures such as confinement" (142). At the Canada–US border, she argues, the 2001 Smart Border Declaration contributed significantly to the development of the North American border into a multiplicity of sites for surveillance (143). Amoore, Marmura, and Salter (2008) likewise argue that neoliberalism has led to a sort of social sifting on the basis of social categories such as class, income, and ethnicity; that sifting, which has infiltrated both sides of the border, offers little room for contestation.

Are we seeing the end of sovereign borders? Certainly not, but we have seen their transformation, especially with regard to North American borders. As we have seen, Newman (2005) suggested that borders need to be understood as a continuum, as simultaneously deterritorializing and reterritorializing.

As we have already seen, Balibar's (2002) concern with state violence and unlawful confinement is further developed by Amoore, Marmura, and Salter (2008), who see how there is inherent conflict in traditional border imageries that both "appeal to the limits in politics and of political community, and a technology of limits—a means of defining what is possible in the governing of life itself. Yet, even as border management has taken on a renewed emphasis for policy makers, assessing the border's status as a definable, concrete entity or process has become increasingly problematic" (96). Coté-Boucher (2008) argues that the exceptional exercise of state sovereignty "as an apparatus of state control has currently been replaced by a security paradigm, which relies upon 'normalization' of security powers so that they operate as everyday or 'ordinary techniques of government' and by an intelligence paradigm whereby the diffuse border also rests upon the national and international sharing of information by security agencies along circuits of information exchange" (149).

In other words, an ever-present contradiction between the state and state-lessness is inherent in modern border management. Agamben (2005) suggests that while sovereignty is no longer seen as a matter of protecting territorial limits managed by discrete borders, states can continue a state of exception, exercising full sovereign control, by deciding where and how law is to be suspended (e.g., in relation to unlawful human rights violations in detention centres). In this sense, diffuse borders do not detract from the power of the state; rather, they extend it inwards as well as onwards and outwards.

So in North America, post-9/11 borders have been repositioned and represented in ways that include quasi-military and policing functions. But it is important to understand here that current bordering practices and technologies promote increasingly diffuse and extended boundaries and foster "cooperation" through intelligence sharing. Walls in North America exist to build or force compliance with near neighbours (Nicol, 2011): "US security policies are imple-mented through agreements and border controls meant to incorporate neigh-bours rather than exclude them, but to incorporate them under the terms of U.S. domestic security agendas instead of through foreign policies, diplomacy or broader treaties and international agreements" (263). New border technologies, that is, provide a means to encompass, contain, and control beyond the range of state borders, even if they are embedded within borders.

But what is diffuse or extraterritorial about such technologies? Are not the guards and the fences, the checkpoints and the bridges, found in or bounded by finite spaces? As we discussed in Chapter 5, for Walters (2006), whose concern is the delocalization of borders through technology, the real issue is that "today, it seems, borders are becoming more and more important not as military or economic practices but as spaces and instruments for the policing of a variety of actors, objects and processes whose common denominator is their 'mobility' ... or more specifically, the forms of social and political insecurity that have come to be discursively attached to these mobilities" (188).

The theme of mobility informs all current border management as well as the development of technologies to screen mobility. It is becoming clearer and clearer that globalization and its impacts will not make borders go away but *will* reconfigure borders in order to marry the imperatives of security and mobility (Nicol and Townsend-Gault, 2005). We are told that in North America after 9/11, security trumped trade, but this was an oxymoron: security *is* trade, the two are co-constitutive, and trade was securitized as a means of promoting security. So the issue at hand has been how to *manage* mobility—that is, how to capture data about flows of people and goods in ways that maintain if not strengthen the "exceptional" sovereignty claims of states (Salter, 2008). The pinnacle of achievement of modern globalization efforts has been to appear open while closed.

Many scholars, including Balibar (2002) and Rumford (2008), suggest that borders are everywhere—that they are not contained by sites of control but operate through individuals and social relations, through data sets and practices, through the act of living itself. Such techniques, implemented by highly sophisticated technologies and databases, are seen as the "alternative" to profiling along racial or ethnic grounds, although the data they scrutinize are codified by race, ethnicity, economic status, and other indicators. In their erasure of the individual and their focus on the "dividual," they make the individual insignificant and meaningless. Having been detached from identity and territory, the "dividual" prised apart in the data code can be manipulated to fit appropriate risk scenarios—in effect, to justify them. In this way, the data themselves create risk categories, which in turn define security threats. Those data also define the community of scholars, policy-makers, specialists, and other actors, who refine and promulgate the appropriate responses to risks in ways that are self-referencing and premediated.

Yet borders themselves, as spaces of enclosure, have not vanished. They continue to be sites of security "threats." And they are where normative assessments of risk are made, whether at airports or land crossings, at ports or even embassies. External borders, whether in the EU or the United States, are more numerous and daunting than ever. This is not to say that borders as sites of control and surveillance have not become much more diffuse: they have. The point here is that the distinction between control and disciplinary society has been linked to how data are now collected and processed at borders. Following from Walters and Deleuze, the institutional agencies concerned with border management must now be more diffuse and less institutionally situated in hierarchical governmental structures. They must operate *within* the state as well as at its margins, and indeed their reach is extraterritorial at times. They extend beyond borders and work in ways that are independent of international borderlines in the classic sense. They create large and powerful government institutions that operate *along* as well as outside the line (see Nicol, 2011).

The cooperation discourses that have been so typical of the post-9/11 era have been fostered by border technologies that promote and further US hegemony in the form of networked empire, in ways both biopolitical and extraterritorial. Those discourses have also been promoted in ways that securitize and normalize the everyday challenges of policy harmonization, cultural differences, and political diversity. We also need to remember that although the contemporary meaning of borders has been appropriated by securitization discourses focused on halting immigration and illegal movements of people and goods, borders have historically functioned as more than sites for managing mobility. Only recently have border management agencies been appropriated as securitization actors.

One of the tangible outcomes of this creation of what might arguably be called a cross-border management regime has been the development of an "understanding" among those who advocate for technological solutions to border management issues. A distinctive North American approach has developed that is very different from that of the EU in terms of the technicalities of agreements and the way in which the EU has created an overarching border agreement with considerable traction (the Shengen Agreement). This has not happened in North America. Papademetriou and Collet (2011), writing for the Migration Policy Institute in Washington, suggest that these differences can be evaluated in terms of four areas: collecting and sharing travellers' data; using new technologies to verify individual identity; employing new technologies to monitor physical borders; and building partnerships to achieve border management goals. They conclude that a single global system is required that would universalize security architectures and goals.

Today, however, the meaning of borders is open to contestation. Does their joint management symbolize partnership or contestation? Does it mean the delimitation of space or the conditions for hegemony? Are border landscapes repressive or facilitative? For whom? Are they economic gates or panoptic sites, or both? While these questions have always been salient, it would be accurate to say that the multiple functions of international borders evolved with the multiple technologies of state control. Initially it was not the borders themselves that mattered—since they were unmarked and "unpoliced"—so much as how they defined the edges of states and regulated territories, how they sent messages that were understood differently on either side of the line. The boundary might be a tattered flag, marking the difference between the "mild and wild wests" described by Katenberg (2003) and deployed as a symbolic plot device in Canadian films such as *Gunless*. Or it might be a real border post manned by customs agents attempting to tax commodities and seize contraband.

The reflexive nationalisms that have been generated by border security are mediated by what Beck (2006) has called the universalisms of "Pax Americana," especially in this current era of globalization. According to Beck (2000, 2006), transnationalism in and of itself is important but does not always promote a blending, hybridity, or cosmopolitanization of culture. Contrary to what some have argued (Beck, Sznaider, and Winter, 2003), Americanization can be the same as globalization, and for that reason it is not simply a homogenizing process; it is also a force of reaction and resistance. Transnationalism can create the conditions for reaction and reflexivity and for methodological nationalisms as well as shared identities and territories. Some have referred to this quality as "ambivalence" (see Thomson and Randall, 1994); others view it as a more grounded and active force than the term ambivalence implies. Moreover, it goes beyond elitist constructs (Granatstein, 1996) in terms of its integration into contemporary popularized geopolitical discourses. This is why, in this volume, I have preferred the term "reflexive" when examining the process. True, transnationalism is an important trigger for the "uncoupling of state and nation" in the development of what has become known in Europe as "cosmopolitan society" (Beck, 2006). And true, it has been encouraged within the EU through funded programs designed to bridge regional spaces. But as Beck notes, transnationalism assumes that there is no "other"—it creates a "both/and" situation rather than an "an/or" situation. It overcomes, also, "us and them" and "transcends the distinctions between aliens and nations, friends and foes, foreigners and natives" (66). Transnationalism also produces blended identities and reduces the impact of separate nationalisms. For Canadians, by contrast, "us" has been a problematic construct in relation to the United States, for the concept of "not-American" is deeply embedded here, while for Americans the recognition of Canada as "us" is tenuous and even problematic—as the Bush administration reminded North Americans only too well after 9/11 (Nicol, 2005; Thompson and Randall, 1994; Granatstein, 1996)

The argument has been made in Europe that a cosmopolitan society of both/and has emerged, or even a new regionalism (Scott, 2005). With regard to North America, Beck (2006) among others contends that no such development has occurred. National borders are becoming taller and thicker, despite calls for common goals and values, for cooperation, and even for a "security perimeter" (see Nicol, 2005; Konrad and Nicol, 2008). The historical role of borders in brokering this specific type of hegemonic transnationalism is indisputable (Nicol, 2012).

Farson (2006) notes that today's national borders are "in many respects the product of the nation-states that emerged in Europe following the 1647 Treaty of Westphalia" (24). This is interesting for North Americans in that these are definitely not the same boundaries, for them, as existed under the Peace of Westphalia. They emerged, true, as boundaries promoting self-determination, but also in contradistinction to the existing boundaries of nation-states that had been imposed on them by Europe's colonial powers. Just as Farson reminds us that "borders do not necessarily mean the same thing to all people or even to the same people in different contexts" (24), we need to remind ourselves that in North America, the states that were foundational in creating the Peace of Westphalia were nowhere to be seen in the twentieth century when boundaries were finalized between Canada and the United States in 1908; and even then, Canada's status as an independent state was contested by the United States. The story since then can be better seen as one in which, despite globalization, classic nation-states still attempt to instrumentalize themselves in North America in the face of a continuing, and perhaps even refreshed, American hegemony project. At the same time, however, there is both accommodation and strong resistance from Canadians and Mexicans to the increased Americanization of mobility, security, and economy, as the US continues to exert its influence in new ways. Overall, the Canada–US border—as idea, metaphor, institution, and site of territorialization—has been an important site and symbol of this uneven, reflexive, and hegemonic relationship. For Canadians the border has become an increasingly important reflexive space for constructing identity and culture over time. Given a history of vivid imagery and popular texts, it is likely to remain so. But it has also, through the same reflexive process, become an institution for facilitating increased US hegemony and is likely to retain this role even as cooperation and cross-border institutions are developed that try to erase the borderline entirely. At the end of the day, the fences and bridges that characterize this relationship, both real and symbolic, do not represent separate and opposite phases but are two sides of the same coin and operate simultaneously.

BIBLIOGRAPHY

Ableson, Donald E., and Duncan Wood, 2007. *People, Security and Borders: The Impact of the WHTI on North America.* Fulbright Foundation.

Abgrall, Jean-François. 2005. *Economic Relations and Cross-Border Organizations along the 49th Parallel.* Government of Canada, Policy Research Institute, Working Paper Series 001.

Ackleson, Jason. 2011. "The Emerging Politics of Border Management: Policy and Research Considerations." *The Ashgate Research Companion to Border Studies,* ed. Doris Wastl-Walter. Farnham: Ashgate. 245–61.

——. 2009. "From 'Thin' to 'Thick' (and Back Again?): The Politics and Policies of the Contemporary US–Canada Border." *American Review of Canadian Studies* 39, no. 4: 336–51.

Adamson, Robert J. 2005. "Law, Sovereignty, and Transnationalism: Delivering Social Goods Using a Functional Approach to Borders." *Holding the Line: Borders in a Global World,* ed. Heather Nicol and Ian Townsend-Gault. Vancouver: UBC Press. 50–60.

Agamben, Giorgio. 2005. *State of Exception.* Chicago: University of Chicago Press.

Agnew, John. 2007. "No Borders, No Nations: Making Greece in Macedonia." *Annals of the Association of American Geographers* 97, no. 2: 398–422.

——. 2005. *Hegemony: The New Shape of Global Power.* Philadelphia: Temple University Press.

——. 2003. *Geopolitics: Re-Visioning World Politics.* New York and London: Routledge.

Aitken, H.G.J. 1959. *The State and Economic Growth.* New York: Social Science Research Council.

Allison, Graham. 2001. "Nuclear Terrorism: It's the Plutonium, Stupid." Press Release, Harvard University, Belfer Center for Science and International Affairs. 18 November 2001. http://belfercenter.hks.harvard.edu.

Amoore, Louis, Stephen Marmura, and Mark B. Salter. 2008. "Smart Borders and Mobility: Spaces, Zones, and Enclosures." *Society and Surveillance* 5, no. 2: 96–101. http://www.surveillance-and-society.org. Accessed 4 August 2012.

Anderson, Benedict. 1991. *Imagined Communities: Reflections on the Origin and Spread of Nationalism.* New York and London: Verso.

Anderson, Kay J. 1995. *Vancouver's Chinatown: Racial Discourse in Canada, 1875–1980.* Montreal and Kingston: McGill–Queen's University Press.

Andreas, Peter. 2005. "The Mexicanization of the US–Canada Border: Asymmetric Interdependence in a Changing Security Context." *International Journal* 60, no. 2 (Spring 2005): 449–62.

———. 2000. *The Wall around the West*. Lanham: Rowman and Littlefield.

Avalon Project. http://avalon.law.yale.edu/subject_menus/18th.asp. Accessed 14 July 2014.

Aydinli, Ersel, and James Rosenau. 2005. *Globalization, Security, and the Nation-State: Paradigms in Transition*. Albany: SUNY Press.

Balibar, Etienne. 2002. *Politics and the Other Scene*. Trans. Christine Jones, James Swenson, and Chris Turner. New York and London: Verso.

Balzacq, Thierry, ed. 2011. *Securitization Theory: How Security Problems Emerge and Dissolve*. London and New York: Routledge.

Beck, Ulrich, 2006. *The Cosmopolitan Vision*. Cambridge: Polity.

———. 2000. *What Is Globalization?* Cambridge: Polity.

———. 1999. *World Risk Society*. Cambridge: Polity.

Beck, Ulrich, and Edgar Grande. 2007. *Cosmopolitan Europe*. Cambridge: Polity.

Beck, Ulrich, Natan Sznaider, and Rainer Winter, eds. 2003. *Global America? The Cultural Consequences of Globalization*. Liverpool: Liverpool University Press.

Behiels, Michael D., and C. Stuart. 2010. *Transnationalism: Canada–United States History into the 21st Century*. Montreal and Kingston: McGill–Queen's University Press.

Bélanger, Damien-Claude. 2011. *Prejudice and Pride: Canadian Intellectuals Confront the United States, 1891–1945*. Toronto: University of Toronto Press.

Bell, Colleen. 2011. *The Freedom of Security: Governing Canada in the Age of Counter-Terrorism*. Vancouver: UBC Press.

———. 2006. "Surveillance Strategies and Populations at Risk: Biopolitical Governance in Canada's National Security Policy." *Security Dialogue* 37 (June): 147–65.

Bender, Thomas. 2006. "The American Way of Empire." *World Policy Journal* 23, no. 1 (Spring 2006): 45–61.

Bengough, John Wilson. 1886. *A Caricature History of Canadian Politics*. Vols. 1 & 2. Toronto: Grip Printing & Publishing, 1886. http://openlibrary.org/books/OL23351871M/A_caricature_history_of_Canadian_politics. Accessed 28 March 2012.

Berland, Jody. 2009. *North of Empire: Essays on the Cultural Technologies of Space*. Durham: Duke University Press.

Beylerian, Onnig, and Jacques Lévesque. 2004. *Inauspicious Beginnings: Principal Powers and International Security Institutions after the Cold War, 1989–1999*. Montreal and Kingston: McGill–Queen's University Press.

Bigo, Didier, 2006a. "Globalized Insecurity: The Field and the Ban-opticon." *Illiberal Practices of Liberal Regimes: The (In)Security Games*, ed. Didier Bigo and A. Tsoukala. Paris: l'Harmattan. 5–47. In English.

———. 2006b. "Internal and External Aspects of Security." *European Security* 15, no. 4 (December): 385–404.

———. 2002. "Security and Immigration: Towards a Critique of the Governmentality of Unease." *Alternatives*, 27, Special Issue: 63–92.

Bonditti, Philippe. 2004. "From Territorial Space to Networks: A Foucaldian Approach to the Implementation of Biometry." *Alternatives: Global, Local, Political* 29, no. 4: 465–82.

Bone, Robert, and Robert J. Mahnic. 1984. "Norman Wells: The Oil Center of the North-west Territories." *Arctic* 37, no. 1 (March): 53–60.

Boucher, Christian. 2005. "Toward North American or Regional Cross-Border Com-munities: A Look at Economic Integration and Socio-Cultural Values in Canada and the United States." Government of Canada, Policy Research Institute, Working Paper Series 002.

Bowman, Isaiah. 1928. *The New World*. Yonkers-on-Hudson: World Book Company.

Bradford, Kristen, et al. 2003. "One Nation under Threat: Securing the United States from the Entry of Terrorists." https://publicpolicy.pepperdine.edu/master-public-policy/content/capstones/terror.pdf. Accessed 14 July 2014.

Brégent-Heald, Dominique. 2012. "Big Spy Country: Film and the U.S.–Canada Borderlands during the Second World War." *49th Parallel* 29 (Summer). https://fortyninthparallel journal.files.wordpress.com/2014/07/3-bregentheald-big-spy-country.pdf. Accessed 27 May 2015.

Brennan, Timothy. 1997. *At Home in the World: Cosmopolitanism Now*. Cambridge: Har-vard University Press.

Brister, Bernard. 2008–9. "William Lyon Mackenzie King: Master Politician or Master Procrastinator?" *London Journal of Canadian Studies* 24: 5–27.

Brunet-Jailly, Emmanuel, et al. 2006. "Leader Survey on Canada–US Cross-Border Regions: An Analysis." Government of Canada, Policy Research Institute, Working Paper Series 012.

Bukowczyk, John J., et al. 2005. *Permeable Border: The Great Lakes Basin as Transnational Region, 1650–1990*. Pittsburgh and Calgary: University of Pittsburgh Press and Uni-versity of Calgary Press.

Buzan, Barry, and Lene Hanson. 2009. *The Evolution of International Security Studies*. Cambridge: Cambridge University Press.

Buzan, Barry, and Ole Waever. 2003. *Regions and Powers: The Structure of International Security*. Cambridge: Cambridge Studies in International Relations no. 91.

Buzan, Barry, Ole Waever, and Jaap de Wilde. 1997. *Security: A New Framework for Analysis*. Boulder: Lynne Rienner.

Camarota, Steven. A. 2001. "Immigrants in the United States—2000: A Snapshot of America's Foreign-Born Population." Center for Immigration Studies. http://www.cis.org/articles/2001/back101.html. Accessed 12 October 2012.

Campbell, Bruce, and Ed Finn. 2006. *Living with Uncle in an Age of Empire*. Toronto: James Lorimer.

Campbell, David. 1998. *Writing Security: United States Foreign Policy and the Politics of Identity*, 2nd ed. Minneapolis and Manchester: University of Minnesota Press and Manchester University Press.

Canada. 2012. "Canada's Economic Action Plan." http://actionplan.gc.ca/en/page/bap-paf/beyond-border-shared-vision-perimeter-security-and-economic-competitivenes. Accessed 15 July 2013.

———. Perimeter Security and Economic Competativeness: Beyond the Border Action Plan: A Shared Vision for Perimeter Perimeter Security and Economic Competi-tiveness. 2011. http://actionplan.gc.ca/grfx/psec-scep/pdfs/bap_report-paf_rapport -eng-dec2011.pdf. Accessed 14 July 2012.

———. 2011. *Perimeter Security and Economic Competitiveness: What Canadians Told Us*. Report on Consultations on Perimeter Security and Economic Competitiveness between Canada and the United States. http://actionplan.gc.ca/grfx/psec-scep/pdfs/BBWG-GTPF_Eng.pdf. Accessed 15 July 2014.

———. 2001. *The Canada/United States Accord on Our Shared Border: A Call to Action for 2001 and Beyond*. 21 February.

———. 2001. "The Canada-U.S. Border: Where the Rubber Hits the Road." Remarks delivered to the Economic Club of Detroit by Michael Kergin, Ambassador of Canada to the United States, Detroit. http://connection.ebscohost.com/c/speeches/5124870/canada-u-s-border. Accessed 15 July 2015.

———. 2000. Canada-United States Accord on Our Shared Border Update. http://publications.gc.ca/collections/Collection/Ci51-95-2000E.pdf. Accessed 12 July 2014.

———. 1995. *The Joint Border Agreement—The Canada-U.S. Accord on Our Shared Border*. http://publications.gc.ca/collections/Collection/Ci51-95-2000E.pdf. Accessed 15 July 2015.

Canada. Department of Foreign Affairs and International Trade. 2011. "Minister Baird's Visit to Washington Highlights Canada's Commitment to Jobs and Economic Growth with United States." http://www.international.gc.ca/media/aff/news-communiques/2011/221.aspx?view=d. Accessed 5 August 2011.

———. 2005. "Forward from the Prime Minister." *A Role of Pride and Influence in the World: Canada's International Policy Statement*. Ottawa.

Canada. House of Commons. 2009. *An Examination of Selected Canada–U.S. Border Issues*. Report of the Standing Committee on International Trade. June. 40th Parliament. 6.

Canada. Library and Archives Canada. 2012. "Guardians of the North." https://www.collectionscanada.gc.ca/comics/027002-3000-e.html. Accessed 15 July 2014.

Canada. Office of Prime Minister Stephen Harper. 2011. "Beyond the Border: A Shared Vision for Perimeter Security and Economic Competitiveness: A Declaration by the Prime Minister of Canada and the President of the United States of America." 4 February 2011. Washington, DC. http://pm.gc.ca/eng/media.asp?id=3938. Accessed 5 August 2011.

———. 2004. News release: "Government of Canada Releases Comprehensive National Security Policy." 27 April. http://pm.gc.ca/eng/news.asp?id=186. Accessed 30 April 2007.

Canada. Senate. 2002. Standing Senate Committee. 2002. *Fifth Report of Canada's Standing Senate Committee on National Security and Defence*. http://www.parl.gc.ca/37/1/parlbus/commbus/senate/com-e/defe-e/rep-e/rep05feb02-e.htm. Accessed 31 August 2010.

Canada–U.S. Smart Border Declaration: Action Plan for Creating a Secure and Smart Border, December 2001.

Canadian Chamber of Commerce. 2008. A Canada–U.S. Border Vision. http://www.chamber.ca/images/uploads/Reports/a-canada-u.s.border-vision.pdf. Accessed 30 July 2012.

Canadian Citizenship and Immigration Resource Centre. 2009. "Securing Canada's Borders." http://www.immigration.ca/permres-gii-securingborders.asp. Accessed 18 August 2009.

CASE. 2006. "Critical Approaches to Security in Europe: A Networked Manifesto." *Security Dialogue* 37 (December): 443–87.

Cavanagh, John, Sarah Anderson, Jaime Serra and J. Enrique Espinosa. 2002. "Happily Ever NAFTA." *Foreign Policy* 132 (September–October 2002): 58–65.

Cavell, Richard, ed. 2004. *Love, Hate, and Fear in Canada's Cold War.* Toronto: University of Toronto Press.

Chalfin, Brenda. "Border Scans: Sovereignty, Surveillance, and the Customs Service in Ghana." *Identities* 11, no. 3: 397–416.

Clark, Campbell. 2010. "U.S. Warned Canadians of Insidious Stereotypes on Canadian TV, Wikileaks Shows." *Globe and Mail,* 1 December 2010. http://www.theglobe andmail.com/news/politics/us-warned-of-insidious-stereotypes-on-canadian -tv-wikileaks-shows/article1318964. Accessed 4 August 2012.

Clarkson, Stephen. 2008. *Does North American Exist? Governing the Continent after NAFTA and 9/11.* Toronto and Washington: University of Toronto Press and Woodrow Wilson Center Press.

Clarkson, Stephen, and Erin Fitzgerald. 2009. "A Special Military Relationship? Canada's Role in Constructing US Military Power." *Journal of Military and Strategic Studies* 12, no. 1: 1–24. http://www.jmss.org/jmss/index.php/jmss/article/viewFile/276/290. Accessed 15 July 2014.

Coates, Ken S., P. Whitney Lackenbauer, William R. Morrison, and Greg Poelzer, 2008. *Arctic Front: Defending Canada in the Far North.* Toronto: Thomas Allen.

Cohen, Andrew. 2005. *Geopolitics of the World System.* Lanham: Rowman and Littlefield.

Condon, Bradly, and Tapen Sinha. 2003. *Drawing Lines in Sand and Snow: Border Security and North American Economic Integration.* Armonk, NY: M.E. Sharpe.

Congressional Quarterly. Cargo and Container Security House Appropriations Committee. 2009. Homeland Security Subcommittee April 2, 2009. CQ Congressional Testimony.

Corrigan, Philip, and Derek Sayer. 1985. *The Great Arch: English State Formation as Cultural Revolution.* Oxford: Blackwell.

Côté-Boucher, Karine. 2008. "The Diffuse Border: Intelligence-Sharing, Control, and Confinement along Canada's Smart Border." *Surveillance and Society* 5, no. 2: 142–65.

Cox, Kevin. 2002. *Political Geography: Territory, State, and Society.* Oxford: Blackwell.

Craig, Béatrice. 2005. "Before Borderlands: Yankees, British, and the Saint John Valley French." *New England and the Maritime Provinces: Connections and Comparisons,* ed. Stephen J. Hornsby and John G. Reid. Montreal and Kingston: McGill–Queen's University Press. 74–93.

Crane, David. 2002. "We Can Resist American Hegemony." *Toronto Star,* 21 July 2002.

Dalby, Simon. 2008. "Imperialism, Domination, Culture: The Continued Relevance of Critical Geopolitics." *Geopolitics* 13, no. 3: 413–36.

Dalby, Simon, and Gearóid Ó Tuathail. 2002. *Rethinking Geopolitics.* New York and London: Routledge.

de Goede, Marieke. 2008. "Beyond Risk: Premediation and the Post-9/11 Security Imagination." *Security Dialogue* 39, nos. 2–3: 155–76.

Delanty, Gerard. 2009. *The Cosmopolitan Imagination: The Renewal of Critical Social Theory.* Cambridge: Cambridge University Press.

———. 2006. "The Cosmopolitan Imagination: Critical Cosmopolitanism and Social Theory." *British Journal of Sociology* 57, no. 1: 25–47.

Deleuze, Gilles. 1990. "Postscript on the Societies of Control." *L'autre journal* 1 (mai 1990). http://abdn.ac.uk/modern/node/109.

Depledge, Duncan. 2013. "Assembling a (British) Arctic." *Polar Journal* 3, no. 1: 163–77. DOI: 10.1080/2154896X.2013.783273.

Dijkink, Gertan. 1998. "Geopolitical Codes and Popular Representations." *GeoJournal* 46, no. 4: 293–99.

Dillon, Michael. 2008. "Underwriting Security." *Security Dialogue* 39, nos. 2–3: 309–32.

Dimmel, Brandon. 2011. "South Detroit, Canada: Isolation, Identity, and the US–Canada Border, 1914–1918." *Journal of Borderlands Studies* 26, no. 2: 197–209.

Dittmer, Jason. 2005. "Captain America's Empire: Reflections on Identity, Popular Culture, and Post-9/11 Geopolitics." *Annals of the Association of American Geographers* 95, no. 3: 626–43.

Dittmer, Jason, and S. Larsen. 2007. "Captain Canuck, Audience Response, and the Project of Canadian Nationalism." *Social and Cultural Geography* 8, no. 5: 735–53.

Dittmer, Jason, et al. 2011. "Have You Heard the One about the Disappearing Ice? Recasting Arctic Geopolitics." *Political Geography* 30 (2011): 202–14.

Dodds, Klaus. 2007. *Geopolitics: A Very Short Introduction.* Oxford: Oxford Univerisity Press,

Donnan, Hastings, and Thomas M. Wilson. 1998. *Border Identities: Frontiers of Identity, Nation and State.* London: Bloomsbury.

Doran, Charles. 1984. *Forgotten Partnership: Canada–US Relations Today.* Baltimore: Johns Hopkins University Press.

Drache, Daniel. 2012. *Big Picture Realities: Canada and Mexico at the Crossroads.* Waterloo: Wilfrid Laurier University Press.

———. 2004. *Borders Matter: Homeland Security and the Search for North America.* Halifax: Fernwood.

Eden, Lorraine, and Maureen Appel Molot. 1993. "Canada's National Policies: Reflections on 125 Years." *Canadian Public Policy* 19, no. 3: 232–51.

Entriken, Nicholas 2004. "Political Community, Identity and Cosmopolitan Place." *International Sociology* 14: 269–82. Reprinted in *Remapping Europe,* ed. Mabel Berezin and Martin Schain. Baltimore: Johns Hopkins University Press, 2004.

Farish, Matthew. 2010. *The Contours of America's Cold War.* Minneapolis: University of Minnesota Press.

Farson, Stuart. 2006. "Rethinking the North American Frontier after 9/11." *Journal of Borderlands Studies* 21, no. 1: 23–45.

FATF-GAFI. 2010. "Detecting and Preventing the Illicit Cross-Border Transportation of Cash and Bearer Negotiable Instruments." Best Practice Paper to Special Recommendation IX (Cash Couriers). http://www.fatf-gafi.org/media/fatf/documents/recommendations/International%20BPP%20 Detecting%20and %20Preventing%20 illicit%20cross-border%20transportation%20SR%20IX%20%20COVER%202012 .pdf. Accessed 15 July 2014.

Findlay, John M., and Kenneth S. Coates eds. 2002. *Parallel Destinies: Canadian–American Relations West of the Rockies.* Seattle: Center for the Study of the Pacific Northwest in Association with University of Washington.

Flint, Colin. 2006. *Introduction to Geopolitics, Tensions, Conflicts, and Resolutions.* London: Routledge.

Fortmann, Michel, and David G. Haglund. 2002. "Canada and the Issue of Homeland Security: Does the Kingston Dispensation Still Hold?" *Canadian Military Journal* 3, no. 1 (Spring): 17–22.

Foucault, Michel. 2007. *Security, Territory, Population: Lectures at the Collège de France, 1978–1979.* New York: Palgrave Macmillan.

———. 2008. *The Birth of Biopolitics: Lectures at the Collège de France, 1978–1979*. New York: Palgrave Macmillan.

Fulford, Robert. 2001. "Anti-American Cant a Self-Inflicted Wound." *National Post*, 22 September. http://www.robertfulford.com/AntiAmericanism2.html. Accessed 25 October 2011.

———. 1998. "Blood and Bondage: Can Americans Rise Above a History Steeped in Past Misdeeds? Review of Paul Johnson's Book *A History of the American People*." *Ottawa Citizen*, 22 March. http://www.robertfulford.com/Johnson.html. Accessed 15 July 2014.

Fukuyama, Francis. 1989. "The End of History?" *The National Interest*, Summer 1989.

Gabriel, Dana. 2011. "Canada–US Deep Integration Agenda Continues Unabated." 28 March. http://beyourownleader.blogspot.ca/2011/03/canada-us-deep-integration-agenda_28.html. Accessed 14 August 2012.

Gattinger, Monica, and Geoffrey Hale. 2010. *Borders and Bridges: Canada's Policy Relations in North America*. Toronto: Oxford University Press.

Gilbert, Emily. 2007. "Leaky Borders and Solid Citizens: Governing Security, Prosperity, and Quality of Life in a North American Partnership." *Antipode* 39, no. 1: 77–98.

———. 2005. "The Inevitability of Integration? Neoliberal Discourse and the Proposals for a New North American Economic Space after September 11." *Annals of the Association of American Geographers* 95, no. 1: 202–22.

Glassner, Martin Ira. 2003. *Political Geography*. New York: John Wiley.

Goldfarb, Anne. 2007, "Reaching a Tipping Point: Effects of Post-9/11 Border Security on Canada's Trade and Investment." Conference Board of Canada, June 2007. http://www.conferenceboard.ca/documents.asp?rnext=2028. Accessed 21 March 2008.

Gramsci, Antonio. 1973. *Letters from Prison*, ed. and trans. Lynne Lawner. New York: Harper and Row.

Granatstein, J.L. 2011. "Our American Friends Are Trouble." *Ottawa Citizen*, 9 October. http://www.ceasefire.ca/?p=8714#sthash.wPwLgtMJ.dpuf.

———. 2010. "Canada's Critical Interest in Mexico." *National Post*, 16 June 2010. http://fullcomment.nationalpost.com/2010/06/16/j-l-granatstein-canadas-critical-interest-in-mexico. Accessed 20 July 2011.

———. 2002. "A Friendly Agreement in Advance: Canada–US Defence Relations Past, Present, and Future." C.D. Howe Institute.

———. 1996. *Yankee Go Home: Canadians and Anti-Americanism*. Toronto: HarperCollins.

Gwyn, Julian. 2005. "Comparative Economic Advantage: Nova Scotia and New England, 1720–1860." In *New England and the Maritime Provinces: Connections and Comparisons*, ed. Stephen J. Hornsby and Jon G. Reid. Montreal and Kingston: McGill–Queen's University Press. 295–314.

Haddal, Chad C. 2010. *Border Security: The Role of the US Border Patrol Specialist in Immigration Policy*. 11 August. Washington: Congressional Research Service. http://fas.org/sgp/crs/homesec/RL32562.pdf,Accessed 15 July 2014.

Haglund, David G. 2007. "A Security Community—'If You Can Keep It': Demographic Change and the North American Zone of Peace." *Norteamérica* 2, no. 1 (January–June 2007): 77–100. http://www.cisan.unam.mx/Norteamerica_anterior/num3/pdf/haglund.pdf. Accessed 15 July 2014.

Hale, Geoffrey. 2011. "Politics, People, and Passports: Contesting Security, Travel, and Trade on the US-Canadian Border." *Geopolitics* 16: 27–69.

Hale, Geoffrey, and Christina Marcotte. 2010. "Border Security, Trade, and Travel Facilitation." In *Borders and Bridges: Canada's Policy Relations in North America*, ed. Monica Gattinger and Geoffrey Hale. Toronto: Oxford University Press.

Hannay, James. 1909. *History of New Brunswick.* Saint John: Bowes.

Hardt, Michael, and Antonio Negri. 2000. *Empire.* Cambridge: Harvard University Press.

Hart, Michael. 1988. "Of Friends, Interests, Crowbars, and Marriage Vows in Canada–
United States Trade Relations." *Images of Canadianness: Visions on Canada's Politics,
Culture, and Economics,* ed. Leen D'Haenens. Ottawa: University of Ottawa Press.
199–220.

Hart, Michael, and William Dymond, 2001."Common Borders, Shared Destinies:
Canada, the United States, and Deepening Integration." Centre for trade Policy and
Law. Ottawa.

Harvey, David. 2009. *Cosmopolitanism and the Geographies of Freedom.* New York:
Columbia University Press.

———. 2003. *The New Imperialism.* London: Oxford University Press.

Harvey, Frank P. 2006. "The Homeland Security Dilemma: The Imaginations of Fail-
ure and the Escalating Costs of Perfecting Security." June. Report prepared for the
Canadian Defence and Foreign Affairs Institute. http://www.cdfai.org/PDF/The%20
Homeland%20Security%20Dilemma.pdf. Accessed 15 July 2014.

———. 2004. *Smoke and Mirrors: Globalized Terrorism and the Illusion of Multilateral
Security.* Toronto: University of Toronto Press.

Hataley, Todd. 2007. "Catastrophic Terrorism at the Border: The Case of the Canada–
United States Border." Homeland Security Affairs, Proceedings of the Workshop on
Preparing for and Responding to Disasters in North America. December. http://
www.hsaj.org/?article=supplement1.2. Accessed 22 October 2012.

Heininen, Lassi, and Heather N. Nicol, 2007. "A New Northern Security Agenda." *Borderlands: Comparing Border Security in North America and Europe,* ed. Emmanuel
Brunet-Jailly. Ottawa: University of Ottawa Press. 133–65.

Helleiner, Jane. 2009. "'As Much American as a Canadian Can Be': Cross-Border Experience and Regional Identity among Young Borderlanders in Canadian Niagara."
Anthropologica 51, no. 1: 225–38.

Herod, Andrew, Gearóid, Ó Tuathail, and Susan M. Roberts. 1998. *An Unruly World?
Globalization, Governance and Geography.* London: Routledge.

Hornsby, Stephen J., Victor A. Konrad, and James J. Herlan, eds. 1989. "The Northeastern Borderlands: Four Centuries of Interaction." Orono and Fredericton: Canadian
American Centre/Acadiensis Press.

Hornsby, Stephen J., and John G. Reid. 2005. *New England and the Maritime Provinces:
Connections and Comparisons.* Montreal and Kingston: McGill–Queen's University
Press.

Horsman, Reginald, 1987. "On to Canada: Manifest Destiny and United States Strategy
in the War of 1812." *Michigan Historical Review* 13, no. 2 (Fall): 1–24.

Hou, Charles, and Cynthia Hou. 2002. *Great Canadian Political Cartoons. 1915–1945.*
Vancouver: Moody's Lookout Press.

———. 1997. *Great Canadian Political Cartoons. 1820–1914.* Vancouver: Moody's Lookout Press.

———. 1998. *The Art of Decoding Political Cartoons: A Teacher's Guide.* Vancouver:
Moody's Lookout Press.

Huntington, Samuel P. 1996. *The Clash of Civilizations and the Remaking of World Order.* New York: Simon and Schuster.

Hurrell, Andrew. 2005. "Pax Americana or the Empire of Insecurity?" *International Relations of the Asia-Pacific* 5, no. 2: 153–76.

Huysmans, J. 2006. *The Politics of Insecurity: Fear, Migration, and Asylum in the EU.* Abingdon: Routledge.

Ilias, Shayerah, Katherine Fennelly, and Christopher M. Federico. American Attitudes toward Guest Worker Policies." *International Migration Review* 42, no. 4 (Winter 2008): 741–66.

Imas, Karen. 2007. "States and Provinces Experiment with Enhanced Driver's Licenses as Alternative to Passport Rules: II Sidebar: Some States Tentative on Enhanced Licenses." Eastern Regional Conference of the Council of State Governments.

Ince, Nathan. 2011. "A Matter of Survival: The Development of Anti-Americanism in 19th Century Canada." School of Canadian Studies, Carleton University. Capstone Seminar Series. http://capstoneseminarseries.files.wordpress.com/2011/03/nathan-2 .pdf. Accessed 10 August 2012.

Ingram, Alan, and Klaus Dodds, 2009. *Spaces of Security and Insecurity: Geographies of the War on Terror.* Farnham: Ashgate.

International Boundary Commission (IBC). 2011. http://www.internationalboundary commission.org/history.html. Accessed 6 March 2012.

IPSOS.com. 2011. "Two in Three (68%) Believe Canada Will Compromise Too Much to Get a Perimeter Security Agreement with the US—Country Split on Whether They Trust Stephen Harper to Negotiate a Deal That Improves Border Access but Doesn't Sacrifice Independence." 19 February. http://www.ipsos-na.com/news-polls/press release.aspx?id=5136. Accessed 14 July 2014.

Isin, Engin F. 2004. "The Neurotic Citizen." *Citizenship Studies* 8, no. 3: 217–35.

Jeffry, Alex. 2009. "Containers of Fate: Problematic States and Paradoxical Sovereignty." *Spaces of Security and Insecurity: Geographies of the War on Terror,* ed. Alan Ingram and Klaus Dodds. Farnham: Ashgate. 42–63.

Jones, Reece. 2012. *Border Walls Security and the War on Terror in the United States, India, and Israel.* New York: Palgrave Macmillan.

Kant, Immanuel. *Political Writings.* Cambridge: Cambridge University Press, 1991.

Katenberg, William H. 2003. "A Northern Vision: Frontiers and the West in the Canadian and American Imagination." *American Review of Canadian Studies* 33, no. 4 (Winter 2003): 543–63. http://findarticles.com/p/articles/mi_hb009/is_4_33/ai_n29061203. Accessed 14 July 2014.

Kilroy, Richard J. 2007. "Perimeter Defense and Regional Security Cooperation in North America: United States, Canada, and Mexico." *Homeland Security Affairs,* Supplement no. 1. http://www.hsaj.org/?special:article=0.1.3. Accessed 14 July 2014.

Kimery, Anthony. 2011. "Northern Border Intel-sharing Deficient, Fed Audit, Officials Say." *HSTODAYUS.* 8 March. http://www.hstoday.us/blogs/the-kimery-report/blog/ northern-border-intel-sharing-deficient-fed-audit-officials-say/42d9c82e1e3675af 884c26396777931b.html. Accessed 14 July 2014.

Knowles, Valerie. 2007. *Strangers at Our Gates: Canadian Immigration and Immigration Policy, 1540–2006.* Toronto: Dundurn Press.

Kohn, Edward Parliament. 2000. "This Kindred People: Canadian–American Relations and North American Anglo-Saxons during the Anglo-American Rapprochement, 1896–1903." PhD diss., Department of History, McGill University.

Konrad, Victor, and Heather Nicol. 2010. "Passports for All." *Canadian–American Public Policy* 74.

———. 2008. *Beyond Walls: Reinventing the Canada–United States Borderlands*. Aldershot: Ashgate.

———. 2004. "Boundaries and Corridors: Rethinking the Canada–United States Borderlands in the Post-9/11 Era." *Canadian–American Public Policy* 60.

Koring, Paul. 2012. "Applicants for Canadian Visas Will Be Checked against U.S. databases." *Globe and Mail,* 4 January. http://www.theglobeandmail.com/news/politics/applicants-for-canadian-visas-will-be-checked-against-us-databases/article6934557. Accessed 19 August 2013.

Kramer, Paul A. 2002. "Empires, Exceptions, and Anglo-Saxons: Race and Rule between the British and United States Empires, 1880–1910." *Journal of American History* 88, no. 4: 1315–53.

Kutcher, Stanley Paul. 1975. "John Wilson Bengough: Artist of Righteousness." MA diss., McMaster University. http://digitalcommons.mcmaster.ca/opendissertations/513. Accessed 14 July 2014.

Kuus, Merje. n.d. "Critical Geopolitics" http://www.isacompss.com/info/samples/critical geopoliticssample.pdf.

Lackenbauer, P. Whitney. 2011. "Canadian Arctic Sovereignty and Security Historical Perspectives." Occasional Paper no. 4. Calgary Papers in Military and Strategic Studies.

Lagassé, Philippe. 2003. "Northern Command and the Evolution of Canada–US Defence Relations." *Canadian Military Journal* (Spring): 15–22.

Lass, William E. 1975. "How the Forty-Ninth Parallel Became the International Boundary." *Minnesota History* 44 (Summer): 209–19.

Laxer, James. 2012. *Tecumseh and Brock: The War of 1812.* Toronto: Anansi.

———. 2003. *The Border: Canada, the US, and Dispatches from the 49th Parallel.* Toronto: Doubleday Canada.

Lazzarato, Maurizio. "From Biopower to Biopolitics." Trans. Ivan Ramirez. *Pli* 13: 100–11.

Lee, Erika. 2006. "A Nation of Immigrants / A Gatekeeping Nation: American Immigration Law and Policy, 1875–Present." *A Companion to American Immigration History,* ed. Reed Udea. Wiley: Blackwell.

———. 2002. "Enforcing the Borders: Chinese Exclusion along the US Borders with Canada and Mexico, 1882–1924." *Journal of American History* 89, no. 1 (June): 54–86.

Lewis, Martin W., and Kären E. Wigen. 1997. *The Myth of Continents: A Critique of Metageography.* Berkeley: University of California Press.

Libraries and Archives Canada. *Guardians of the North.* http://epe.lac-bac.gc.ca/100/200/301/lac-bac/guardians_north-ef/2009/www.collectionscanada.gc.ca/superheroes/index-e.html. Accessed 14 July 2014.

Longley, Ronald Stewart. 1981. *Sir Francis Hincks: A Study of Canadian Politics, Railways, and Finance in the Nineteenth Century.* New York: Arno Press.

Loyd, Jenna M., Matt Mitchelson, and Andrew Burridge, eds. 2012. *Beyond Walls and Cages: Prisons, Borders, and Global Crisis.* Athens: University of Georgia Press.

Lutz, John. 2002. "Work, Sex, and Death on the Great Thoroughfare: Annual Migrations of 'Canadian Indians' to the American Pacific Northwest." *Parallel Destinies: Canadian–American Relations West of the Rockies,* ed. John M. Findlay and Jenneth S. Coates. Montreal and Kingston: McGill–Queen's University Press. 80–103.

Mackey, Eva. 1999. *House of Difference: Cultural Politics and National Identity in Canada.* London: Routledge.

Magnet, Shoshana Amielle. 2011. *When Biometrics Fail: Gender, Race, and the Technology of Identity.* Durham: Duke University Press.

Mahant, Edelgard, and Graeme S. Mount. 1999. *Invisible and Inaudible in Washington: American Policies toward Canada.* Vancouver: UBC Press.

Mann, Michael. 1993. *The Sources of Social Power.* Vol. 2. London: Cambridge University Press.

Mattli, Walter. 1999. *The Logic of Regional Integration: Europe and Beyond.* Cambridge: Cambridge University Press.

McDougall, John. 2006. *Drifting Together: The Political Economy of Canada–US Integration.* Peterborough: Broadview Press.

McDuff, Gerald. 2012. "As the US Becomes Fortress America, Canada Will Have to Pay More Attention to Its Own Interests." http://www.issuesnetwork.com/articles/mcduff20010813.html. Accessed 12 August 2102.

McEwen, Alec. 2001. "The Value of International Boundary Commissions: The Canadian American Experience." http://people.ucalgary.ca/~amcewen/ibc.pdf. Accessed 14 July 2014.

McKenna, Barrie. 2010. "As Border Beefs Up, Security 'Perimeter' Remains a Dream." http://www.theglobeandmail.com/report-on-business/commentary/barrie-mckenna/as-border-beefs-up-security-perimeter-remains-a-dream/article1835011. Accessed 24 October 2011.

Merk, Frederick. 1971. *Fruits of Propaganda in the Tyler Administration.* Cambridge: Harvard University Press.

———. 1963. *Manifest Destiny and Mission in American History: A Reinterpretation.* Cambridge: Harvard University Press.

Mitchell, Don. 2000. *Cultural Geography: A Critical Introduction.* London: Blackwell.

Mitchell, Timothy. 1999. "Society, Economy and the State Effect." *State/Culture*, ed. George Steinmetz. Ithaca: Cornell University Press. 76–97.

Moens, Alexander. 2011. "'Lessons Learned' from the Security and Prosperity Partnership for Canadian–American Relations." *American Review of Canadian Studies* 41, no. 1: 53–64.

Molchanov, Mikhail A. 2005. "Regionalism and Globalization: The Case of the European Union." *Perspectives on Global Development and Technology* 4, nos. 3–4: 4313–46.

Moser, John E. 1998. *Twisting the Lion's Tail: American Anglophobia between the World Wars.* New York: NYU Press.

Mouat, Jeremy, 2002. "Nationalist Narratives and Regional Realities: The Economy of Railway Development in Southeastern British Columbia." *Parallel Destinies: Canadians, Americans, and the Western Border*, ed. John M. Findlay and Kenneth S. Coates. Seattle: Center for the Study of the Pacific Northwest in Association with University of Washington. 123–54.

Muller, Benjamin J. 2010. *Security, Risk, and the Biometric State: Governing Borders and Bodies.* London and New York: Routledge.

Murray, David. 1996. "Criminal Boundaries: The Frontier and the Contours of Upper Canadian Justice, 1792–1840." *American Review of Canadian Studies* 26, no. 3 (Fall): 341–56.

Myers, Gustav. 1914. *A History of Canadian Wealth.* Chicago: C.H. Kerr.

National Security Strategy of the United States. 2006. The White House. http://georgewbush
    -whitehouse.archives.gov/nsc/nss/2006. Accessed 14 July 2014.
National Security Strategy of the United States. 2010. The White House. http://www
    .whitehouse.gov/sites/default/files/rss_viewer/national_security_strategy.pdf.
    Accessed 14 July 2010.
Nava, Mica. 2006. "Domestic Cosmopolitanism and Structures of Feeling: The Specificity
    of London." *The Situated Politics of Belonging,* ed. Nira Yuval-Davis, Kalpana Kan-
    nabiran, and Ulrike Vieten. London: Sage, 42–53.
Neill, Robin. 1991. *A History of Canadian Economic Thought.* Routledge History of Eco-
    nomic Thought Series. London and New York: Routledge.
Newman, David, 2006. "The Lines That Continue to Separate Us: Borders in Our 'Bor-
    derless' World." *Progress in Human Geography* 30, no. 2: 143–61.
———. 2005. "From the International to the Local in the Study and Representation of
    Boundaries: Theoretical and Methodologial Comments." *Holding the Line: Borders
    in a Global World,* ed. Heather Nicol and Ian Townsend-Gault. Vancouver: UBC
    Press. 400–13.
Newman, David, and Anssi Paasi. 1998. "Fences and Neighbours in the Postmodern
    World: Boundary Narratives in Political Geography." *Progress in Human Geography*
    22 (April): 186–207.
Nichols, Roger L. 2010. "The Canada–US Border and Indigenous Peoples in the Nine-
    teenth Century." *American Review of Canadian Studies* 40, no. 3: 416–28.
Nicholson, Norman. 1979. *The Boundaries of the Canadian Confederation.* Montreal and
    Kingston: McGill–Queen's University Press.
Nicol, Heather N. 2012. "The Wall, the Fence, and the Gate: Reflexive Metaphors along
    the Canada–US Border." *Journal of Borderlands Studies* 27, no. 2: 139–66.
Nicol, Heather N. 2012. "Building Borders the Hard Way." *Ashgate Research Companion
    to Border Studies.* Ed. Doris Wastl-Walter. Aldershot: Ashgate. 263–83.
———. 2006. "The Canada–U.S. Border after September 11: The Politics of Risk Con-
    tructed." *Journal of Borderlands Studies* 21, no. 1: 47–68.
———. 2005. "Resiliency or Change? The Contemporary Canada–US Border." *Geopolitics*
    10, no. 4: 767–90.
Nicol, Heather, and Julian Minghi. 2005. "The Continuing Relevance of Borders in Con-
    temporary Contexts." *Geopolitics* 10, no. 4: 680–87.
Nicol, Heather N., and Ian Townsend-Gault. 2005. *Holding the Line: Borders in a Global-
    izing World.* Vancouver: UBC Press.
Nugent, William. 2009. *Habits of Empire: A History of American Expansionism.* Random
    House Digital.
O'Donnell, John H. 1909. *Manitoba as I Saw It from 1869 to Date.* Toronto: Musson.
O'Hanlon, Michael E. 2006. "Homeland Security: Border Protection Testimony." House
    Committee on Homeland Security, Subcommittee on Intelligence, Information Shar-
    ing, and Terrorism Risk Assessment. 28 June. http://www.brookings.edu/research/
    testimony/2006/06/28defense-ohanlon. Accessed 9 August 2012.
Ó Tuathail, Gearóid. 2000. "The Postmodern Geopolitical Condition: States, Statecraft,
    and Security into the Twenty-First Century." *Annals of the Association of American
    Geographers* 90, no. 1: 166–78.
———. 1992. "Putting Mackinder in his Place: Material Transformations and Myth."
    Political Geography 11: 100–18.

Ó Tuathail, Gearóid, and John Agnew. 1992. "Geopolitics and Discourse: Practical Geopolitical Reasoning in American Foreign Policy." *Political Geography* 11, no. 2: 190–204.

Ó Tuathail, Gearóid, Simon Dalby, and Paul Routledge. 1998. *The Geopolitics Reader.* London: Routledge Press.

Ó Tuathail, Gearóid, and Timothy Luke. 1998. "Global Flowmations, Local Fundamentalism, and Fast Geopolitics: 'America' in an Accelerating World Order." In *An Unruly World? Geography, Globalization, and Governance,* ed. Andrew Herod, Gearóid Ó Tuathail, and Susan Roberts. New York and London: Routledge.

O'Sullivan, John. "Annexation." *The United States Democratic Review* 17, no. 85 (July–August 1845): 5.

Orchard, David. 1998. *The Fight for Canada: Four Centuries of Resistance to American Expansionism.* Toronto: Stoddart.

Papademetriou, Demetrios, and Elizabeth Collet. 2011. *A New Architecture for Border Management.* Washington: TransAtlantic Council on Migration, Migration Policy Institute.

Partridge, Christina. 2011. "Canadians and American Less Concerned about Security Issues and Provincial Premiers Rated." http://pollingreport.ca/updates/?p=321. 8 September. Accessed 24 October 2011.

Payan, Tony, 2006. "The Three US–Mexico Border Wars: Drugs, Immigration, and Homeland Security." Praeger Security International.

Perras, Galen Roger. 2006. "Future Plays Will Depend on How the Next One Works: Franklin Roosevelt and the Canadian Legations Discussions of January 1938." *Journal of Military and Strategic Studies* 9, no. 2 (Winter): 1–3.

Popescu, Gabriel. 2012. *Bordering and Ordering the Twenty-First Century: Understanding Borders.* Lanham: Rowman and Littlefield.

Pratt, Anna, and Sara K. Thompson. 2008. "Chivalry, 'Race' and Discretion at the Canadian Border." *British Journal of Criminology* 48, no. 5 (September): 620–40.

Pratt, Julius W. 1925. "Western War Aims in the War of 1812." *Mississippi Valley Historical Review* 12 (June): 36–50.

Public Safety Canada. 2013. "2013 Public Report on the Terrorist Threat to Canada." http://www.publicsafety.gc.ca/cnt/rsrcs/pblctns/trrrst-thrt-cnd/index-eng.aspx.

Rabidoux, Ethan Georges. 2010. "Street Gospels: Political Cartoons and Their Role in Canadian Democracy." *Canadian Journal of Media Studies* 8, no. 1.

Rankin, David M. 2004. "Borderline Interest or Identity? American and Canadian Opinion on the North American Free Trade Agreement." *Comparative Politics* 36, no. 3 (April): 331–51.

Rebuilding America's Defenses: Strategy, Forces and Resources for a New Century. 2000. Washington: Project for the New American Century.

Reimer, Chad. 2002. "Borders of the Past: The Oregon Boundary Dispute and the Beginnings of Northwest Historiography." *Parallel Destinies: Canadian-American Relations West of the Rockies,* ed. John M. Findlay and Kenneth S. Coates. Seattle: Center for the Study of the Pacific Northwest in Association with University of Washington.

Roach, Kent. 2003. *September 11: Consequences for Canada.* Montreal and Kingston: McGill–Queen's University Press.

Roberts, Susan, Anna Secor, and Matthew Sparke. 2003. "Neoliberal Geopolitics" *Antipode* 35, no. 5: 886–97.

Rodrigue, Barry. 1997. "The Canada Road Frontier: From Mythical Reportage to Analytical Reconstruction." *Histoire Mythique et Paysage Symbolique: Mythic History and Symbolic Landscape.* Actes du projet d'échange Laval–Queen's, octobre 1995, octobre 1996, rencontres de Québec et de Kingston. Sous la direction de Serge Courville et Brian Osborne. Quebec City: CIEQ.

Ross, Douglas, and Anil Hira. 2006. "Canada, a Land of Deep Ambivalence: Understanding the Divergent Response to U.S. Primacy after 9/11." University of Maine, Canadian American Public Policy Series No. 68.

Rudmin, Floyd. 1993. *Bordering on Aggression: Preparations against Canada.* Hull: Quebec: Voyageur.

Rudolph, Christopher. 2008. "A Smart Border? The American View." *Immigration Policy and the Terrorist Threat in Canada and the United States.* Ed. Alexander Moens and Martin Collacott. Fraser Institute. http://www.fraserinstitute.org. Accessed 4 August 2012.

Rumford, Chris. 2008. *Cosmopolitan Spaces, Europe, Globalization, Theory.* New York and London: Routledge.

Said, Edward. 1978. *Orientalism.* London and New York: Vintage.

Salter, Mark B. 2008. "When the Exception Becomes the Rule: Borders, Sovereignty, Citizenship." *Citizenship Studies* 12, no. 4: 365–80.

———. 2006. "The Border as State of Exception." *Exceptional Measures for Exceptional Times: The State of Security Post 9/11.* Ed. Colleen Bell and Tina Managhan. Centre for International and Strategic Studies, York University.

———. 2004. "Passports, Mobility, and Security: How Smart Can the Border Be?" *International Studies Perspectives* 5, no. 1 (February): 71–91.

———. 2003. *Rights of Passage: The Passport in International Relations.* Boulder: Lynne Rienner.

Sands, Christopher. 2002. "Fading Power or Rising Power: 11 September and Lessons from the Section 110 Experience." *Readings in Canadian Foreign Policy: Classic Debates and New Ideas.* Ed. Duane Bratt and Christopher J. Kukucha. Toronto: Oxford University Press. 249–64.

Sapolsky, Harvey M. 2005. "Canada: Crossing the Line." *Breakthroughs* 14 (Spring): 31–37.

Sciacchitano, Katherine. "From NAFTA to the SPP. Here Comes the Security and Prosperity Partnership, but—What Security? Whose Prosperity?" http://www.dollarsand sense.org/archives/2008/0108sciacchitano.html. Accessed 12 August 2012.

Scott, James W. 2009. "Bordering and Ordering the European Neighbourhood: A Critical Perspective on EU Territoriality and Geopolitics." *TRAMES* 13, no. 3: 232–47.

———. 2005. "The EU and 'Wider Europe': Toward an Alternative Geopolitics of Regional Cooperation?" *Geopolitics* 10, no. 3: 429-54.

Security and Prosperity Partnership of North America (SPP). 2009. "SPP, Myths vs. Facts." http://www.spp.gov/myths_vs_facts.asp. Acessed 25 January 2009.

Seghetti, Lisa M. 2004. "Border Security: U.S.–Canada Immigration Border Issues." CRS Report for Congress. RS21258. 28 December.

Sharp, Paul F. 1947. "The American Farmer and the 'Last Best West.'" *Agricultural History* 21, no. 2 (April): 65–75.

Sharpe, Joanne. 1996. "Hegemony, Popular Culture, and Geopolitics: The *Reader's Digest* and the Construction of Danger." *Political Geography* 15, nos. 6–7: 557–70.

Slater, David. 2008. *Geopolitics and the Post-Colonial: Rethinking North–South Relations.* New York: Wiley-Blackwell.

Smith, David R. 2005. "Structuring the Permeable Border: Channelling and Regulating Cross-Border Traffic in Labor, Capital, and Goods." *Permeable Border: The Great Lakes Basin as Transnational Region, 1650–1990,* ed. John J. Bukowczyk et al. Pittsburgh and Calgary: University of Pittsburgh Press and University of Calgary Press. 121–51.

Smith, Joshua M. 2005. "Humbert's Paradox: The Global Context Smuggling in the Bay of Fundy." *New England and the Maritime Provinces Connections and Comparisons,* ed. Stephen J. Hornsby and John G. Reid. Montreal and Kingston: McGill–Queen's University Press. 109–24.

Smith, Neil. 2003. *American Empire: Roosevelt's Geographer and the Prelude to Globalization.* Berkeley: University of California Press.

Sohoni, Deenesh. 2006. "The 'Immigrant Problem': Modern-Day Nativism on the Web." *Current Sociology* 54, no. 6 (November): 827–50.

Sokolsky, Joel, and Lagassé, Phillipe. 2006. "Suspenders and a Belt: Perimeter and Border Security in Canada–US Relations." *Canadian Foreign Policy* 12: 15–30.

Sparke, Matthew, 2006. "A Neoliberal Nexus: Economy, Security, and the Biopolitics of Citizenship on the Border." *Political Geography* 25, no. 2: 151–80.

——. 2005. *In the Space of Theory: Postfoundational Geographies of the Nation-State.* Minneapolis: University of Minnesota Press.

——. 2004. "Passports into Credit Cards: On the Borders and Spaces of Neoliberal Citizenship." *Boundaries and Belonging: States and Societies in the Struggle to Shape Identities and Local Practices,* ed. Joel S. Migdal. West Nyack, NY: Cambridge University Press.

Stana, Richard. 2010. "Border Security: Enhanced DHS Oversight and Assessment of Interagency Coordination Is Needed for the Northern Border." GAO Report to Congressional Requesters. Darby: Diane.

Stuhl, Andrew. 2013. "The Politics of the 'New North': Putting History and Geography at Stake in Arctic Futures." *Polar Journal* 3, no. 1: 94–119.

Sullivan, Peter, David Bernhardt, and Brian Ballantyne. n.d. "The Canada–US Boundary: The Next Century." http://www.internationalboundarycommission.org/docs/ibc-2009-01-eng.pdf Accessed 14 July 2014.

Sutherland, D.A. 2005. "Nova Scotia and the American Presence: Seeking Connections Without Conquest, 1848–1854." *New England and the Maritime Provinces: Connections and Comparisons,* ed. Stephen J. Hornsby and Jon G. Reid. Montreal and Kingston: McGill–Queen's University Press. 144–58.

Taylor, Joseph E., III. 2002. "The Historical Roots of Canadian–American Salmon Wars." In *Parallel Destinies: Canadians, Americans, and the Western Border,* ed. John Findlay and Ken Coates. Seattle: Center for the Study of the Pacific Northwest in Association with University of Washington. 155–80.

Thompson, John Herd, and Stephen J. Randall. 1994. *Canada and the United States: Ambivalent Allies.* Athens: University of Georgia Press.

Thorner, Thomas, and Thor Frohn-Nielsen, eds. 1998. *A Country Nourished on Self-Doubt: Documents in Post-Confederation Canadian History.* Toronto: University of Toronto Press.

Tinic, Serra. 2009. "No Rerun Nation: Canadian Television and Cultural Amnesia." *Flow*, 12 June 2009. http://flowtv.org/2009/06/no-rerun-nation-canadian-television-and-cultural-amnesia-serra-tinic-university-of-alberta. Accessed 8 December 2012.

Torpey, John. 2000. *The Invention of the Passport: Surveillance, Citizenship, and the State.* Cambridge: Cambridge University Press.

Turbeville, Daniel E., III, and Susan L. Bradbury. 2005. "NAFTA and Transportation Corridor Improvement in Western North America: Restructuring for the Twenty-First Century." *Holding the Line: Borders in a Global World.* Ed. Heather Nicol and Ian Townsend-Gault. Vancouver: UBC Press. 268–90.

United States. 2012. "US Defence Strategy." http://thehague.usembassy.gov/issues_in_focus2/us-defense-strategy-2012.html.

——. 2011. Declaration by President Obama and Prime Minister Harper of Canada—Beyond the Border. Issued by the White House, Office of the Press Secretary. https://www.whitehouse.gov/the-press-office/2011/02/04declaration-president-obama-and-prime-minister-harper-canada-beyond-bord.

——. 2006. "Fencing the Border: Construction Options and Strategic Placement." Joint Hearing before the Subcommittee on Economic Security, Infrastructure Protection, and Cyberspace of the Committee on Homeland Security [Serial no. 109–92] with the Subcommittee on Criminal Justice, Drug Policy, and Human Resources of the Committee on Government Reform [Serial no. 109–254]. House of Representatives, 109th Congress, 2nd sess., 20 July 2006.

United States. Department of State. 2008. "Western Hemisphere Travel Initiative." http://www.dhs.gov/western-hemisphere-travel-initiative.Accessed 15 July 2014.

United States Government Accountability Office, 2010a. "Statement for the Record to the Committee on Homeland Security and Governmental Affairs, US Senate Secure Border Initiative: "DHS Has Faced Challenges Deploying Technology and Fencing along the Southwest Border." Statement for the Record of Richard M. Stana, Director, Homeland Security and Justice Issues. GAO-10-651T. http://trac.syr.edu/immigration/library/P4705.pdf Accessed 15 July 2014.

——. 2010b. GAO Report to Congressional Requesters. "Border Security: Enhanced DHS Oversight and Assessment of Interagency Coordination Is Needed for the Northern Border." http://www.gao.gov/new.items/d1197.pdf. Accessed 14 July 2014.

Vance, Anneliese, 2008. "Strategic Responses by Canadian and US Exporters to Increased US Border Security Measures: A Firm-Level Analysis." *Economic Development Quarterly* 22, no. 3 (August): 239–51.

van Houtum, Henk. 2012. "The Mask of the Border." *Ashgate Research Companion to Border Studies*, ed. Doris Wastl-Walter. Aldershot: Ashgate: 49–62.

Vertovec, Steven, and Robin Cohen, eds. 2002. *Conceiving Cosmopolitanism: Theory, Context, and Practice.* Oxford: Oxford University Press.

Vertovec, Steven, and Robin Cohen, eds. 2002. "Introduction." *Conceiving Cosmopolitanism: Theory, Context, and Practice*, ed. Vertovec and Cohen. Oxford: Oxford University Press. 1–22.

Walsh, James P. 2010. "From Border Control to Border Care: The Political and Ethical Potential of Surveillance." *Surveillance and Society* 8, no. 2: 113–30.

Walters, William. 2006. "Border/Control." *European Journal of Social Theory* 9: 187–204.

Wark, Wesley. 2006. "National Security and Human Rights Concerns in Canada: A Survey of Eight Critical Issues in the Post—9/11 Environment." Ottawa: Canadian

Human Rights Commission, 2006. http://www.chrc-ccdp.ca/sites/default/files/ ns_sn_en_1.pdf. Accessed 14 July 2012.

Warner, Judith. 2010. *U.S. Border Security: A Reference Handbook*. Santa Barbara: ABC-Clio.

Widdis, Randy W. 1998. *With Scarcely a Ripple: Anglo-Canadian Migration into the United States and Western Canada, 1880–1920*. Montreal and Kingston: McGill–Queen's University Press.

Wilkinson, Bruce D. 1986. "Bilateral Free Trade with the United States." *Southern Exposure: Canadian Perspectives on the United States*, ed. David H. Flaherty and William R. McKercher. Toronto: McGraw-Hill Ryerson. 95–105.

Williams, Michael C. 2011. "The Continuing Evolution of Securitization Theory." *Securitization Theory: How Security Problems Emerge and Dissolve*, ed. Thierry Balzacq. London and New York: Routledge. 212–22.

Wimmer, Andreas, and Glick Shiller. 2002. "Methodological Nationalism and Beyond: Nation-State Building, Migration, and the Social Sciences." *Global Networks* 2, no. 4: 301–34.

Winterdyk, John A., and Kelly W. Sundberg. 2010. "Assessing Public Confidence in Canada's New Approach to Border Security." *Journal of Borderlands Studies* 25, nos. 3–4: 1–18.

Wood, Patricia K. 2002. "Borders and Identities among Italian Immigrants in the Pacific Northwest, 1880–1938." *Parallel Destinies: Canadians, Americans and the Western Border*, ed. J. Findlay and K. Coates. Seattle: University of Washington Press. 104–22.

Woodcock, George. 1989. *The Century That Made Us: Canada 1814–1914*. Toronto: Oxford University Press.

Wylie, Lana. 2010. *Perceptions of Cuba: Canadian and American Policies in Comparative Perspective*. Toronto: University of Toronto Press.

Wynn, Graeme. 1987. "Forging a Canadian Nation." *North America: The Historical Geography of a Changing Continent*, ed. Robert D. Mitchell and Paul A. Groves. Lanham: Rowan and Littlefield. 373–409.

Zeller, Suzanne, 1987. *Inventing Canada: Early Victorian Science and the Idea of a Transcontinental Nation*. Toronto: University of Toronto Press.

INDEX

www.ingramcontent.com/pod-product-compliance
Lightning Source LLC
Chambersburg PA
CBHW060028030426
42334CB00019B/2224